The Culture of Denial

SUNY Series in Environmental Public Policy
David W. Orr and Harlan Wilson, Editors

THE CULTURE
OF DENIAL

Why the Environmental Movement
Needs a Strategy
for Reforming Universities and Public Schools

C. A. BOWERS

State University of New York Press

Published by
State University of New York Press, Albany

For information, address State University of New York
Press, State University Plaza, Albany, N.Y., 12246

Production by Diane Ganeles
Marketing by Bernadette LaManna

Library of Congress Cataloging-in-Publication Data
Bowers, C. A.
    The culture of denial : why the environmental movement needs a
strategy for reforming universities and public schools / C.A.
Bowers.
        p.   cm. — (SUNY series in environmental public policy)
    Includes bibliographical references and index.
    ISBN 0–7914–3463–X (alk. paper). — ISBN 0–7914–3464–8 (pbk. :
alk. paper)
    1. Environmental education.   2. Environmental ethics—Study and
teaching.   3. Environmentalism.   4. Public schools.   5. Universities
and colleges.   I. Title.   II. Series.
GE70.B677   1997
363.7′0071—dc20   96–43769
                                                                CIP

10 9 8 7 6 5 4 3 2 1

CONTENTS

PREFACE

This book is about how our public schools and universities continue to reinforce the conceptual and moral foundations of what should be understood as a culture of denial. The denial takes many forms: that our consumer life-style has an adverse impact on the future viability of natural systems; that the power of science and technology may prove tragically limited in reversing global environmental trends; and that modern people can learn from cultures that have emphasized the development of networks of community reciprocity. For most North Americans, the denial that the prospects of future generations are being threatened is supported by carefully orchestrated visual images of plenitude—in the shopping malls and through the media. The problem, as represented in the media, does not appear as a limitation of nature's "resources," but as a dilemma in how to expand the level of consumerism while the number of unemployed increases from technologically-driven economic restructuring and downsizing. That the long term consequences of this cruel dilemma are not being recognized is also part of the culture of denial reinforced in our educational institutions.

The denial that our modern cultural beliefs and practices are forcing adaptations in the environment that do not bode well for the future of the Earth is also made easier by the large number of cultural distractions that have become, in many instances, personal obsessions that range from surfing the Internet to following the latest weight reducing diet. Even the increasing number of books and media choices serve to divert attention from considering the cultural implications of the ecological crisis, and thus help sustain the culture of denial. In writing about how public schools and universities promote the high-status forms of knowledge that are based on the modern myths that legitimate technological progress and individual centeredness, while treating as low-status the forms of knowledge and relationships that contribute to viable community and human/nature relationships, I have had to consciously resist the mesmerizing effect of these cultural distractions. Indeed, I have written this book with the full awareness that it will be seen by many people, especially within public schools and universities, as yet another point of view competing for their attention. This diversity, which is largely a result of the commodification of knowledge and relationships, is now the source of nihilism that emphasizes the authority of subjective judgment and the relativity of moral norms. I have also written with a deep awareness of the complexity and slowness of the process of cultural change, and of the educational establishment's record of lagging behind other sectors of society when it comes to adopting fundamental changes related to moral and social justice issues. Many of the cultural patterns that are contributing to the degradation of the environment are experienced at a taken-for-granted level of awareness and have led me to give special attention to the way in which ecologically problematic cultural patterns are encoded and thus reproduced through the language processes mediated by public school teachers and university professors.

Even the conventions of the English language contribute to the taken-for-granted attitude toward denying (or ignoring—which has the same effect) the interdependencies that are the most critical and inescapable aspects of human life. As I point out in another book, *Educating for an Ecologically Sustainable Culture* (1995), humans are nested in cultural systems, and cultural systems are nested in natural systems. We are dependent upon the use of cultural symbols for our sense of meaning, self-identity, and communication with others; that is, we are cultural beings and give varying degrees of personalized expression to these shared cultural patterns. We are also dependent upon our environment for both the chemical exchanges that sustain human life and the physical reference points that are the basis of our symbolic systems (which is not to suggest that our cultural maps accurately represent the most important characteristics of the environment). In spite of these actual dependencies and patterns of co-development, I have found that the English language only makes available words and phrases that convey the sense of separation as expressed in the phrases "individual and culture" and "culture and natural systems." In places I have tried to reframe this sense of basic difference and separation by using "individual/cultural" as a way of conveying the idea that the individual is a cultural being. I have also used variations on "human/biotic community" and "culture/ecosystems" as a way of suggesting dependencies and structural couplings. But the linguistic conventions of our anthropocentric culture prevailed in too many instances, with the result that words that should have conveyed what I wanted to foreground in the discussion of ecosystems (e.g., individual behavior, cultural patterns, etc.) were kept separate through the use of a conjunction that suggests the linkage of distinct entities. Writing about the "human and biotic community" and "human relations with nature" retains the cultural convention of thinking about distinct entities and attributes. The word "and" totally misrepresents how we should understand the energy and information exchanges that occur as individuals (as cultural beings) interact with natural systems. The many misrepresentations this word introduces into the analysis has made me even more aware of the need for new metaphors that foreground processes and relationships (what Bateson refers to as the "patterns that connect") rather than distinct entities and attributes—which seem to be part of the legacy of our literate and decontextualized pattern of thinking.

I was encouraged to write this book by constant reminders that the pressures influencing the direction of educational change at both the public school and university levels are motivated primarily by elite groups who are concerned with promoting technological and economic competitiveness. I am especially grateful to Doug Tompkins, Quincey Tompkins

Imhoff, and Jerry Mander of the Foundation for Deep Ecology for a grant that allowed me to reduce my teaching load at Portland State University. Without the grant the book could not have been completed. I am also indebted to Richard Gale, Director of the Environmental Studies Center at the University of Oregon, for enabling me to have full access to the University of Oregon library. Charlene Spretnak's insightful suggestions contributed to a more accurate representation of recent intellectual trends within the university. Laird Christensen's careful reading of the entire manuscript led to changes that improved the clarity of my arguments. And, as in the past, the research and writing of this book was made easier by the constant support of my wife, Mary Katharine Bowers.

Chapter 1

INTRODUCTION

Public school and university education have long been viewed as a panacea for the variety of conditions relating to individual and social advancement. Before World War II, formal education was identified with the advancement of democracy; more recently it has been justified on the grounds that it is essential to the nation's economic interests. Indeed, there is significant evidence that these expectations have been partially met. But what has not been adequately recognized is that in advancing knowledge (the university's chief claim to legitimacy) and disseminating it (the public school's primary role), a powerful sorting process was occurring that separated the multiple forms of cultural knowledge into high and low-status categories. Basically, high-status knowledge is associated with modern assumptions, values, and ways of knowing; knowledge which is not associated with the modern individualistic and technologically oriented culture of change has been viewed as low-status—and largely excluded from the nation's classrooms. While this invidious distinction is more clearly recognized today by certain traditionally oriented ethnic groups, it now needs to be challenged for environmental reasons.

The introduction of millions of tons of toxic chemicals into the environment, as well as the impact of modern technologies on fisheries, forests, topsoil, aquifers, and weather systems, now make it increasingly difficult to ignore the connections between the high-status forms of knowledge promoted by public schools and universities and the ecological crisis. The rapid increase in human population, along with the spread of moral disintegration among previously

1

stable and relatively self-reliant cultures, are also important contributors to the decline of the Earth's natural systems. Both of these world-wide trends have also been
heavily influenced by the West's high-status forms of knowledge. In effect, the changes in the Earth's chemistry and
biological processes, which are on a downward trendline,
bring into question in the most profound and urgent way
the forms of knowledge that our educational institutions
equate with modern progress.

The ecological crisis now forces us to acknowledge the
intellectual and moral double binds in what is being taught
in our public schools and universities. As one of these double binds is that few public school teachers and university
professors recognize how modern values and behavioral
patterns are connected to the ecological crisis, it will become
increasingly necessary for environmentally conscious groups
to challenge what is being taught in our educational institutions. The question of why the various groups that make
up the environmental movement should take on this task,
as well as the forms of resistance they will encounter, will
be addressed in later chapters. For now it is important to
obtain a clearer overview of the intellectual and moral double binds that characterize the relationship between the
high-status knowledge being promoted in our educational
institutions, the global commoditization and thus Western-
ization of knowledge and relationships within different cultures, and the degradation of the life-supporting natural
systems that all species (including humans) depend upon.

Whenever the democratic process has been undermined
by special interest groups or by the failure of citizens to
fully participate, it has been thought that what the public
needed was an increased exposure to public education. Similarly, when the economy lagged more formal education was
seen as essential to improving the efficiency and reliability
of the work force. Today, it is argued that educating the elite
scientists and technologists who design the computer-based
machines that are increasingly displacing the human worker
should be one of our nation's top priorities. But as we learn
more about changes occurring in degraded natural systems,
as well as how human activities are changing weather sys-

tems that will in turn alter the distribution of species (and thus our patterns of dependence), framing the solution to the crisis in a way that does not involve a radical change in the conceptual and moral foundations of the educational process will only add to our problems. This is a classic double bind situation where the promotion of our highest values and prestigious forms of knowledge serve to increase the prospects of ecological collapse.

A strong case can be made that the cultural assumptions underlying the high-status forms of knowledge, which were supposed to ameliorate the shortcomings of democracy and the economy, actually contribute to increasing the political power of economic and technological elites that continue to undermine, as Tom Athanasiou documents in *Divided Planet: The Ecology of Rich and Poor* (1996), democracy by destroying the traditional basis of self-reliant communities. Critics who have been able to keep the failures of modernization in perspective have largely been ignored or misunderstood by the university educated segment of the population. And while more people sink into economic, moral, and political poverty, politicians continue to use the media and bureaucratic agencies to keep social unrest from becoming a destabilizing political force. Today, the scale and multiple dimensions of the ecological crisis make the politics of self-deception both more difficult to sustain over the long-term and infinitely more dangerous. If we continue to take seriously the formulaic arguments about the ameliorative effects of high status forms of knowledge now being promoted by politicians and spokespersons of the educational establishment, we will face ecological consequences that cannot be hidden by the rhetoric of politicians or visually smoothed over by the media.

That these privileged forms of knowledge contribute to the double bind where modern progress leads to environmental degradation can be seen by comparing the characteristics that appear to be shared by ecologically centered cultures with the deep cultural assumptions that underlie the entire range of public school and university curricula. The identification of patterns of ecologically centered and, until recently, sustainable cultures should not be inter-

preted to mean that they share identical beliefs and daily
practices. Careful consideration of such indigenous cultures
as those of North and South America, or of the cultural syn-
thesis worked out by the Balinese, reveals tremendous diversity in how their shared cultural patterns are expressed.
Unfortunately, in deliberately denigrating these ecologically
centered approaches to dwelling in very different environments, Western cultures have failed to recognize that many
indigenous cultures had worked out the symbolic frameworks for answering questions of long-term survival that all
cultures must address: namely, how to live in a sustainable
relationship with an environment that cannot be taken for
granted. This cultural development of a symbolic reference
system, I will argue, exerts a powerful influence over a cultural group's ability to live within the limits of its bioregion,
rather than being dependent upon the resource base of
other cultural groups. These areas of symbolic development
should also be considered essential to putting modern cultures on a more sustainable pathway.

Briefly, the areas of cultural development that are present in ecologically centered cultures, and which exist only in
limited or distorted form in modern cultures, include the
following:

1. Mythopoetic narratives (meta-narratives that explain
origins and fundamental relationships) that represent humans and other forms of life that make up the natural
world as equal participants in a sacred, moral universe.

2. A metaphorical language and thought process (which involves all cultural forms of metaphorical expression—in the
arts, design of buildings, layout of social space, clothes, etc.)
that is rooted in the natural world. That is, natural phenomena are used as analogs for understanding human relationships, the everyday and transitional events in human
life, as well as human relationships with nature. Nature
based metaphorical languages often lead to interspecies
communication and combine, with the mythopoetic creation
stories, to make reciprocity with nature a moral absolute.

3. A sense of temporality (how the culture organizes the
experience of time) where the past and future are sources

of authority that influence how decisions in the present are made. This sense of time involves both a complex way of understanding and experiencing tradition, and a deep sense of the connectedness and responsibility for the well-being of future generations.

4. A well-developed tradition of transgenerational communication where elders, both women and men, take responsibility for passing on and renewing knowledge essential to just and self-reliant human communities, and to sustainable human/nature relationships.

5. Forms of community where conviviality, mutual aid, ceremonies (expressed through dance, song, narrative), patterns of civic responsibility and reciprocity ensure that economic production and exchange do not become the dominant force in everyday life.

6. Technological approaches to dwellings, food production, healing, and other aspects of community life exhibit a deep local knowledge of the elements of ecological design. This local knowlege, built up and refined over countless generations, takes account of the characteristics of natural systems, the skills and needs of the community, the need to minimize waste and destructive effects, as well as how to integrate technology into the cultural group's symbolic world of moral and spiritual connectedness.

7. An ideology (the modern word for guiding beliefs, values and episteme) that can be described (again, in modern terminology) as cultural/bio-conservatism; that is, an ideological orientation that emphasizes conserving cultural values, beliefs, and practices that contribute to sustainable relationships with the environment. Unlike the various expressions of Western liberalism, which are anthropocentric and contribute to an experimentally oriented culture, cultural/bio-conservatism is based on the recognition that humans are dependent upon the viability of natural systems. Critical thought and technological innovation that help carry forward ecologically sustainable cultural patterns are as important to cultural/bio-conservatism as are the wisdom based traditions handed down and renewed over generations.

The form of modern culture that public schools and universities have helped to create and legitimate is also based on powerful mythopoetic accounts of how life began, and of the fundamental relationships that must be observed. It also has its own distinct metaphorically based languages, a complex way of representing the temporal dimensions of life, and a guiding and legitimating ideology. But these areas of cultural development are radically different from what characterizes cultures that have survived over hundreds, even thousands of years, without destroying the prospects of future generations. One of the great ironies today is that the knowledge of relationships that ecologically centered cultures have developed is considered by modern individuals to be "primitive," backward, and unworthy of advanced, progressive cultures. And in terms of the status system that is dogmatically reinforced in public school and university curricula, the symbolic achievements of these ecologically centered cultures fall into the category of low-status knowledge—except in departments of anthropology and linguistics where there is a long tradition of documenting the belief systems and practices of "primitive" cultures (originally, to ensure that libraries and museums would have accurate accounts of cultures considered to be on the verge of extinction). The different minority cultures within North America that still retain some of the characteristics of highly developed ecologically centered cultures (e.g., elders, a sense of connectedness to the features and rhythms of the land, respect for traditions that have sustained the sense of community responsibility and mutual support, and so forth) may also be studied in schools and universities, but primarily as fitting into the category of folklore, which occupies the lowest rung on the status ladder in English departments.

The double bind that our educational institutions are helping to put us in can be seen even more clearly by identifying the cultural assumptions (guiding root metaphors) that underlie the high-status knowledge that must be learned before the diploma or degree is awarded. These assumptions provide the basic orientation and legitimating framework for the creation of the new knowledge, which in turn will be translated in the technologies used for updating and extending the commodification of human relationships and activities—including relationships with the environment. And the Western universities that are chiefly responsible for the designation and promotion of high-status knowledge educate many of the members of the elite classes in Third World countries to the Western model of economic development. These assumptions are also being promoted in Third World systems of higher education that are based on these Western models of what a university should be. These assumptions include:

1. A view of the individual as the basic social unit (indeed, increasingly the gene is represented as the unit that determines both biological and cultural development). This leads to thinking of intelligence, creativity, and moral judgment as individual attributes. The pursuit of self-interest and the sense of being separate from nature follow from this view of the autonomous individual.

2. An anthropocentric view of the world that leads to organizing knowledge and constituting values from a human perspective and need. Relationships with the natural world are thus framed variously by instrumental values and rational approaches to problem solving, the stance of the objective observer, and the cultural categories of public and private property.

3. Change is viewed as inherently progressive in nature. Thus, values, ways of knowing, and technologies that foster change have the highest status in our educational institutions. The assumption that connects all changes with social progress, and the messianic drive to spread progress throughout the world, leads to the globalization of these values, ways of knowing, and technologies.

4. Traditions, except for family holidays, patterns, and events, are seen as inhibiting progress. They are also viewed as irrelevant to a modern, experimentally oriented culture. The promoters of high status knowledge only recognize traditions (including the earlier achievements within a field of knowledge) when it helps to represent how far and rapidly we have progressed. Within the high status knowledge community, tradition is synonymous with banality and backwardness.

5. The world is understood as secular in nature, with spirituality either being limited to the experience of the individual or explained in functional terms. The division between the secular and the spiritual was partly a result of the agreement of the "fathers" of modernity to separate church and state, to privatize religion, and to promote a form of education that would encourage the belief that the individual's rational process, when properly informed, is the ultimate basis of authority.

6. Social development is understood in economic and technological terms. Development (progress) takes the form of turning knowledge, relationships, and cultural achievements into commodities—thus expanding the influence of economic values into more aspects of community life. The globalization of commoditized knowledge and relationships (with computers being the latest expression of this market place mentality) is justified in evolutionary terms, with the elite elements of Western culture (technology, science, consumer lifestyle) being represented as the most fully evolved.

7. Machines, which were the basis of metaphorical thinking in the early years of modern science, continue to serve as the analog for understanding life processes—from the molecular to the cosmic. Witness the following statement by Hans Moravec, a leader in the high-status field of artificial intelligence:

> Our culture still depends utterly on biological human beings, but with each passing year our machines, a major product of the culture, assume a greater role in its maintenance and continued growth. Sooner or later our machines will become knowledgeable enough to handle their own maintenance, reproduction, and self-improvement without help. When this happens, the new genetic takeover will be complete. *Our culture will then be able to evolve independently of human biology and its limitations, passing instead directly from generation to generation of ever more capable intelligent machinery.* (italics added, 1988, p. 4)

One consequence of this metaphorical language is that machines are increasingly viewed as superior to humans—in the areas of work, intelligence, entertainment, and healing.

8. Technologies are created by experts who think in terms of standardized designs that can be replicated anywhere in the world, the use of materials that will maximize profits and ensure centralized control over the use of the technology, and a short replacement time by more advanced technologies.

9. There is an increasing reliance on science as the most powerful and legitimate source of explanations of the origin and "evolution" of human life, and all other life processes — including the genetic basis of cultural developments.

Collectively, the assumptions encoded in high-status knowledge put modern cultures on a highly experimental pathway, while at the same time providing the conceptual and moral guarantee of progress. The encoding of these assumptions in the language and thought process further ensures that aspects of cultural experience that can be interpreted by this cultural grammar will be recognized as "real"; at the same time, what cannot be understood or recognized in terms of this cultural schemata ceases to have any standing. For example, the pitfalls facing experimentally oriented cultures are obvious to people who do not have an economic, political, or identity-based-interest in promoting the current cultural trajectory of modern high-status forms of knowledge that the Earth's ecosystems cannot sustain. Members of cultures based on the ecologically centered patterns identified earlier are more apt to recognize that the main issues facing all humans concern the destruction of the environment and the loss of traditional knowledge of how to live symbolically rich lives without undermining the prospects of future generations. Yet, those who protect high-status knowledge from being challenged, and promote its further development (not to mention obtaining copyrights on the technological advances it leads to), are unable to recognize the environmental evidence that brings into question their deepest assumptions. The extent of this collective myopia will be documented in the chapters that focus directly on what is being taught in the nation's educational institutions.

Generalizations about the differences between high and low-status forms of knowledge need to be interpreted as referring to the dominant characteristics that can be found on the opposite ends of the continuum of the cultural groups that make up American society. There is overwhelming evidence of a dominant elite whose power and legitimacy are based on the privileged forms of knowledge promoted in our educational institutions—particularly in universities. There is also an abundance of evidence relating to the marginalized and exploited cultural groups who are seen by the advocates of modernization as backward and inferior in intellectual and moral terms. But generalizations about the ecological consequences of high and low-status forms of knowledge also have to take account of the cultural patterns and beliefs found more in the middle reaches of this continuum of cultural orientations. It needs to be kept in mind, for example, that not all traditional cultures are models of ecological citizenship. Nor should all low-status forms of knowledge that underlie the cultural practices of marginalized groups be considered as immune from criticism and reform efforts. Furthermore, it needs to be remembered that solutions to the cultural aspects of the ecological crisis are not attainable simply by borrowing (appropriating) from the many approaches that ecologically centered cultures have taken to the creation of inclusive mythopoetic creation stories, transgenerational communication, cultural/bio-conservatism, and so forth. Indeed, this last warning may be relevant only to New Age activists, as it is nearly impossible to imagine the keepers of high-status knowledge even acknowledging that modern culture might have taken the wrong pathway of development. It is just as impossible to imagine them recognizing that the educational process should include the careful study of the earth wisdom of traditional cultures, and questions of how to reconstitute the conceptual and moral foundations of modern life. But this observation, which is based on more than twenty-three years of personal interaction with the keepers of high-status knowledge (at a university that prided itself on being a liberal institution), again frames the discussion in terms of the dominant elite that occupies the extreme end of the continuum.

Generalizations about this group also need to be framed against the background of the efforts of educators and private foundations that occupy a central position on this continuum. That is, they possess the credentials necessary to participate in the symbolic world of high-status knowledge but have traditionally been concerned about the plight of marginalized, low-status groups. While their efforts to "green" educational institutions, from developing more efficient approaches to energy use in campus buildings to bringing about changes in the content of courses, must still be viewed as having a limited influence, they nevertheless need to be kept in the foreground of any discussion of educational reform strategies. Their efforts serve as reminders that significant cultural change often occurs through the efforts of dedicated people who start working from the margins of established power groups. They also serve both as models that can inspire similar efforts in other educational institutions, and as examples that must constantly be scrutinized in terms of internal contradictions. This last point is especially important as many environmental activists, both within and outside educational institutions, continue to embrace liberal assumptions that they acquired earlier without recognizing that these very assumptions provided both the conceptual and moral basis of the Industrial Revolution.

Perhaps the most visible and promising effort to reorient higher education toward the goal of an ecologically sustainable future was the Campus Earth Summit for Higher Education, held in 1995 at Yale University. Sponsored by the Heinz Family Foundation, the conference brought together 450 faculty, staff, and students from twenty-two countries, including representatives from all fifty states. The three day conference resulted in the publication of the *Blueprint for a Green Campus*, which contained the following recommendations:

(1) Integrate Environmental Knowledge into All Relevant Disciplines; (2) Improve Undergraduate Environmental Studies Course Offerings; (3) Provide Opportunities for Students to Study Campus and Local Environmental Issues; (4) Conduct a Campus Environmental Audit; (5) Institute Environmentally Responsible Purchasing Policies; (6) Reduce Campus Waste; (7) Maximize Energy Efficiency;

(8) Make Environmental Sustainability a Top Priority in Campus Land-Use, Transportation, and Building Planning; (9) Establish a Student Environmental Center; (10) Support Students Who Seek Environmentally Responsible Careers (Heinz Family Foundation, 1995, pp. 2–3).

That these recommendations were the main achievement of the meeting indicates a general concern on the part of the attendees that higher educational institutions are continuing to operate as though the ecological crisis exists only as a media event. Like the Declaration of Independence, the *Blueprint* represents an attempt to awaken the most influential leaders within the educational establishment. More importantly, its recommendations identify the different areas in which higher education needs to initiate basic changes—with the curriculum being only one area.

While there are many small colleges, foundations, and individual professors attempting to foster environmentally oriented reforms, two programs stand out in terms of their national visibility and ability to provide leadership, as well as to channel resources to promising reform efforts. In 1990, Tufts University established the Environmental Literacy Institute with the goal of educating the entire student population of the university to become "environmentally literate." The leadership behind this commitment came from the combined efforts of Tufts President, Jean Mayer, and the Dean of Environmental Programs, Anthony Cortese. One of the key features of the Institute is a two-week summer workshop at which faculty from different disciplines engage in an intensive study of environmental issues and discuss how these issues can be integrated into their courses. Faculty are then encouraged to teach their revised courses the following year. Institute faculty then review the course syllabi before making them available to universities across the country. In addition, Tufts University is also the home base for the Secretariat of University Presidents for a Sustainable Future. One of the key features of this group is The Tallories Declaration, which commits the signatory to provide institutional leadership both in introducing environmental awareness into all facets of university life and in developing partnerships with community organizations working toward environmental renewal. To date, the Declaration has been signed by 223 university presidents representing institutions in North and South America, Asia, Africa, and Western and Eastern Europe.

The other noteworthy national effort is the Second Nature Institute started in 1993 by Cortese and Bruce Droste. The name of the Institute, according to its founders, was chosen to highlight that its central purpose was to make environmentally sound living "second nature" to the next generation of educational leaders. Most notable is its support of a consortium of seventeen historically African American and Native American institutions that are providing leadership training in how to introduce environmental literacy into the educational process.

There are many other efforts being made across North America to introduce environmental issues into courses, conduct campus energy audits, and convince departments to adopt more long-range strategies for collaborating with community action groups. The Green University Strategic Plan for George Washington University, the Eco-Justice Task Force established by the School of Theology at Claremont Graduate School, La Verne University's faculty-wide effort to green its entire curriculum, and Portland State University's School of Education graduate program, which focuses on the connections between education, culture, and ecology at the master's level and community and environmental renewal at the doctoral level, are just a few of the reform efforts taking place on what must be acknowledged as the outer fringes of higher education.

But even the success of establishing environmental studies programs at most major universities across North America must be viewed as an expression of grudgingly granted tokenism—like the establishment of ethnic and women's studies departments. That is, environmental studies is being accepted as an area of academic study, but its presence on campuses has had no significant influence on what is taught in departments such as psychology, political science, philosophy, history, economics, sociology, and so forth. While there may be one or two environmentally ori-

ented faculty members within liberal arts and professionally oriented departments who are attempting to clarify
how relationships between humans and nature traditionally have been represented in these disciplines, or who are
exploring the implications of changing the conceptual and
moral priorties within the discipline, they are always in the
minority. More importantly, they are seen by their more or-
thodox colleagues as being engaged in trendy and thus not
really scholarly pursuits. These marginalized faculty are
also penalized in the academic reward system when they
volunteer their time to help the usually underfunded environmental studies program survive. The low level of support,
as well as the inability of the more traditional academics to
recognize the implications of the ecological crisis for their
own disciplines, should be kept clearly in mind when considering why these promoters of high-status knowledge cannot be relied upon to reform themselves.

The growing number of private foundations supporting
efforts to develop ecological literacy is somewhat more encouraging. However, the experience of participating in foundation sponsored conferences, where everybody shares
similar views about the need to make the environment the
main focus of educational reform, can indeed be mislead-
ing—particularly when conversations with colleagues at
one's home institution seldom touch on environmentally related issues. This type of experience, along with the reform
efforts cited above (including the Yale University Campus
Earth Summit), can create a deceptive sense of the impact
that conferences, foundation grants, and networking among
environmentally concerned educators really have on mainstream public schools and universities. To make this point
in the context of the earlier discussion of high and low-status knowledge, these reform efforts are taking place in that
part of the continuum where there are few leverage points
for effecting real change. That is, the reform efforts lack
academic legitimacy, as well as a political and economic
power base within the institution.

Putting these reform efforts in proper perspective requires admitting that they are taken seriously by only a
small minority of university presidents and faculty, and by

an even smaller number of public school teachers. Aside from the more progressive public school science teachers who now base their environmental science courses on the constructivist view of intelligence (which is the latest reinterpretation of Industrial Revolution/Enlightenment assumptions about the connection between individual empowerment and social progress), it is safe to say that it is the unique public school teacher indeed who understands either the surface or deeper implications of David Orr's observation that *"all education is environmental education"* (1992, p. 90). Even the first recommendation of the *Blueprint for a Green Campus* on the "Need to Integrate Environmental Knowledge into All Relevant Disciplines" is framed in a way that recognizes that environmentally oriented faculty have no real power to effect changes in what is being taught in university classrooms and rewarded as significant research. While the document recommends integrating "environmental knowledge into all relevant courses," it provides examples of integration that do not lead to fundamental reform in the conceptual foundations of the disciplines, but are "add-ons" that merely give the appearance of relevance. Instead of citing an example of, say, an economics professor who helps students rethink the assumptions about scarcity, competition, and the causal connections that are supposed to exist between free market forces and human progress, the *Blueprint* cites the example of an economic professor at Tufts University who revised his course to include homework problems on articles from the *New York Times* about the poaching of elephants and the debate over grazing fees in the American West. A second example involved a drama professor who revised her theater technology course to teach students about resource flows of chemicals used in theater production (1995, p. 10).

Specific recommendations on how faculty should approach the integration of environmental knowledge into all areas of the university curriculum also suggest an add-on approach. High on the list is the need to "discuss with peers, faculty in your department, program, or related field, the environmental perspectives and components of your academic field." The *Blueprint* also recommends "making an

environmental course, or a course with a focus on environmental topics, part of the core curriculum or distribution requirement." Indeed, these recommendations appear far-
reaching and essentially sound when one considers the lack
of environmental awareness in the discourse and reward
system of most academic departments. With more of their
research funding now coming from environmental, rather
than defense related governmental agencies and industries,
certain areas of the sciences are becoming notable exceptions to the kind of environmental denial that exists in most
departments.

Given the widespread indifference that still pervades
most departments, it is wishful thinking to base the kind of
fundamental changes needed in the cultural assumptions
that underlie the advancement of high-status knowledge
on the hope that faculty who now benefit from the present
system will be willing to engage in a serious discussion of
how to introduce an environmental perspective into their
courses and research. Adding an environmentally oriented
course, even if it had a deep cultural perspective on human
and nature relationships, to the core curriculum or set of
distribution requirements seems to ignore that the real
problem is in what is being taught in the existing core
courses. Universities have long prided themselves on encouraging diversity of thinking—as long as the diversity
was based on the same deep cultural assumptions. Unfortunately what students learn from this intellectual equivalent
of a shopping mall is how to compartmentalize their own
moral and intellectual commitments in ways that fit the
ideological and epistemological orientation of the different
disciplines. Learning to compartmentalize as one moves
from one course to another dulls the awareness of contradictions—especially contradictions that obscure the fact
that the environment can only tolerate so much human stu-
pidity before its internal changes call people to account. It
also conditions students to accept moral and intellectual
relativism as a necessary part of participating in institutional settings governed by high-status forms of knowledge.
But what is most problematic about this add-on approach to
integrating environmental knowledge into the university

curriculum is that the basic double binds remain unchallenged—if they are even recognized.

There is an important parallel between the present inability of academics to recognize that high-status knowlege is built upon a set of anthropocentrically oriented cultural myths, and their earlier inability to recognize the racism and sexism in this privileged form of knowlege. University professors and public school teachers only became aware of the connections between what they were teaching and the symbolic and structural nature of racism and sexism after years of street demonstrations, court battles, and media attention. Even now there are powerful sectors in the academic community that do not yet recognize that the intellectual norms of "objectivity" and rigor also encode the epistemic orientations of the English language (if that is the language of the scholar/researcher). Nor do they recognize that it is at the level of epistemic code reproduced in the language that all forms of inquiry and knowledge construction become political, and this raises the issue of cultural domination—particularly when the language of the academic or expert explains the problem and solution that other cultural groups are expected to accept. The most obvious example of the cultural myopia that surrounds the myth of objective inquiry is evident in the ways that scientific explanations subvert the moral relationships that are integral to how many indigenous cultures understand "natural" phenomena.

It took feminists over a hundred years of political activism before public schools and universities began the slow and still uneven process of examining how the curriculum, hiring practices, and reward system favored men—often to the total exclusion of women. Our educational institutions have an even more dismal record in recognizing the racist assumptions that were often the basis of a field of inquiry (psychology and anthropology come easily to mind). Their attempts to rectify this deep-seated tradition, particularly in the area of curriculum reform, have largely taken the form of academic tokenism where the problem is isolated by setting up a special department of ethnic studies. But these institutions are beginning to respond to outside political pressures to address these social justice issues. And this may be the point that is most significant in terms of whether our educational institutions continue to take a tokenism approach to environmentalists, or begin to address the more deeply embedded cultural assumptions that are the basis of the high-status forms of knowledge that continue to ignore the problem of long-term sustainability. The evidence, I think, is overwhelming that the latter will only occur in response to outside political pressures.

This leads me to state the central purpose of this book, which is to foster a critical and sustained discussion of why it is absolutely imperative that what is learned in public schools and universities be made a central concern of the environmental movement. A second purpose is to suggest workable strategies for integrating the educational process into the larger task of changing from a culture that exploits the environment to one that can live within sustainable limits. When we consider the power of public education to obfuscate fundamental human/environment relationships, to delegitimate certain forms of cultural knowledge while conferring high status on other forms, to determine who has access to the credentialing process essential to positions of power within society, and to renew the deepest held mythologies of the dominant culture, the need to develop an educational strategy becomes as important as any challenge now facing the environmental movement. Indeed, a strong case can be made that the need for political action directed toward preserving wild lands, slowing the rate of pollution of land and water, and winning support for a specific piece of environmental legislation, has its roots in the environmentally destructive cultural beliefs and practices that are mostly passed on from generation to generation through the media and educational institutions. Unless the culture of modernism is fundamentally altered, which in part means altering what students learn in public schools and universities, there will be an unending series of environmental problems that will keep attention focused on the immediate consequences of these cultural beliefs and practices, and not on the source of the problem. This is the classic double bind situation that now needs to be addressed; that is, if the world's natural systems do not first collapse from the increased pressure caused by the continuing expansion of the human population.

However, before considering the key issues that must be addressed as part of the process of developing an educational strategy, it is necessary to identify possible reasons for the environmental movement's current indifference to the double binds now being exacerbated by the modernizing orientation of our public schools and universities. The suggestion that education and culture are as bound together as culture and natural systems is fairly obvious when stated in this way. So the question becomes, Why have intelligent people who are aware of environmental problems ignored by vast numbers of Americans been unable to recognize the critical importance of the primary relationships between education, culture and ecosystems? Obviously, they are not intellectually limited or morally atrophied. The reasons, I suspect, are as varied as they are complex. But they need to be taken into account as we start to think about the purpose and strategy for an ecologically sound approach to educational reform.

The three most obvious reasons that educational institutions are ignored include the fragmented nature of the environmental movement, the marginal status of a deep cultural perspective in the education of the people who become environmental writers and activists, and the ideological orientation that many members of environmental groups share with the educational community. A brief consideration of each complex set of reasons will help us recognize that developing an educational reform strategy will require giving as careful consideration to the dynamics and varied nature of what I have loosely referred to as the "environmental movement" as must be given to the even more complex nature of the educational establishment.

Reasons for Laissez Faire Attitude toward Public Schools and Universities

Fragmented Nature of the Environmental Movement

The use of the phrase "environmental movement" may suggest intellectual laziness or a general lack of understanding on the part of the person who uses it. It may also suggest an awareness that it is the only label sufficiently broad to encompass a wide range of interest groups who, in some instances, share little in common except the need to include the word "environment" in their promotional literature and appeals for funding. As I am attempting to reach interest groups who represent the entire spectrum of environmental writers and activists (including corporate leaders who recognize the danger of pushing beyond critical ecosystem thresholds), the latter explanation accounts for my use of this admittedly inaccurate phrase. I could have used the more conventional distinction that separates environmentalists from deep ecologists. According to this approach, the environmentalists include groups who utilize science and technology as a means of managing the environment as a natural resource that can be exploited on a long-term basis. Thus, most scientists, free-market environmentalists, and elements of the business community interested in "sustainable economic development" would fit into this category. Among the more prominent groups challenging the conceptual and moral basis of our ecologically destructive cultural patterns are the deep ecology philosophers, social ecologists, and ecofeminists. Following the lead of Arne Naess and George Sessions, deep ecology thinkers have attempted to identify an alternative set of guiding philosophical principles that avoid the dangers of the anthropocentric assumptions that underlie modern culture. Social ecology, as represented in the ideas of Murray Bookchin and Janet Biehl, takes a more systemic approach to understanding the roots of the ecological crisis. Thus, social ecologists are critical of deep ecology thinkers for emphasizing the influence of philosophical ideas rather than the role of capitalism in reducing nature to an exploitable resource. But their prescriptions for a post-capitalist form of culture share much in common with the current expression of libertarian thinking that emphasizes "self-managing, face-to-face communities." While critical of both deep ecology and social ecology (for very different reasons), ecofeminists in the words of Charlene Spretnak offer as "an alternative to the Western patriarchal worldview of fragmentation, alientation, agonistic dualisms, and exploitative dynamics . . . a radical reconceptualization that honors holistic integration:

interrelatedness, transformation, embodiment, caring, and love" (1994, p. 187).

I find that the distinctions between environmentalists and the groups who take a more critical approach to systemic and cultural beliefs to be useful in certain circumstances. But we should be looking for a shared basis of interest in addressing the complex problem of developing a strategy for awakening the educational establishment to its role in perpetuating ecologically destructive cultural beliefs and values. Thus, I shall continue to use the more inclusive label of "environmental movement," while recognizing that the various groups encompassed by this label will approach any serious consideration of an educational strategy in terms of their distinctive interpretative frameworks. With regard to the more doctrinaire members of these different groups, my expectations have been scaled back to the point of hoping merely to shift their focus from an incidental interest in educational issues to a more sustained discussion. For people in the environmental movement who are open to addressing changes that will affect the mainstream of American society, and to considering educational institutions as one of the most viable leverage points, I have greater expectations for success.

To return to the main issue under discussion here, it is this diversity of groups within the environmental movement that accounts, to a large degree, for the reason why educational reform has been ignored. In the early 1900s, environmental groups came into existence in response to how specific environmental issues were perceived at the time. The early conservation movement worked to save large tracts of land from economic development by having them set aside as national parks. As human demand and technological developments began to degrade the environment in other ways (threat of species extinction, loss of forest cover, degraded fish habitat, etc.) environmental groups continued to form for the purpose of dealing with specific environmental problems. It is this problem-specific orientation of most environmental groups (protecting rain forests, saving whales, restoring degraded habitats, enacting legislation that address specific environmental abuses) that has pre-

vented them from considering how the cultural assumptions passed on through the different levels of formal education contribute to the problems that become their primary
concern. Focusing on environmentally specific issues has
also been essential to the survival of groups operating on
limited budgets, and who have had a better chance of obtaining continued outside funding if they remained focused
on the environmental issues that other people shared an interest in. If these groups had launched a broad-based effort
to reform the cultural orientation taught in the classrooms,
they would have jeopardized, in many instances, their
sources of financial and political support—as well as lost
the central focus essential to their success. Furthermore,
the crisis nature of many environmental problems has required immediate action, such as responding to the spill of
radioactive waste or other toxic chemicals, the need to block
the sale of what remained of an old growth stand of trees,
and the need to take action that would reverse the rapid
decline of a particular species. This need to respond to environmental crises, which now characterize many environmental groups, makes sustained reflection on the broader
cultural issues more difficult. Understanding the deep cultural assumptions, where they came from and how they are
encoded and reenacted in daily practices, also requires a different form of knowledge than what is required in the rapid
marshalling of public attention, economic resources, and
scientific/technological expertise essential to restoring the
viability of an ecosystem or to protecting existing environmental legislation from being dismantled. And this brings
us to the second set of reasons the connections between education, culture, and the ecosystem have been largely ignored: namely, the lack of a deep understanding of culture
that environmental groups share with other segments of society who were educated in America's public schools and
universities.

Marginalization of Culture

In one sense, environmental writers and activists cannot avoid dealing with culture as it is integral to how they
think about environmental issues and to their use of tech-

nologies. Contrary to popular opinion and what is taught in various subfields of science, the scientific way of understanding natural phenomena is based on a culturally specific epistemology. This is often overlooked partly because of the legitimating ideology that few people are able or willing to question, and partly because the cultural epistemology shared by scientists has become so widespread around the world that it has taken on the mythic status of a culture-free mode of inquiry. In effect, the word "culture" encompasses everything humans think, value, communicate, and in other ways act out. Even the more biological aspects of human and other forms of life are influenced by cultural practices.

Given the pervasiveness of culture, one might well question the claim that environmentalists have ignored the role culture plays, and thus the importance of education, in the increasingly problematic relationship between humans and the environment. The reason for my concern is that most of our culture is learned and reenacted at a taken-for-granted level. Indeed, cultural patterns, such as the subject-verb-object ordering of our language and thought processes, are part of our natural attitude. Most of our experience is based on taken-for-granted patterns that contribute to communication, meaning, and in other ways enable people to negotiate relationships and resolve everyday issues. In effect, these implicit cultural patterns serve as the conceptual and moral background knowledge that enables us to deal with the more explicit uncertainties; but when these patterns lead to problematic relationships, such as the perception of the environment as a natural resource or computers as a culturally neutral technology, they then need to be made explicit—which is often the first step in the process of effecting change in the culture. Making explicit the gender bias in language, and in our everyday relationships, is an example of cultural change that involves the revision of previously held taken-for-granted patterns.

The primary reason that environmentalists tend not to think of environmental issues in terms of cultural patterns, but to use other categories and metaphorical language that further marginalizes an awareness of the influence of culture, is that their own education occurred in institutions that treat culture as the specific interest of anthropologists. When students take an anthropology class they are learning about culture; but their psychology, history, literature, and biology classes are represented as bodies of knowledge, theories, individual scholarly achievement and creativity, that do not require an understanding of how they are an expression of a particular culture. Furthermore, the organization of knowledge in each of the disciplines is based on philosophically grounded assumptions that had their origins in the formative development of the modern mind-set when philosophers and social theorists did not understand how culture influenced their own ways of thinking. The result of this inability to recognize the constitutive role of culture is that the assumptions that underlie the modern way of thinking reproduce misunderstandings of these earlier thinkers. For example, currently held assumptions that represent the individual as the basic social unit, intelligence and creativity as attributes of the individual, language as a neutral conduit, the rational process as yielding "objective" and thus culture-free knowledge, and change as inherently progressive in nature, would more easily be recognized as culturally specific if differences in cultural epistemologies were understood.

As these modern and culturally specific assumptions underlie most areas of the public school and university education, few graduates of these institutions are able to recognize the constitutive role (and taken-for-granted status) of culture in human experience—except when specific cultural patterns become existentially problematic. Having been educated to base their own thoughts, values, and technological practices on the assumptions underlying modern consciousness, most environmentalists simply reproduce the way of understanding that continues to disregard the influence of culture. Some environmentalists, such as Wendell Berry and Gary Snyder, come very close to writing directly about the hidden influence of culture. The writings of Richard Nelson, Gregory Cajete, Jerry Mander, and Helena Norberg-Hodge are even more explicit. But most environmentalists share the proclivity either to ignore culture or to equate culture with modernity, which may account, in part, for why they have ignored how educational institutions re-produce the double binds of the culture.

As I will be basing my analysis and suggestions for ed-ucational change on a way of understanding culture that is not widely shared, a brief explanation of what I mean by culture might help prevent misinterpretations of critical parts of my argument. The anthropologist Clifford Geertz suggests that the word "culture" should be seen as "denot-ing an historically transmitted pattern of meanings embod-ied in symbols, a system of inherited conceptions expressed in symbolic forms by means of which men communicate, perpetuate, and develop their knowledge about and atti-tudes toward life" (1973, p. 89). After listing a number of dif-ferent ways that culture influences human experience, Ward H. Goodenough summarized in the following way how everyday experience involves the expression of culturally shared patterns: "culture, then, consists of standards for de-ciding what is, standards for deciding what can be, stan-dards for deciding how one feels about it, standards for deciding what to do about it, and standards for deciding how to go about doing it" (1981, p. 62). I will be using the word culture in the same inclusive way, but will stress more how cultural patterns are learned at a tacit and contextual level, and thus experienced as taken-for-granted—or what can be called our "natural attitude" toward everyday life. I will also be emphasizing how past forms of cultural intelli-gence and moral sensitivity, particularly as they relate to human relationships with the environment, are encoded and reproduced through different forms of communication that sustain people's taken-for-granted experience—from the metacommunication of body language to the cultural encoding and reproduction characteristics of computer me-diated thinking and communication.

When this more complex view of culture is used as the *basis* of thinking about environmental issues, and not as an incidental issue that might be brought into the discussion as an afterthought, it then becomes easier to recognize the patterns of modern thinking that characterize most current criticisms of modernity. This more complex view of culture also makes it easier to bring into the discussion of ecological

sustainability a comparative perspective that is less distorted by the modern bias against more traditionally oriented cultures. In short, the foregrounding of the cultural
nature of human experience (including the recognition that
cultural patterns are given individualized expression)
makes it easier to avoid the modern form of discourse that
misrepresents the individual, whether in the role of theorist
or as the object of analysis, as culturally autonomous.

For example, in making the case that educational institutions are perpetuating a double bind by educating students to high-status cultural assumptions and practices that
threaten the viability of ecosystems, an important distinction needs to be kept clearly in mind. Understanding how
culture is part of our taken-for-granted patterns of thought
and behavior is essential to being able to consider the second
area of concern: namely, the ecologically problematic cultural patterns that need to be given specific attention. One of
the most difficult cultural processes to recognize is how the
languages of a cultural group encode and continue to reproduce the patterns of metaphorical thinking that occurred at
an earlier time in the history of the cultural group. This is
essential to understanding why environmentalists continue
to perpetuate the double binds of modern culture by relying
upon the patterns of thinking that contributed to the ecological crisis in the first place. The way in which cultural
patterns are learned at a taken-for-granted level of understanding is also important if the process of making explicit
and reconstituting problematic cultural patterns is to be carried beyond what is already obvious and immediate. How
cultural patterns, which always have a human origin, become reified and thus experienced as having an objective
(even universal) status is another aspect of everyday experience that needs to be understood. Particularly relevant to
our concerns here is how taken-for-granted patterns tend to
be projected onto other cultural groups as their basis of understanding. This leads to misunderstanding the differences
between cultural groups, and often to the unintentional imposition of practices and beliefs—in the name of progress.

The other aspect of culture that we shall return to in
later chapters has to do with the questions that environ-

mentalists need to raise in considering any aspect of culture. The questions fall into two categories: "Which cultural patterns are contributing to the ecological crisis?" and "What are the characteristics of cultural patterns that contribute to long-term sustainability?" Both questions are essential to a critical assessment of the form of culture being learned in public schools and universities.

The Shared Ideological Orientation

The diversity within the environmental movement suggests that it would be impossible to obtain agreement on a guiding set of ideological principles. The eight "Basic Principles" of Deep Ecology articulated by Bill Devall, George Sessions, and Arne Naess (1985, p. 70) did not lead to an increase in collaboration between social ecologists, ecofeminists, and deep ecologists. Nor have the principles been embraced by environmentalists ranging from eco-capitalists, who want to present a green image to consumers, to scientific environmentalists who still embrace the belief that a more rational understanding of the dynamic characteristics of ecosystems will enable us to manage them on a long-term basis. In spite of the fundamentally different perspectives on what deserves attention, and how respective self-interests are to be served by the approach taken to environmental problems, a strong case can be made that there is a common set of assumptions shared by most environmentalists, and that these deeply held and mostly taken-for-granted assumptions can best be understood as an ideology. It is an ideology that frames how basic aspects of human experience are to be understood and acted out.

But the differences between environmental groups reflect differences in which shared assumptions are given more prominence. For example, those groups that want to manage the environment on a more scientific basis foreground the liberal assumption of the ability of rationally based thought to exercise control over the uncertainties of the future. Environmentalists who want to save rain forests or the spotted owl from economic exploitation foreground a different liberal assumption—namely, that liberation from exploitation now needs to be extended to the non-human world. While certain assumptions are given prominence in the thinking of a given environmental group, many of the other assumptions basic to the ideology continue to be shared at a more tacit level of understanding. There may even be fundamental differences about the efficacy of specific ideological assumptions, such as those which lead ecofeminists to distance themselves from what they perceive to be patriarchal patterns in other environmental groups, or those which set the anti-anthropocentric stance of some groups at odds with those who advocate the use of science as the basis of environmental management. These differences, however, often seem not to affect the tacit acceptance of other assumptions that bind these groups to a common ideological orientation.

As more attention will be given later to the connection between the liberal ideology of modernism and the double bind that educational institutions are creating for present and future generations, I will only summarize here why the ideology shared by different groups within the environmental movement has contributed to their indifference toward what is being taught in the nation's educational systems. Simply put, the environmentalists' indifference toward educational institutions results, in part, from sharing with the educational establishment many of the assumptions that underlie modern liberalism. That is, taken-for-granted assumptions and practices tend to go unnoticed until behavior is challenged by a different set of assumptions. As we shall see in the next chapter, the language of mainstream classroom teachers and university academics is derived from and, in turn, reproduces the same ideological assumptions that are taken for granted by most environmental writers and activists. This common grounding in the same deep patterns of thinking also helps account for the ability of environmentalists to stay focused on specific problems.

It is ironic that the ideological assumptions that provided the liberal, conceptual, and moral framework for the development of the Industrial and now the Information-Revolution continue to be the basis of thinking for most environmentalists. Again, it needs to be emphasized that I am not suggesting that *all* the liberal assumptions are em-

braced by *all* environmentalists. It also needs to be emphasized that even when there are fundamental differences
over certain assumptions, the differences often do not lead
to rethinking other liberal assumptions that are still taken
for granted. The following examples are intended to demonstrate both points: the sharing of liberal assumptions and
the inability to question and revise key aspects of modernist
liberal assumptions in the face of radically divergent thinking about human/nature relationships.

I would like to start with an observation by Roderick F.
Nash that supports my argument. In *The Rights of Nature*,
Nash writes:

> The alleged subversiveness of environmental ethics should
> be tempered with the recognition that its goal is the im-
> plementation of liberal values as old as the republic. This
> may not make modern environmentalism less radical, but
> it does place it more squarely in the mainstream of Amer-
> ican liberalism, which, after all, has had its revolutionary
> moments. (1989, p. 12)

In a later passage Nash identifies one of the connections between the philosophical underpinnings of the liberal view of
freedom and how deep ecologists think about the rights of
nature:

> It is significant for the link between Western liberalism
> and environmental ethics that Naess and other deep ecol-
> ogists based this axiom on the 'inherent,' 'intrinsic,' or, as
> older philosophers might have said, 'natural' rights of all
> beings to life, to freedom from excessive human interfer-
> ence, and to the opportunity to pursue their own definition
> of happiness. Here, of course, was an explicit application of
> the familiar tripartite foundation of American liberalism,
> dressed in new ecological language and extended not only
> to all living things but, as Sessions and Naess explained
> after a 1984 camping trip to Death Valley, California, to
> 'rivers, landscapes [and] ecosystems.' (p. 147)

Different liberal assumptions are clearly present in
Arne Naess's emphasis on individuals developing their *own*

guiding ecological principles (1989, p. 37), and Murray
Bookchin's stress on the importance of "individual autonomy" within the context of what libertarians envision as
small scale, participatory communities. Bookchin's revi-
sionist brand of liberalism can be seen in the following
warning—one that demonstrates the modernist liberal tendency to ignore the nature of cultural embeddedness as well
as the diversity of cultural ways of understanding such primary relationships as the individual's relationship to the
human and biotic community:

> A tyranny of consensus, like the famous 'tyranny of struc-
> turelessness,' demeans a free society. It tends to subvert
> individuality in the name of community and dissent in the
> name of solidarity. Neither true community or solidarity
> are fostered when the individual's development is aborted
> by public disapproval and his or her deviant ideas are 'nor-
> malized' by the pressure of public opinion. (1990, p. 176)

As these references to Naess and Deep Ecology may
lead some readers to misinterpret me to be putting the eight
guiding principles of Deep Ecology into the category of liberalism, it is important to make several important distinctions. The eight principles formulated by Arne Naess and
George Sessions are not in themselves an expression of liberal thinking. But the rational approach to articulating the
principles, as well as the emphasis on each individual deciding how to interpret them, are expressions of the liberal
tradition of presenting universal principles that ignore how
ideas reproduce a specific cultural epistemology and moral
code. Naess's statement that individuals must decide their
own approach to a guiding ecosophy does not reflect the
deep influence of Buddhism and Hinduism on his thought
as it does his Western liberal emphasis on individuals interpreting how the guiding principles are to be actualized.
Witness the following explanation by Andrew McLaughlin:

> Even the *kinds* of reasons which might persuade a person
> to adopt a version of the platform (the eight principles)
> may range from rational to nonrational to irrational. For
> example, acceptance might be based on philosophical re-

flection, religious conviction, personal experience, intuition, mystical experience, aesthetic perception, or some
other basis. *Allowing for a variety of paths to the same position is precisely the intent of the Deep Ecology platform.*
(1995, p. 91)

This rational formulation of principles does not take account
of how different cultures have embedded their own understanding of ecological principles in their meta-narratives. It
reflects instead the liberal assumption about the universal
efficacy of abstract rational thought.

Other environmental writers have advocated futurist
thinking (that is, a highly experimental orientation toward
cultural engineering), fostering the ability to "break away
from old patterns of thinking," a subjectivist approach to experiencing the landscape, and social decision-making based
on "communicatively rationalized political debate." Indeed,
the greening of liberal assumptions has created a more ecologically attuned vocabulary that nearly obscures the legitimating role these assumptions played in the creation of an
industrial, and now information based, society. But if the
reader examines closely the conceptual/moral framework
currently being reworked to account for environmental concerns, it is still possible to recognize the essential elements
of liberal ideology: the efficacy of rational thought, the view
of the individual as the basic social unit (now embedded in
information and energy webs), the progressive nature of
new ideas and values, the rejection of forms of authority
grounded in tradition and cultural norms, and so forth.
However, the average reader who shares these basic liberal
assumptions (even readers who reject today's extreme com-
mercialized and nihilistic expression of these assumptions)
is not likely to be aware of the presence of these assumptions in the writings of environmentalists—nor, by extension, in the writings of educators.

Another way to assess the explanatory power of these
generalizations about the liberal ideology that are taken for
granted within both the environmental movement and the
educational community is to consider how the members of
both groups react to the suggestion that, in terms of a guid-

ing ideology, some form of cultural conservatism may be better suited to addressing the complex challenges of living within ecological limits. That is, how many environmentalists and educators would be comfortable with the idea that the survival of the world's cultures within the context of viable ecosystems will require evolving a set of guiding ideological assumptions that are oriented toward conserving ecologically sustainable cultural practices and beliefs? And how many would be comfortable with the further suggestion that the educated elite of American society can learn from the ecologically centered conservatism of other cultures, and from the cultural conservatism of many ethnic groups in American society? Another test that often leads environmentalists and educators to make explicit their liberal assumptions is to suggest that one of the problems we face is an inability to accumulate and transgenerationally communicate ecologically sustainable beliefs, values, technologies, and ceremonial practices.

The argument that some form of conservative ideology may be more appropriate to evolving an ecologically sustainable form of culture presents another kind of challenge to the taken-for-granted assumptions of liberal thinkers. For example, the accumulation and transgenerational communication of ecological wisdom will require that the elderly in our society learn to take on a radically different set of responsibilities in order to play their part as elders. Today's youth will also have to learn how to participate in the process of transgenerational communication if they are to contribute to the process of ecological/cultural renewal, and later to assume the responsibility of elders. I will conclude this overview of how the shared ideological orientation contributes to environmentalists' laissez-faire attitude toward high-status forms of knowledge and the nihilistic values being reinforced in the classroom with a quote from Dave Foreman that recognizes, in a limited way, the nature of the ideological double bind sketched in the last paragraphs. In his book, *Confessions of an Eco-Warrior*, he acknowledges that "it may well be debated whether allying environmentalism with liberalism in general was a positive change. But that is a topic deserving analysis on its own. I am teasing a different rattlesnake here" (1991, p. 197). His analogy of how many environmentalists would react to the connection with conservatism is an apt one that we shall return to in later chapters.

Overview of the Many Dimensions of An Educational Strategy

My suggestion that environmentalists should give attention to the double binds that their own liberal and modernist patterns of thought put them in may sound like another expression of wishful thinking about the power of the printed word. But as the globalization of modern cultural practices (including the use of chemicals and other Western technologies, more widespread centering of daily life on consumerism, etc.) further impact the environment, it will become increasingly obvious that environmentally degrading cultural beliefs and practices themselves will have to be addressed. The subsequent chapters represent an attempt to focus attention on the need to reform the symbolic foundations of modern culture, and thus on what is being learned in public schools and universities, before existing environmental challenges become catastrophic in nature. The differences that characterize the various groups that make up the environmental movement, and the difficulty of reconstituting the deep cultural assumptions that are in conflict with the need for immediate technological solutions to environmental problems, may limit the effort to develop strategies for marshalling the political energy necessary for effecting radical educational reform. However, identifying the complexities of the problem is the first step that needs to be taken in initiating a serious discussion about how public schools and universities can play a more central role in helping to reduce the impact of modern culture on the environment.

The following chapters provide an overview of how university departments continue to promote the modern view of the individual as the basic social unit, an anthropocentric way of understanding human/nature relationships, and the assumptions that underlie the quest for new ideas, values, and technologies. The wide conceptual diversity that appears to exist within and between departments continues to be based on these modernist assumptions, which are in radical opposition to the forms of human relationships with nature that ecologically centered cultures have made their primary concern. This overview of the many expressions of high-status knowledge will help clarify the questions that need to be asked by environmentalists, as well as help demystify the specialized language of different disciplines that makes outside criticism difficult. The other chapters will address issues relating to the need to align educational reform with an ecologically centered ideology, to understand how culture is stored and reproduced (often at the unconscious level) through the language processes that frame teaching and learning, to consider the range of strategies that can be used to avoid a tokenism and add-on approach to reforming the curricular foundations of high-status knowledge, and to understand the connections between reforming teacher education and the greening of public schools.

My hope is that this book will help raise the level of awareness within the environmental movement about the danger of ignoring the educational process, as well as lead to the emergence of a new type of environmental activist— one who has a deep understanding of how culture is encoded, stored, and reproduced in the communicative patterns of everyday life, and in the educational process. It is also the intention of this book to bring the characteristics of ecologically sustainable cultures into the discussion of educational reform. Unless environmentalists have a clear understanding both of how the educational process fits into the more complex dynamics of cultural change, and of cultural patterns that are sustainable, they will have no way of knowing how the educational process is undermining their efforts to create a sustainable future.

Chapter 2

UNIVERSITIES AND
THE CULTURE
OF DENIAL

The theme that gives a sense of coherence to the conflicting images presented through the popular media is
that the world is undergoing rapid change. Images of street
violence are nearly balanced with the use of violence as the
centerpiece of family entertainment. The seemingly endless media presentations of human suffering are framed
against images of what beautiful and successful people con-
sume. Downsizing of the work force is juxtaposed against
announcements of the latest technologies that hold out the
promise of even greater empowerment in the fight to control the uncertainties of nature and to enhance productivity. Against the background of increasing human setbacks
and tragedies is the media message that the peoples of the
world are becoming modern in their expectations, consumer habits, and dependence on technologies that are
taken for granted in the West. Occasionally the media will
report on unemployment caused by changes in the environment, the momentary danger of a toxic spill, and political
stand-offs between environmentalists and economic interest groups, but coverage of the disappearance of local
knowledge that has enabled cultural groups in various
parts of the world to live relatively stable and ecologically
sustainable existences is non-existent. Rather, the process
of globalizing the technological infrastructure that will
transform centuries-old cultural traditions into societies of
modern individuals is represented as the inevitable march
of progress. The loss of cultural diversity in approaches to

community self-sufficiency thus becomes framed as irrelevant and a hindrance to attaining the benefits of the modern lifestyle.

Within some of the groups that make up the environmental movement there appears to be an increasing awareness of the connections between the spread of Western technologies and economic policies such as the General Agreement on Tariffs and Trade, the North American Free Trade Agreement, the International Monetary Fund, the loss of local contextual knowledge upon which different cultural groups have built sustainable lives, and the downward trendline in the ability of ecosystems to remain viable. Indeed, the modern prejudice against traditional subsistance-oriented cultures is beginning to be replaced by an awareness that they represent genuine alternatives, and even sources of resistance, to the globalization of the modern consumer lifestyle (Sachs, 1992; Shiva, 1993). The spread of monoculture is thus being viewed as ecologically disruptive as is the spread of mono-agriculture. This awakening to the differences in how cultures have learned to live within the limits of natural systems now needs to be accompanied by a similar awakening to the role that public schools and universities play in promoting the global spread of modern consciousness and the consumer lifestyle.

The worldwide spread of the culture of modernism reflects the growing concentration of power in elite groups who share similar educational backgrounds. These elites control the Western style corporations, banks, and governmental agencies that are transforming cultures in the Middle East, India, Asia, South-East Asia, South America, and Africa. They are generally graduates of leading North American and British universities, or of their own national universities that have adopted Western approaches to science, technology, and business practices. Economic gains made in different parts of the world are often attributed to the fact that the national leaders responsible for modernizing reforms are graduates of prestigious universities such as the University of Chicago or Harvard University.

The power of elite groups in American society is having a similar transformative effect on the sense of community in rural and urban settings, including the loss of ethnic traditions and the introduction of increasingly destructive technologies into the environment. Multinational corporations now electronically "network" the remotest parts of the country into a vast and increasingly international consumer market. Decisions made in corporate headquarters increasingly disrupt the interdependencies of entire communities by downsizing the workforce. And their advertising budgets lead to shaping the most basic sense of an individual's taken-for-granted "reality" to fit the technologically based vision of progress and, in the process, delegitimate traditional beliefs and practices that represented an alternative basis of community life. A similar commoditizing mentality and concentration of power permeates governmental institutions, the medical establishment, and public schools and universities. While there is considerable variation in the economic and political dynamics that characterize how different elites interact and exert control over their respective domains of social life, the common element shared by all elite groups promoting the globalization of modernization is the form of formal education they received. Ironically, the connections (well understood among many environmental groups) between the modern technologically oriented consumer lifestyle, the destabilization of viable communities, and the degradation of ecosystems, have not led to a critical consideration of how the high-status forms of knowledge promoted through public schools and universities are exacerbating the many crises we now face.

Thus, the primary purpose of this chapter is to identify specific examples of forms of knowledge (including modes of inquiry) that are privileged in public schools and universities, and to clarify their connection to the culture of modernism that is having such a devastating impact on the life-sustaining characteristics of ecosystems. A second purpose is to identify the forms of knowledge, many of which are more locally based and attuned to the characteristics of the bioregion, that are being undermined and, in many instances, destroyed in the name of progress. It is hoped that this critical examination of the Janus face of formal educational institutions will lead environmentalists and others concerned with the future of the human/biotic community to address the complex challenge of radically reforming public schools and universities.

The Modernizing Orientation of Universities

Whereas American public schools inculcate students with the more romantic aspects of the ideology of modernism, it is the universities that provide students with the disciplinary perspectives essential to being able to reinterpret and build upon the mythic, symbolic foundations of modern culture. That is, most students graduate from high school with such a limited knowledge base that they are able to do little more than be compliant consumers and to work in low-status jobs. A university education, particularly the higher levels of graduate study, provides students with the symbolic ability necessary for developing new economic and technological expressions of modernity. Increasingly, their knowledge is used to identify niches in the fabric of cultural life that have not yet been brought into the market economy, and to create the products that will meet the needs artificially created by the media. For this reason we shall focus primarily on the forms of knowledge learned in universities, and on how these forms of knowledge serve as the basis of an experimentally oriented culture that ignores the ecological imperative of living in a balanced and interdependent relationship with the environment.

This experimental orientation began, according to Karl Polanyi, with the Industrial Revolution, when labor and land were transformed into commodities that were subject to market forces. The commoditization of knowledge and relationships previously influenced by non-economic values is now being globalized under the slogan of "development" (Sachs, 1992). Genetic material, water, food, entertainment, interpersonal communication, mentoring, and all aspects of a university education (from the packaging of courses into economic units to the integration of the curriculum into current market trends) have now been turned into commodities. What Polanyi referred to as the "Great Transformation" might be better understood today as the "Great Experiment," as the growing dominance of technological and economic activity both undermines the moral foundations of communities and contributes to the growing problem, among others, of recycling toxic wastes through the environment. At what point this cultural experiment, in bringing the world's cultures and natural systems under the control of market principles and expert systems, leads to catastrophic and irreversible consequences is a question that now occupies the attention of an increasing number of people. In identifying the many ways in which high-status knowledge learned in universities reinforces the cultural assumptions that underlie this global experiment, it should be kept in mind that the low-status cultural patterns now being marginalized and subverted are not driven by economic forces or marketed as commodities— but exist as reciprocal networks of community life.

Science as Ideology and Source
of Cultural Experimentation

The privileged and nearly sacrosanct status accorded to the sciences within the university faculties, which can be seen in the tendency of other disciplines to emulate the scientific mode of inquiry that enables them to claim objective status for their findings, suggests the starting point for considering the cultural and educational aspects of the ecological crisis. Ironically, if we were to focus only on the vast body of scientific knowledge accumulated in recent decades by university educated scientists, including what scientists are now helping us understand about changes occurring in different ecosystems, we might be inclined to accept uncritically the statement Carl Sagan made to the guests attending a dinner held at Vice President Gore's Washington, D. C. residence. In defending the value of a conflict model of inquiry, which he saw as essential to the continued advancement of science, Sagan reminded the guests that "science provides the most adequate basis for understanding that humans possess." Indeed, the list of scientific achievements might even lead to viewing it as one of the few positive characteristics of modernity—and thus as existing in a special category where criticism is seen either as an expression of ignorance or as motivated by a romantic desire to return to the past. But the many scientific achievements, including those that have improved the quality of human life, should not be used as an excuse for continuing to ignore how our cultural uses of science have strengthened the most eco-logically destructive tendencies of modern culture—and by extension are helping to transform the world's cultural di-versity into a Western style monoculture of consumer mar-kets and interlocking technologies.

Universities are the primary sites for educating scien-tists, as well as for supporting basic scientific research. Thus, concerns about the influence that science has had on the direction that modern culture is taking should also lead to raising questions about the narrowness of graduate edu-cation in the various sciences, and about the source of the hubris of the scientific community that has resulted in the lack of self reflection about their role as agents of cultural change. The following concerns, I will argue, have a direct connection with the modern addiction to change, to the use of consumerism as a substitute for meaningful communal and environmental relationships, and to the spread of nihilism.

Science as a Form of Cultural Experimentation. The view of science as an experimental mode of inquiry that uni-versity students acquire under the guidance of mentors is astonishingly limited when one considers the larger cul-tural context. As the funding of scientific research is in-creasingly tied to the development of technologies that can be utilized for commercial, military, and humanitarian pur-poses, the distance between basic research and cultural ap-plications has largely disappeared. Even in the early days of science the technological applications of new discoveries re-sulted in profound alterations in the basic fabric of cultural life. The research that led to the development of the inter-nal combustion engine changed cultural patterns in irre-versible ways—and profoundly influenced the path of modern development. The more recent results of scientific research that led to the development of television, comput-ers, and bio-technology are further evidence that the exper-

imental orientation of science cannot be restricted to the research lab. Jerry Mander's *Four Arguments for the Elimination of Television* (1978) identifies the many ways this
technology has altered what and how humans learn, their
patterns of family interaction, and the ability of elites to
manipulate mass audiences. Similarly, we are just beginning to recognize some of the unanticipated consequences of
the biotechnology revolution that are now introducing radical changes into the culture, including how life itself is
being understood, and who has the right to define what constitutes "normal" life. Indeed, a basic characteristic of Western science is that it is part of an endogenous cultural
process that introduces radical and highly experimental
changes into other areas of cultural life that seemingly are
far removed from the focus of the original research. As the
introduction of the Green Revolution in Third World countries and the worldwide adoption of computer-based technologies demonstrate, what are hailed as the achievements
of science also set in motion exogenous changes (experiments) in other cultures. And where the scientific practice
of commoditizing the genetic basis of life forms, including
the patenting of genetic material by scientific-corporate
elites, takes us is anybody's guess. But the current direction
of this form of experimenting with the foundations of cultural life suggests that it will lead to economic benefits for a
small segment of society, and misery for vast numbers of
people who will be put in the new scientifically determined
caste system that will separate the genetically defective and
thus unemployable from the rest of society.

     In spite of the fact that scientists are educated to view
themselves as the chief guardians of rationally based experimental knowledge, they have failed to recognize that
the influence of their experiments does not stop at the
door of their research facility. This myopia, in effect, is reflected in the scientific community's failure to recognize
that the ripple effect of scientific discoveries on the quality
of cultural life, and on how the cultural uses of the technology affect the viability of natural systems, should also
be part of the inquiry process. A few scientists are beginning to express doubts in public about whether specific

areas of scientific research should be continued, but the dominant ethos is that the scientist is responsible only for discovering new knowledge, and not for its cultural use. If scientists were to extend the ecological paradigm now used to investigate the characteristics of natural systems to include an understanding of changes their form of knowledge brings about in different cultures, they might understand their responsibilities in an entirely different way. That is, if they can overcome their cultural habit of framing scientific inquiry as inherently progressive in nature. The following statement by Francis Crick, who along with James Watson, was a co-recipient of the Nobel Prize, for the discovery of the molecular structure of DNA, is characteristic of nearly the entire scientific community. In explaining how brain research is influencing developments in the architecture of parallel processing computers, Crick articulates the scientist's attitude toward experimentalism as the foundation of further progressive cultural developments. His statement also deepens my concern about the scientist's cultural tendency to use the myth of progress as an excuse for not recognizing their responsibility for the disruptive and often disastrous cultural changes that result from their discoveries.

> Thanks to all these new concepts one can now at least glimpse the possibility that some day it will be possible to model the brain in a biologically realistic way, as opposed to producing biologically implausible models that only capture somewhat limited aspects of brain behavior. Even now these new ideas have sharpened our approach to experimentation. (1994, p. 199)

While Crick's reference raises the question of whether it makes any sense to represent the brain (including the form of intelligent and moral behavior) as a culture-free entity (or thinking as a culture-free process), a more critical concern here has to do with how equating experimentation with progress makes it appear unnecessary to consider the nature of the changes that scientifically based experimentation introduces into the culture. The form of science education that contributes to this combination of myopia and uncritical acceptance of the cultural myth as the basis for legitimating the pursuit of scientific knowledge should be a deep concern of many groups—including environmentalists.

Science Undermines the Meta-Narratives
that are the Basis of Moral Authority.

A number of observers, including a few well-known scientists, have claimed that the ecological crisis is partly attributable to the unrecognized crisis in moral and spirtual values. A public statement signed by Stephen Jay Gould, Hans Bethe, Stephen Schneider, Carl Sagan, and Peter Raven, among others, and issued at a recent international conference on the environment and economics, contained the following passage:

> As scientists, many of us have had profound personal experiences of awe and reverence before the universe. We understand that what is regarded as sacred is more likely to be treated with care and respect. Our planetary home should be so regarded. Efforts to safeguard and cherish the environment need to be infused with a vision of the sacred. (Suzuki and Knudtson, 1992, p. 227)

While not a scientist, Wendell Berry identifies the moral and spiritual roots of the ecological crisis with even greater clarity. In referring to the misuse of energy, which is only one of the more obvious dimensions of the crisis, he observes that:

> . . . the basic cause of the energy crisis is not scarcity; it is moral ignorance and weakness of character. We don't know how to use energy, or what to use it for. And we cannot restrain ourselves. . . . If we had an unlimited supply of solar or wind power, we would use it destructively, too, for the same reasons. (1986, p. 13)

With the exception of the Western approach to moral judgments, which is understood either as the rational or emotive judgment of supposedly autonomous individuals, the moral knowledge of cultural groups traditionally has been transmitted from generation to generation through their narrative traditions that explain fundamental human-with-human, and human-with-nature relationships. These narratives generally have been rooted in mythopoetic accounts of creation, human destiny, and the consequences that result from moral transgressions. The understanding of the moral and spiritual nature of relationships varies widely from culture to culture, and admittedly not all traditional cultures have been ecologically centered; still, the moral and spiritual frameworks that dictate what constitutes appropriate attitudes, behaviors, and communal ceremonies are often finely articulated to the ecological characteristics of the bioregion that is the cultural group's source of existence. Whether we take the example of what remains of the mythopoetic account of Distant Time of the Koyukon of interior Alaska, the ancient Creation Time of the Murngin who still dwell in Arnhem Land (Australia), or the Hopi account of successive creations and human failure, the basis of their shared moral and spiritual sense of order has not been based on the symbolically restrictive form of intelligence given legitimacy by Western scientists. Nor are the increasingly fragile moral frameworks that guide human-with-human and human-with-nature relationships within Western cultures based on the empirical, experimental way of knowing that science demands.

Public schools and university-level science classes indoctrinate future scientists to accept the radical separation between the domain of empirical observation and the domain of moral judgment. Thus, scientists readily acknowledge that their approach to knowledge cannot be applied to settling moral questions. While the fact/value distinction continues to exist as a minor myth within the scientific community, the influence of science continues to be extended beyond the classroom and laboratory in ways that undermine and de-authorize different cultural groups' basis of moral authority. It is this modernizing process of accepting scientific explanations of life processes that led Carolyn Tawangyowma, a spokesperson for the Sovereign Hopi Independent Nation, to observe that "the moral values we once followed have now become make-believe living, like playthings we use" (from press release reprinted in Moody, 1988, pp. 189–190). The continuing effort to provide a scientific explanation for more and more aspects of life represents a form of reductionism in ways of understanding and experiencing. The loss of a sense of the sacred is often the first expression of the moral attrition that results when Western science gains a dominant standing within a culture. In effect, the incessant search for a scientific understanding of all aspects of life—which often leads to developing technologies for manipulating all aspects of life—contributes to the spread of nihilism wherein everything becomes morally relative. The spread of nihilism is furthered when aspects of human experience, especially ways of knowing that become culturally elaborated over time into coherent taken-for-granted moral frameworks that cannot be explained scientifically, are dismissed as expressions of superstition, folk knowledge, and prescientific thinking. The delegitimation of traditional explanatory and moral frameworks, which vary from culture to culture, also weakens the resistance to the modern myth that increasingly utilizes sophisticated advances in science and technology as the moral basis for legitimating the commoditization of all aspects of individual and community life.

Crick's confidence in the progressive mission of science highlights the double bind where a reductionist way of thinking results in both marginalizing and delegitimating cultural ways of understanding human/nature relationships as moral, even spiritual in nature. According to Crick:

> The aim of science is to explain *all* aspects of the behavior of our brains, including those of musicians, mystics, and mathematicians. I do not contend that this will happen quickly. I do believe that, if we press the attack, this understanding is likely to be reached some day, perhaps some time during the twenty-first century. The sooner we start, the sooner we shall be led to a clear understanding of our true nature. . . .We can hope to understand more precisely the mechanisms of such mental activities as intuition, creativity, and aesthetic pleasure, and in doing so grasp them

more clearly and, it is hoped enjoy them more. (1994, pp. 259, 261)

The scientific efforts to explain the "mind as full of elaborate machinery, actively and vigorously constructing concepts (Marler, 1994, p. 72), as the "interaction of nerve cells . . . and molecules associated with them (Crick, 1994, p. 7), or the result of the particular individual sequencing of genetic code, represent the seemingly endless reductionist process that serves to buttress the elite groups who depend upon the spread of nihilism to promote the economic agenda of modernization. The scientist's way of understanding how things "work"—that is, the cause or reason that a person thinks in a certain way, has a criminal record, or experiences what in prescientific terms was called love and moral responsibility—undermines the traditional ways of understanding that enabled people to live in relatively coherent and stable communities. Increasingly, the traditional scientific claim that separated the domain of empirically based inquiry from the domain of values is now disappearing as scientists attempt to account for the latter in terms of individual genetic and species history. But how do we recover the moral frameworks of cultural groups who over centuries worked out complex understandings of the interdependency of natural phenomena and spiritual practices after these moral frameworks have been dismissed as pre-scientific and thus based on ignorance? And how do modern cultures evolve taken-for-granted moral codes that limit individual freedom in relationship to the natural world for the sake of preserving for future generations a viable ecological community? How do we derive a coherent moral human/biotic community from an understanding of the electrochemical impulses that govern the behavior of neurons?

The power of scientific explanations, and of the resulting technologies that are being more widely adopted because of the loss of the authority of shared moral frameworks, have another consequence beyond that of undermining the mythopoetic foundations of a culture's moral code. The scientific method, in marginalizing the significance of a culture's symbolic systems that are the source of meaning and value that guide behavior, reinforces the modern view of the individual as the basic social unit. And the explanation now coming from scientists is that individuals are not really morally responsible beings; rather, consciousness (and thus moral choices) is now being explained as a by-product of the simultaneous firing of neurons in different parts of the brain.

For environmentalists who take seriously Berry's observation that human abuse of natural systems reflects moral ignorance, and who recognize that moral codes attuned to the characteristics of specific bioregions are not created by purely autonomous and experimentally oriented individuals, the increasing dominance of scientific knowledge in shaping the direction of the modernizing process should be a matter of critical concern. The daunting challenge facing the environmental movement is to pressure for the reform of science education in ways that help future scientists recognize that addressing the problem of moral ignorance of relationships, particularly human/nature relationships, may be more important and complex than understanding the chemistry that will enable them to engineer new forms of life. But the starting point is in recognizing the ways in which the reductionist orientation of science undermines the cultural beliefs that are the basis of moral behavior.

Consequences of Marginalizing the Importance of Culture. One of the great ironies, as well as source of the tragedies now being played out in the spread of Western modernism, is that science education ignores that all expressions of human thought and behavior are influenced by the culture's symbolic systems. Scientists themselves think and communicate in culturally specific languages that encode and reproduce the epistemic orientation of their cultural group. As previously pointed out, unless their research findings are locked away in a desk drawer, scientists' discoveries lead eventually to the development of technologies that often result in profound changes in their culture—and often even more cataclysmic changes in other cultures. With the exception of anthropologists and cultural linguists who claim to take a scientific approach to the study of other cultures (but who can never escape introducing their own cultural episteme into their descriptions and interpretations), scientists graduate from the most prestigious educational institutions without being expected to have any deeper understanding of culture than the average person on the street. The result is that scientists, while often able to make insightful observations about current cultural trends (just as other intelligent people do), are unable to recognize how their own activities and justifications are shaped by their own culture. And their understanding of other cultures too often reflects not only the general ignorance shared by the rest of an ethnocentric society, but an open hostility toward what is seen as primitive and inferior ways of thinking.

That scientists can never escape entirely from the influence of their own culture can be seen in the language they use to explain natural phenomena, and in the justifications they give for the importance of their work. The widespread use of mechanistic metaphors to explain life processes (an epistemic pattern that goes back to Johannes Kepler [1571–1630] and other founders of modern science), and the habit of continually framing discoveries within the modern sense of temporality that represents change as the manifestation of a linear form of progress, are just two of the many expressions of the scientists' unrecognized cultural orientation. Carl Sagan's comment at a recent public presentation at the University of Oregon is typical. In responding to a question relating to the environment, Sagan told the audience that "we should do the widest range of social experiments to see what works." He did not suggest that we should begin to listen to the wisdom of our elders, or that we should renew what remains of family and community traditions that do not have an adverse impact on the environment. A statement by Roger Sperry, a Nobel Prize-winning brain biologist, reflects both a lack of understanding of his own cultural assumptions and of the cultural and religious traditions he thinks modern science can help to reconstitute. As Sperry put it: "The task can be likened in some respects to that of trying to deduce what form of religion the teachings of Christ, Mohammed, Buddha, Confucius, and other founders might have taken if Copernicus, Darwin, Einstein, and all the rest had come before their time instead of after" (1985, p. 28).

Another example of the special combination of the scientist's hubris and ignorance of culture is expressed in the following observation of Crick, which he made after claiming that spear wounds are the leading cause of death among tribes living in the remote parts of Ecuador:

> The ability (to use language) leads to another strikingly human characteristic, one that is seldom mentioned: our almost limitless capacity for self-deception. The very nature of our brains—evolved to guess the most plausible interpretations of the limited evidence available—makes it almost inevitable that, *without the discipline of scientific research*, we shall often jump to wrong conclusions, especially about rather abstract matters. (italics added, 1994, p. 262)

He might have informed his readers about the extensive tribal knowledge of the medicinal properties of local plants, which scientists are beginning to study (partly for economic reasons and partly to overcome the dead end of medical research in certain areas). He also might have referred to the elaborate tribal knowledge of edible plants. Instead, Crick represents tribal people as so primitively developed that their most notable characteristic is that they go around spearing their enemies. When this level of cultural understanding is characteristic of an elite group who now exert a profound influence on the global process of modernization, we face especially bleak consequences.

The two most important consequences are the distortions in the public's understanding of the nature of the ecological crisis, and the role that science plays in the loss of local knowledge of how to live in relatively stable and self-sufficient communities. The recent statement presented to the General Assembly of the United Nations by the Union of Concerned Scientists (which was signed by 1600 scientists from seventy countries, including over one hundred recipients of the Nobel Prize) is a prime example of how the scientists' lack of understanding of culture led them to present a highly distorted way of understanding the scope of the ecological crisis. Their warning to humanity, which included the prediction that we may have as little as forty years to

correct current trends of environmental abuse, was based
on an overview of the deteriorating condition of a number of
natural systems. The diverse cultural beliefs and practices
that have contributed to moral ignorance in how humans
interact with natural systems was not even mentioned.

By framing the ecological crisis in terms of what scientists understand, the solutions are also framed in an overly
narrow and technologically biased way. For example, the
special issue of *Scientific American* on "Managing Planet
Earth" (September 1989) presented what were then the
latest scientific findings on changes occurring in the atmosphere, climate, availability of fresh water, human population, and agricultural practices. But the critically important
role that different cultural belief systems play in contributing to the alarming scale and rate of changes in the environment was not mentioned; nor were there references to
cultures that have developed complex symbolic systems in
order to minimize human impact on local environments.
While readers should have been told that the modern capitalistic, scientifically based cultures were contributing dis-
proportionately to the problem, when it was necessary to
indicate that environmental changes were a result of human
activity the scientists chose such ambiguously neutral terms
as "people," "world's population," "institutions," "society,"
"governments," and so forth. The increasingly dominant role
scientists play in shaping the public's understanding of the
ecological crisis makes the scientists' lack of understanding
of culture an especially critical issue. It also distorts the public's understanding of the connections between the myths
underlying modern culture, the continued exploitation of the
environment, and the role that public schools and universities play in perpetuating the high-status forms of knowledge
based on these ecologically problematic myths.

The second major consequence of the scientists' lack of
understanding of the complexity of culture is that the symbiotic relationship between scientific discoveries and the dependency of modern cultures on a steady stream of new
technologies (essential to creating new markets) contributes
to the loss of local knowledge. Unlike the experimental and
progressive orientation that underlies modern scientific
knowledge, local knowledge is built up over generations of

careful observation and communal refinement of technological practices within the context of a bioregion that the
inhabitants are absolutely dependent upon. Not all traditional cultures have been equally successful in developing
moral codes and technologies that meet the test of long-
term sustainability. But the forms of local knowledge that
have been proven essential to cultural/bio-system sustainability outside the globalized orbit of modern technogically
oriented consumer culture are disappearing at an increasing rate. The following observation by Vandana Shiva clarifies how modern science contributes to the loss of local
knowledge, and how this loss is related to the deepening
crisis:

> The disappearance of local knowledge through its interac-
> tion with the dominant western knowledge takes place at
> many levels, through many steps. First local knowledge is
> made to disappear by simply not seeing it, by negating its
> very existence. This is very easy in the distant gaze of the
> globalising dominant system. The western systems of
> knowledge have generally been viewed as universal. How-
> ever, the dominant system is also a local system, with its
> social basis in a particular culture, class, and gender. It is
> not universal in an epistemological sense. It is merely the
> globalised version of a very local and parochial tradition.
> Emerging from a dominating and colonising culture, mod-
> ern knowledge systems are themselves colonising. (1993,
> p. 9)

The denigration of local knowledge is only recently being
recognized as a problem by a small segment of the scientific
community. For the most part, the scientists' cultural tradition of explaining change as an evolutionary process leads
to their judging cultures in terms of their progress in developing scientific and technological knowledge. This residual
Social Dawinism prevents them from recognizing that cultures have taken different developmental pathways, and
should not be judged against the criteria used by Western
elites for measuring progress.

    If scientists understood their own cultural history of
globalizing traditions of thought that were originally local
to the West, and if they understood the multi-layered na-

ture of the symbolic worlds of other cultures that have led to different ways of understanding the natural world (and to making discoveries that have eluded Western scientists), perhaps then they would be able to represent more accurately the limits of scientific knowledge. It would also help them clarify when the introduction of scientifically based technologies into cultures that are relatively self-sustaining is a constructive or destructive force. But broadening the scientist's education to include an in-depth understanding of culture will not be successful if their study is limited to encounters with professors who teach the Western achievements and thinkers within a generally unrecognized Social Darwinist framework that represents the West as the most evolved form of culture. We shall return to this problem when discussing how the humanities contribute to the globalization of modern consumer culture.

The issues identified in this brief discussion of science point to a fundamental problem that environmentalists need to give serious thought: namely, that the Janus nature of science is not likely to be recognized by scientists. As the culture/science connection presently is little understood within the scientific community, it will be necessary for outside groups to articulate what is missing in the education of the next generation of scientists. Furthermore, as the world-modernizing project that is putting the environment at increasing risk is dependent upon new scientific discoveries, it becomes even more imperative for environmentalists to take on the challenge of helping to reform the foundations of science education. And the first step will be to expose its many deep cultural biases, and to explain how these biases contribute to the modern form of culture now being globalized in the form of a technologically based consumer lifestyle.

"Let Them Eat Data": the Globalization
of the Information Age

The statement attributed to Marie Antoinette that conveyed contempt for an earlier revolution in political relationships now heralds, with minor modification, the future basis of human relationships around the world. Cultural changes precipitated by computer-based technologies, even if they fall far short of what some computer visionaries are promising, will make the French Revolution look like a rather bloody and rambunctious local affair. "Information superhighways," "virtual libraries," "hypertexts," "cyberspace," "ubiquitous computing," and "global electronic classrooms," are just a few of the context-free metaphors that computers have introduced into our vocabulary. But how the computer revolution will change the cultures of the world, particularly regarding their ability to reduce their adverse impact on local ecosystems, is not understood. Instead, university-educated interpreters and prophets of the Information Age are nearly unanimous in representing computer technologies as a quantum leap in human progress.

The few critics who have come forward, such as Theodore Roszak and Joseph Weizenbaum, have been nearly drowned out by the range and volume of positive claims about how computers will improve every aspect of daily life. For example, the CEO of a major software company promises that the "information highway will democratize information;" and the director of the Xerox Palo Alto Research Center's computer science laboratory predicts that "computers will be as available as electricity—wherever you are, a little gadget in your pocket can plug you into the global digital flow" (quoted in Wolkomir, 1994, p. 82). The following excerpt from an interview that appeared in *The Chronicle of Higher Education* typifies the way computers are being viewed by people ranging from university presidents to artists. According to Richard A. Lanham, a professor of humanities at UCLA, "in this new society clearly the humanities are going to be essential, because their business is creating new attention structures. *No one knows what they are going to be yet*, but somebody is going to *discover* a way to let people manage information in the new world, much as printed books do today" (italics added, Wilson, 1994, p. A22).

Lanham's lack of caution about endorsing the most fundamental changes in the basis of cultural life without knowing either their human or environmental consequences is echoed in the questions raised by an academic committee established jointly by Stanford University, Carnegie Mellon University, the Massachusetts Institute of Technology, and several other equally prestigious universities for the purpose of considering the educational and political implications of computers for higher education. In an article titled "The Coming Revolution" that appeared in The *Chronicle of Higher Education*, it was reported that the committee was concerned with the following questions: "How . . . will colleges respond when other institutions start offering electronic classes to their students? Are campuses necessary? How many faculty members will be needed? Will large lectures survive? Who will pay for the technology?" (Jacobson, 1994, p. A28).

The administrative concerns expressed in these questions indicate that the committee members had already accepted the assumption that computers represented the next step in the evolution in human learning. Public statements by artists, museum directors, bankers, doctors, business spokespersons, and leaders from every other major sector of society echo the dominant sentiment that computers will transform life as we know it. While we don't understand what cultural norms and practices will be lost, we are nevertheless being urged to join the ranks of the revolutionary technocrats who are sweeping away the old order. The irony is that in a world that is supposedly becoming more organized through the rational use of data, the mythic dimensions of modern culture appear to be even more deeply ingrained in the thinking of the educated elites.

The computer scientists, software developers, and most users of computers received the professional basis of their education in universities. Their inability to recognize the cultural implications of the computer revolution they are helping to further, as well as the lack of a critical perspective in the public discourse surrounding the expanding use of computers, again points to the pivotal role universities play in failing to provide the conceptual frameworks necessary for communicative competence in addressing the most fundamental changes now taking place on a global scale. The Western myth of progress, which is learned through the media and in the public schools, continues to mesmerize academics in the disciplines most connected to the development and application of computer based technologies, with the result that questions about how their understanding of intelligence can be reconciled with the characteristics of an ecologically sustainable culture are not addressed. And in overlooking this question in terms of their own professional writing and research, they are unable to help students frame the questions essential to freeing them from basing their own lives on a myth that is increasingly becoming disconnected from ecological realities.

As a way of emphasizing two key points—that universities play a central role in providing the high status knowledge that enables elite groups to develop and promote the globalization of computer based technologies, and that universities should not be ignored by environmentalists just because they also offer a few environmental courses—I will identify a number of the cultural amplification characteristics of this revolutionary and supposedly progressive technology. Each amplification characteristic deserves more extended treatment if we are to grasp the full implications of these cultural changes in how people understand their relationship to the environment. However, this overview of eight fundamental changes in forms of cultural knowledge, communication patterns, and moral relationships will help clarify how computer-based modernization represents the new commoditized form of Western colonization—one that is even less sensitive to the actual experiences of people whose traditional patterns (including sources of livelihood) are undermined by the electronic integration of world markets, flow of capital, and consumer trends.

The popular image of a technology that facilitates the individual's ability to solve difficult problems more efficiently, communicate instantaneously over long distances, and "navigate" through the increasingly vast sea of stored data, is partly correct. Computers enable us to simulate what is occurring in natural systems, to design solutions to complex problems, communicate globally with people who share similar interests, and to store and access phenomenal amounts of data. However, hidden behind these many important uses, and behind the rhetoric that celebrates each technological advance as elevating humankind to an even higher level, is the fundamental fact that the technology is not culturally neutral. In mediating how the individual participates in the complex symbolic ecology we call culture, the computer amplifies certain cultural (including ideological and epistemological) orientations and patterns while undermining others. That is, just as a stick amplifies a person's ability to reach the fruit high in the tree's branches while reducing the ability to feel, taste and smell the fruit, the computer selects for amplification certain forms of cultural knowledge and communication. When the computer is used in a non-Western setting, it undermines traditional forms of moral authority by reinforcing the Western way of representing the individual as the morally responsible agent, just as it represents the individual as constructing knowledge on the basis of data. In effect, computers select for amplification the cultural orientations of the people who created the technology, while reducing (marginalizing and undermining) the forms of culture that cannot be accommodated by this Cartesian machine. The following list of cultural amplification and reduction characteristics needs to be considered not only in terms of how computer-based technologies are altering human relationships (and thus their sense of community— as Berry understands the term), but also individual and cultural relationships with the environment.

1) Computer-based technologies amplify forms of cultural knowledge that can be made explicit, digitalized, and communicated as context-free data and images. They reduce (leave out of the computer-mediated communication/storage/thought process) forms of cultural knowledge that are tacit, contextual, and kept alive as personal memory. These forms of knowledge are usually passed on as part of the narratives that are the basis of a community of memory. These are also the forms of knowledge learned in mentor relationships.

2) Computer-based technologies amplify the Western cultural orientation (learned primarily in public schools and universities) that represents thinking as based on data. These technologies reduce the possibility of recognizing that "thinking" is deeply influenced by the cultural epis-

teme encoded in the metaphorical languages of the cultural group. It also helps to obscure the role language plays in the process of cultural domination, and in the loss of cultural diversity.

3) Computer-based technologies amplify the Western cultural orientation that represents the individual as the basic social unit. That is, it fosters the view of the individual as an autonomous rational agent who is empowered by being able to access and manipulate data. These technologies reduce (portray as irrelevant) the tradition of transgenerational communication. Elders are replaced by the storage capacity of the CD-ROM and Hypertext, and by the promise that individuals will be able to navigate through the data and images in ways that allow them to construct their own stories.

4) Computer-based technologies amplify the Western cultural view of temporality that frames the individual's experience of time in terms of what is seen as relevant to the immediate problem or personal sense of meaning. These technologies undermine the experience of time that encompasses the distant past and future as integral dimensions of the present. By undermining the authority of living traditions and the moral claims of future generations, these technologies strengthen a highly experimental form of culture that is guided by an increasingly short-term perspective. Furthermore, as the human sense of time is reduced to fit the ever shorter time frames of computer technology, there is an even greater separation of human experience from the time cycles that characterize the different forms of life found in ecosystems.

5) Computer-based technologies amplify a conduit view of language which is essential to the self-universalizing characteristics of modern consciousness. That is, the conduit view of language, like the metaphor of an "information superhighway," creates the illusion that what is being communicated between computers is culturally neutral (i.e., objective, context-free data). These technologies reduce (distort) the awareness that the language/thought connection is inherently metaphorical in nature, and that the metaphorical constructions of "reality" are framed by the root metaphors of the cultural group. Many ecologically centered cultures are based on root metaphors (mytho-

poetic narratives) that explain the interdependency of life forms and the consequences that result when these interdependent relationships are not respected.

6) Computer-based technologies amplify a print form of consciousness. While voice communication is becoming an increasingly important part of technologically mediated communication, the essential characteristics of print based consciousness are still being reinforced: communication where the spoken or printed word is separated from contextual and communal sources of meaning; printed texts that require "individual" analysis and action; communication with members of an abstract public that share similar interests (the new community of abstract interests that reaches over vast distances); and a decontextualized pattern of thinking that is increasingly insensitive to local contexts, cultural patterns, and ecosystems. The cultural mediation process reduces the experience of participatory communal relationships where context, memory, and mutual responsibility for renewing relationships are carried on through face-to-face communication.

7) Computer based technologies amplify the use of language that encodes a human-centered and instrumental way of understanding moral relationships toward others, and toward the environment. As I point out in a recent book (1995, pp. 23–40), language is used to communicate about relationships, and it encodes the language community's way of understanding the moral nature of these relationships. For example, genderized language based on a patriarchal root metaphor both framed how differences between men and women were to be understood and what constituted morally appropriate ways of relating to each other in different social settings. Similarly, computer-mediated languages that represent what is, in fact, a cultural way of understanding in terms of objective facts and data reinforce the Western cultural way of viewing the individual as an objective and autonomous problem-solver. Lost in computer-mediated communication processes are the metaphorically constructed languages of cultural groups that represent humans as interdependent and thus as morally responsible for not acting in selfish and individually centered ways. Many cultures have developed the complex lan-

guages of music, dance, and narrative as ways of storing and renewing the group's understanding of relationships and celebrating the life-enhancing patterns that have evolved over generations of collective experience. These morally and ecologically centered languages are being undermined as the instrumental, scientific (and supposedly "objective") problem-solving language that computers are designed to accommodate become more globalized.

8) Computer-based technologies amplify the Western cultural tradition of understanding life forms in mechanistic terms—indeed, they are renewing this tradition by becoming the new machine metaphor. References to the body in terms of pumps, circulation systems, fluids, and parts are being replaced by neural networks, genetic determinants, genetic engineering, biotechnology, and so forth. Indeed, one of the goals of computer scientists is to create a machine that will represent the next stage in human evolution; that is, a machine that surpasses humans as thinking beings. The literature of computer visionaries never refers to humans as moral or cultural beings. In addition to Moravec's book (quoted earlier), *The Anthropic Cosmological Principle* by John Barrow and Frank Tipler (1988) and *Metaman: The Merging of Human and Machine Consciousness* by Gregory Stock (1993) are representative of how computers are now being viewed as the next stage in the evolutionary process. What is being undermined by this technology, and by the scientists who are attempting to make this technology the basis of a new cosmology, is an organic, ecological understanding of life—a way of understanding that is not well developed in Western cultures. The wisdom in the more complex ways of understanding human/nature relationships that are based on the mythopoetic narratives of traditional cultural groups is even more likely to go unrecognized as the new mechanistic, biologically deterministic way of thinking gains more prominence through the spread of modernization.

Just as the scientific community has been unable to recognize that its own educational base is too narrow for understanding how their cultural epistemology and legitimating ideology subvert the symbolic foundations of other

cultural groups, the experts developing computer technology are caught in a similar double bind of not possessing a
deep understanding of culture—their own as well as other
cultural ways of knowing. The result of this double bind is
that they remain unaware of the distinctive cultural mediating characteristics of the computer technology they are
developing. That is, they are so deeply embedded in the
Western tradition that takes for granted the conduit view
of language, the culturally autonomous and individually
centered view of the rational process, and the radical reduction of knowledge to data, that they are unable to recognize
the limited and culturally disruptive nature of computer-
mediated knowledge. Unfortunately, as academics from
non-technological fields become increasingly involved in
the special interest groups on the Internet (there are now
over two thousand interest groups, ranging from eco-theol-
ogy to Greek archaeology), there is less likelihood that a
more cautious and reflective attitude will emerge about the
increasingly widespread use of computers in the educational process. The ability to communicate with other
scholars around the world about mutual research interests
fosters a sense of participating in an intellectual community that is often lacking at the departmental level where
the history of political strife can make substantive conversation difficult. E-mail also allows for scholarly communication without the inhibiting effects of status differences
and is fast becoming an alternative medium within which
a scholar can establish a reputation. The perceived benefits, which largely remove the limitations of time and space
that made previous forms of communication both slow and
laborious, are leading otherwise non-technically oriented
academics to embrace computers as a necessity of their
profession. Indeed, there are few academic offices that are
not equipped with a computer. Unfortunately, as the academic community increasingly becomes "connected" they experience, from their relatively well-paid vantage point,
only the positive aspects of the globalization of the modern
mind-set. And the growing dependency of being "on-line"
makes it increasingly difficult for them to be serious critics
of computer-mediated communication.

Humanities and Social Sciences:
Anthropocentrism, Fads, and Nihilism

Although departments in the humanities and social sciences offer an occasional course that introduces an environmental perspective into the discipline, these departments are in special need of radical reform. Professors who teach courses with an environmental focus are generally viewed by their colleagues as working on the periphery of the discipline, and are tolerated only as a ritualistic means of maintaining the appearance of addressing current social concerns—a tolerance that parallels the incorporation into existing courses of a few feminist and ethnic authors. The traditionalists within the disciplines (e.g., literature, philosophy, sociology, history, etc.) continue to renew the disciplines by allowing competing interpretative frameworks to serve as the basis of overturning the authority of previous scholarship. If a course addresses environmental issues, its educational significance is undermined when it is perceived as just another interpretation competing for attention. What environmentalists need to understand is that the internecine strife over research methodology, interpretive frameworks, and relevance of past scholarship does not lead to questioning the deeper anthropocentrically based assumptions shared by the warring factions within the department. Just as Marxism and capitalism appear to be poles apart in the areas of social values and forms of political organization and yet share an even deeper set of cultural attitudes regarding an anthropocentric universe and the progressive nature of science and technology, the diversity of intellectual approaches within university departments represent a similar surface phenomenon that obscures the deeper and more critically important cultural assumptions upon which the disciplines are based.

Regardless of whether we are considering the latest development in literary criticism, postmodern analysis, macro-economics, or class analysis, the way of thinking is based on the interlocking set of Eurocentric cultural assumptions that have given modernity, and the high-status forms of knowledge it is based upon, its particular messianic ethos. For example, inquiry in both the traditional departments as well as in the new interdisciplinary fields such as women's studies, cultural studies (which often is seen as encompassing any course that addresses how relations of power contribute to social injustice), and ethnic studies, is based on an human-centered view of the universe. That is, the environment (if it is even considered as relevant in terms other than economic) is viewed from a human perspective—with the added assumption that whatever significance academics accord to the environment should be regarded as a superior form of understanding to what is learned from daily experience. And the academic's way of understanding the human condition is considered a quantum leap beyond indigenous groups' knowledge of what Edward Goldsmith refers to as the natural economy of local systems (1992, pp. 298–300).

Much of the higher education curriculum introduces students to the traditions and achievements of humans since the rise of literacy, to the various expressions of hubris that have doomed people to misery and death, and to the refined rituals for heaping criticism on the writings of other scholars. The reinforcement of the anthropocentric perspective learned earlier in public schools helps to ensure that the vast majority of scholarship and classroom teaching will go unquestioned, except for the marginalized voices of a small number of environmentally oriented academics who have managed to gain a foothold.

How psychologists explain human intelligence and behavior is typical both of the conflict model of thinking so highly valued by academic scholars, and of the anthropocentric way of thinking. For the prominent Yale University psychologist, Robert J. Sternberg, a theory of intelligence must take into account "the relationship between (1) intelligence and the *internal* world of the individual; (2) intelligence and the *external* world of the individual, or the use of these *mental mechanisms* in everyday life in order to attain an intelligent fit with the environment; and (3) intelligence and experience, or mediating role of one's passage through life between the internal and external worlds of the individual (italics added, 1992 edition, p. 268). Sternberg's theory of mental mechanisms that operate inside the mind (or brain) as the individual keeps both the internal and external world under intelligent control is not sufficiently scientific for University of Hawaii's Arthur W. Staats, who describes himself as a third-generation behaviorist. Although his interpretation of "psychological behaviorism" situates the individual's behavior within an environment that is seen as reinforcing certain behaviors (what Skinner earlier referred to as "selecting" the behavior), his radically different theory of human behavior retains the same anthropocentric framework for representing how humans are situated in the world (1994, pp. 93–114).

After decades of research, scholarly writing and debate, and the expenditure of immense sums of money, the field of psychology has produced a vast number of theories that are as reductionist as the opposing theories of Sternberg and Staats, and oriented toward enhancing the control of experts over human thought and behavior. And they have all been equally morally bankrupt. The anthropocentric bias, which has its roots partly in the attempt to study human intelligence and behavior "scientifically", has helped to eliminate for the majority of people an awareness of how different cultural groups renewed the ecological wisdom acquired over generations of learning from their environments. This modern approach to the study of intelligence and behavior, which is abstracted from the ecology of cultural and natural systems that everybody is rooted in, should be of concern to every environmentalist.

Anthropocentrism is also the foundation upon which other academic disciplines are based. Indeed, the "humanities" clearly suggest that humans are the main focus of study—that is, humans after the rise of literacy. A careful examination of the debate among academics from a variety of fields over what constitutes the canon essential to the "educated" person will reveal that the writers and practitioners of a more ecologically responsive form of existence are largely absent from their lists of notable authors. For example, the core of Allan Bloom's argument, which attracted a large readership a few years ago, needs to be reexamined in terms of his ignorance of the contribution that

his intellectual and spiritual heroes made to a form of consciousness that equated progress with bringing nature
under rational control. As Bloom put it, "the tiny band of
men (Plato, Aristotle, Descartes, Bacon, Locke, Newton)
who participated fully in this way of life are the soul of the
university" (1987, p. 271). Anthropocentric thinking is also
the basis of Harold Bloom's recent book, *The Western
Canon: Books and Schools for the Ages* (1994). Bloom is eru-
dite, caustic toward his academic enemies, and totally silent
with regard to literary and oral forms of representing humans as members of a sustainable moral and natural ecology. The authors selected by Bloom (Saul Bellow, Norman
Mailer, John Updike, and a 156 other notables) have written with great sensitivity and insight about human relationships, but have ignored the more elementary feature of
human life; namely, how humans fit into the cycle where
the waste products of one process serve as the raw material
for renewing life in other processes, to paraphrase Goldsmith (1992, p. 299). Gary Snyder is more direct in explaining the cycle that humans cannot escape—except in the
culturally circumscribed thinking of the authors promoted
by academic humanists like Bloom. As Snyder reminds us:

> Everyone who ever lived took the lives of other animals,
> pulled plants, plucked fruit, and ate. Primary people have
> had their own ways of trying to understand the precept of
> nonharming. They knew that taking life required grati-
> tude and care. There is no death that is not somebody's
> food, no life that is not somebody's death. Some would take
> this as a sign that the universe is fundamentally flawed.
> . . . Subsistance people live without excuses. . . . A subsis-
> tance economy is a sacramental economy because it has
> faced up to one of the critical problems of life and death:
> the taking of life for food. (1990, pp. 183–184)

Anthropocentric thinking is clearly evident in the way
departments of economics reduce natural systems to "in-
puts" in the production system, and to "natural resources"
that are to be exploited by market forces. And philosophy
departments continue the long legacy of endless (many
would say "pointless") reflections that alternate between ab-

stract representations of how the human world is known and morally constituted and the more trivial and arcane questions that philosophers address. Like academic psychologists, recent philosophers have made remarkably few contributions to improving the quality of human life, or even to understanding it in ways that would make sense to an intelligent person. One measure of the degree of intellectual self-indulgence that characterizes the state of philosophy on campuses across the country can be found in the kind of subjects that are addressed in books and articles that appear in professional journals. Journal articles such as "Indeterminism and Control," "Does Theological Fatalism Rest on an Equivocation?" and "On Middle Knowledge" are typical of the increasingly specialized intellectual exchanges within the field.

The philosophers' concern with definitions and rational consistency in the development of an argument, as well as their willingness to argue about the most arcane issues imaginable, manifest a pronounced lack of awareness that their own ways of thinking are culturally influenced, and that other cultural groups have evolved radically different approaches to answering questions about how to live in ecologically respectful relationships. What students encounter in most philosophy courses, with the exception of the environmental ethics course that may occasionally be offered, will also demonstrate the philosophers' total lack of awareness that the ecological crisis raises fundamental questions about the dominant culture's way of knowing, its moral values, and its way of understanding human/nature relationships.

The extreme anthropocentrism of Western philosophy (a generalization that applies to mainstream philosophers such as Plato, Marx, Dewey, and to more recent developments in Britain, France, Germany, and North America) can be clearly seen in the conclusions that Richard Rorty reaches in a book intended to illuminate how to live personally meaningful lives that are also lived in "solidarity" with other human beings in the modern world. "To sum up," as arguably America's most highly visible philosopher puts it, "the citizens of my liberal utopia . . . would be liberal ironists" (1989, p. 61). Rorty then goes on to explain the essential moral, intellectual, and political characteristics of his ideal citizen:

> I shall define an ironist as someone who fulfills three conditions: (1) She has radical and continuing doubts about the final vocabulary she currently uses, because she has been impressed by other final vocabularies, vocabularies taken as final by people or books she has encountered; (2) she realizes that arguments phrased in her present vocabulary can neither underwrite nor dissolve these doubts; (3) insofar as she philosophizes about her situation, she does not think her vocabulary is closer to reality than others, that it is in touch with a power not herself. (p. 73)

Rorty further adds that his ideal citizen would:

> spend her time worrying about the possibility that she has been initiated into the wrong tribe, taught to play the wrong language game. She worries that the process of socialization which turned her into a human being by giving her a language may have given her the wrong language, and so turned her into the wrong kind of human being. But she cannot give a criterion for wrongness. (75)

Indeed, his nihilist hero would be too self-absorbed to recognize the radical transformations taking place in the Earth's ecosystems, too modern to recognize that some form of culturally based self-limitation for the sake of others (both humans and members of the biotic community) is essential to reversing the current trendlines, and too ethnocentric to recognize that her existential uncertainties are not characteristic of cultures that have maintained their narrative traditions.

Two other examples of anthropocentric thinking may help suggest just how widespread this cultural orientation is within universities—and that this orientation is shared equally by liberal and conservative thinkers. The recent book by Benjamin R. Barber, a liberal political scientist at Rutgers University, contains an insightful discussion of how our approaches to education must be based on a different way of understanding human temporality if they are to contribute to greater participation within a self-renewing community. Recalling an earlier way of understanding how individual lives are embedded in the continuities of time (what Shils refers to as "living traditions"), Barber makes the following observation:

> Thus all useful education begins with and circles back to historical understanding. Since time gives knowledge a narrative structure, self-knowledge means storytelling. And when the self-knowledge is collective, the storytelling is shared. Education is systematic storytelling. No wonder there is such tumult surrounding the attempt to identify the right stories! As storytelling, education disclosed temporal connections and compels an encounter between unreflected present, reconstructed past, and contrived future. History is not some specialized subject in technical education, it is liberal education: it is an account in the narrative mode of our being a people, as a 'public.' Defined and understood, the 'I' entails a 'We,' and 'We' is always a story whose end points bring new beginnings and whose outcome is conditioned (though not necessarily limited) by history. (1992, pp. 21–22)

When the anthropocentric bias is taken for granted, Barber's statement appears to possess a degree of insight that is missing in most recent discussions of the connections between education, freedom, and community. But when the reader takes account of how all aspects of community and thus individual well-being (psychological and physical health, ability to participate in viable economic relationships, participatory decision-making, etc.) are being affected by the degradation of the environment, Barber's human-centered perspective can be seen as part of the problem.

The last example of anthropocentrism I shall cite, partly because it reflects the myopia shared by conservative thinkers, can be found in William Bennett's list of stories that he considers essential to revitalizing the process of moral education in the schools. As a former professor of philosophy and Secretary of Education (1985–1988), Bennett argues that children need to hear the culture's stories that exemplify how moral people thought and behaved in difficult, even dangerous situations. Bennett believes that without a knowledge of how moral behavior is actually expressd, students will be left to invent their own moral behavior—which he sees as often destructive to themselves and to their community. Bennett argues that if we want children to know what courage is, we should tell them the story of Harriet Tubman and the Underground Railroad. If we want them to understand persistence in the face of adversity, we should tell them about Lincoln during the Civil War, and the experience of the Donner Party. His list also included stories of exemplary historical figures who possessed special moral traits: honesty, respect for the rights of others, loyalty, kindness, and so on (1988, pp. 77–90). But absent from his list are the stories of humans acting morally in their relationships toward the land, and toward non-human forms of life.

These examples of anthropocentrism are not intended to represent a full account of the extent and depth of the problem of passing on high-status knowledge that serves as the basis for further development in modern technologies and consumer expectations. Rather, it is to establish that the mainstream traditions of thought (even the latest revisions in departmental orthodoxies) are based on a deeply rooted set of cultural assumptions that represent the fate of humans as separate from that of the environment. The widespread existence of this cultural bias needs to be carefully considered as part of any political strategy to make public and university education more environmentally responsive.

But scrutiny of humanities and social science departments should not be limited to the problem of anthropocentrism. For all their varied theoretical perspectives, these departments continue to reinforce the Western myth that represents change as progressive in nature. New theories of inquiry and explanation are quickly embraced as opening new ways of understanding, with the expectation that even newer theories will shortly displace them. Even post-modernism, the most recent intellectual fad, represents change, the relativism of all perspectives and interpretations, and the de-authorization of all values and truths as the norm that should guide the thoughtful person's life. Academics still wedded to modern assumptions continue to promote the conflict model of inquiry as the most viable way of ensuring social progress and overcoming the threat of ideas and values congealing into dogma (the irony is that in spite of their commitment to the conflict model of inquiry, most academics would like to see their theory become the accepted norm for thinking). For these modernist academics (whom postmodernists regard as dangerously outdated relics), the individual, a linear view of causality, and the basing of claims to truth and moral knowledge on a form of thinking that emphasizes rationality and literacy, serve as their tradition of overturning traditions.

The possibility of stasis, where a new explanatory framework is recognized as providing the standards of interpretation that define politically correct thinking within the discipline is soon overturned by the academic's drive to find a new and more adequate basis of understanding. It is important to note that the periods of stasis, and the revolts against what each new generation of academics perceive as the outmoded explanatory framework, are never judged in terms of how adequate they are for contributing to the quality of everyday life. Rather, the hubris of academics, their continual need to discover new knowledge in order to meet the publication requirements for academic promotion, and a deep belief in the ideology that equates the search for truth with the overturning of traditions, better account for their addiction to the treadmill of change.

Postmodernism is one of the latest intellectual fads to sweep through humanities and social science departments, and it has carried the relativizing process of critical interpretation to the extreme where nihilism is being viewed as the only intellectually and morally honest stance for academics to take. Nihilism, as Nietzsche pointed out, involves a state of consciousness where nothing has any more value than anything else; where knowledge has no basis of authority (and thus is little more than personal preferences— which really don't matter); and where the sense of relativism and purposelessness of life undermines making personal commitments. In short, nihilism involves a way of experiencing in which everything is meaningless and without value. But for the postmodernist academics, who continue under the sway of French intellectuals of the sixties and seventies (whom the present generation of French intellectuals are largely ignoring), nihilism must be embraced if they are to avoid succumbing to the illusion of progess that modernist academics still base their theories upon.

Influenced by such writers as Roland Barthes, Jacques Derrida, Michel Foucault, and Jacques Lacan, among others, postmodernist members of humanities and social science departments have laid a theoretical basis for the relativizing of all cultural norms by arguing that the conventions of language are historically and culturally relative. Since we can only know the world through the constituting characteristics of language, what we can know and experience is relative—that is, an interpretation based on deeper and largely unrecognized layers of interpretation that extend back in time. Thus the world as we can know it is no more deserving of being accorded any more status of being real or having authority than any other linguistically constructed world. Using concepts such as "de-centering," "difference," "intertextuality," and "simulacrum," postmodernist academics have "deconstructed" the assumptions that underlie facts, individuals, subjective experience, authors, texts, readers, linear causality, and other authoritative and taken-for-granted reference points in the thinking of their modernist colleagues. In effect, postmodernist thinkers have declared the conceptual foundations of modernism to be obsolete and groundless. As Pauline Marie Rosenau observes, "the postmodernists are satisfied to conclude that what is actually going on can never be stated definitely; in any case, it matters little because there is no single meaning for any text, for any political, social, economic event. An infinite number of interpretations of any scenario is possible" (1992, p. 41). Similarly, the modern notion of time (as linear) and space (as geography) are relativized, with both time and space becoming reconstituted and lived on a personal basis. Indeed, the postmodernist's understanding of "hyper-space" is the imaginary space that allows for the simulation of an infinite number of scenarios.

Postmodernists' relativistic interpretations of the constituting and storage role of language, as well as their understanding of the interconnected and interactive ("intertextual") nature of all relationships, events, and cultural artifacts, leads to viewing claims for the authority of values and truths as meaningless. Personal interpretations and perspective, which are themselves subject to constant change, are the postmodernists' alternatives to the "power plays" of individuals who uphold the authority of values and truths. And as individuals are no longer seen as having a biographically distinct center and identity, but as constantly changing through interaction with surrounding events and beings, they are not accountable for being morally consistent. For postmodernists, morality is also a matter of personal interpretation. More correctly, the notion of immoral behavior is meaningless to them. Indeed, they would view it as a reactionary way of thinking—an atavism of a more primitive and less reflective form of existence. As Rosenau notes, "the postmodern individual is . . . an active human being *constituting his / her own social reality*, pursuing a personal quest for meaning but making no truth claims about the results" (italics added, 1992, p. 52). This relativistic, self-absorbed, "live and let live" stance corresponds to the qualities Rorty identifies as essential to the "ironist" whom he upholds as the ideally developed human being. The social practice of this nihilistic stance can be seen in the writings of Derrida. For example, in the "Envois" section of *The Post Card: From Socrates to Freud and Beyond*, Derrida's sense of meaningless leads him to omit sections of sentences, thus leaving it to the reader to fill in the missing thoughts as personal whim or creative imagination dictates (1987, pp. 162–256). As there are no fixed reference points in the language games that frame and reframe "reality," there is no basis for privileging a system of cultural coding over complete silence. The only certainty is that the process of continual deconstruction makes everything momentarily possible.

As pointed out earlier, modernist academics, who ironically now refer to themselves as "conservatives," continue to rely upon conceptual categories that ignore the primacy of culture in human experience. For them, the individual is to be regarded as the basic social unit that thinks rationally, and texts are to be read as containing the authoritative judgments of scholars (experts) who explain the actual nature of events and causal relationships in human history. These modernist thinkers use their classrooms to reinforce a number of other certainties: the superiority of literacy over oral-based cultures, the reliability of words, principles, and generalizations that are context-free (that is, they can be universalized) over the local, contextual, and idiosyncratic; the anthropocentric and secular interpretation over the ecological and spiritual; individually-centered rational and moral judgments over knowledge and moral codes that are renewed and handed down over generations; and the valuing of the new and experimental over traditional forms of authority, technologies and wisdom.

Certain aspects of postmodernist thinking represent a real advance over these certainties: the recognition of the constitutive role of language; the realization that what humans experience is a cultural construct; the acknowledgment that events, facts, individuals, etc., are not self-contained autonomous entities, and so forth. There is even a radically different emphasis given to postmodernism by thinkers such as David Ray Griffin, Charles Jencks, and Charlene Spretnak who see in the dereification of modern assumptions the possibility of constructing more viable human communities and relationships with the natural world. But these constructive postmodernist thinkers do not represent the mainstream of postmodernist thinking, which now appears to be reinventing itself as a branch of "cultural studies." However, the ongoing change of labels and jargon has not altered the double bind of basing a critique of modernity on even more deeply held modern assumptions. For example, the postmodernists' critique of their modernist colleagues fails to take account of how people experience their everyday world of shared cultural patterns. Perhaps this critically important oversight results from the proclivity of academics to treat previously held explanatory frameworks as distinct and self-contained, and thus to be ignored when a new explanatory framework becomes the current intellectual fashion.

Phenomenology, imported from Europe by an earlier generation of academics, provided a theoretical account of how most of the patterns of life in the world are experienced at a taken-for-granted level by the individual—that is, as part of the individual's "natural" attitude. However the postmodernists' failure to retain this earlier theoretically based insight into the nature of how humans (in all cultural settings) experience their world is excused, they can still be criticized for failing to recognize that their own taken-for-granted cultural patterns contradict their postmodern theories. Derrida, for example, continues to write books, order his sentences in the left-to-right pattern characteristic of Western cultures, use conventional spellings, and conform to the cultural norms expected of a professor at the Ecole des Hautes Studes en Sciences Sociales in Paris. Lesser known postmodernists also live schizophrenic lives where their intellectual efforts to deconstruct the conceptual and moral foundations of modern consciousness are kept quite separate from their own desire to attain the standard forms of institutional recognition and reward (including promotion and tenure), and to live the bourgeois lifestyle of the university professor.

A second reason the constructive potential of the postmodern thinkers' sensitivity to the complexity of the language processes has not been realized is that they retain in their thinking the modern bias toward tradition. The project of relativizing all beliefs, values, and other cultural norms would not have been undertaken in such a messianic manner if postmodern theorists had actually experienced the social and economic disorder, physical violence, and the myriad forms of deprivation experienced in places such as Sarajevo, and even in our own urban centers. While not acknowledging it, postmodern academics base their theoretical deconstructions on the assumption that change will always work out in ways that are progressive—or at least, do not involve real life-and-death consequences.

At the same time, postmodernists retain the modernists' Enlightenment bias that represents tradition as a source of

oppression that must be overturned. If they understood tradition as everything handed down from the past to the present (that is, as having survived because the traditions were
found useful and worthy of being reenacted and passed on to
each successive generation) perhaps they would have recognized that some traditions have contributed to the quality of
daily life: traditions in food preparation and preservation,
music, civil liberties, technologies that facilitate communication, and so forth. They might also have recognized that
instead of creating the intellectual and moral justifications
for the life of the self-absorbed nihilist, their efforts should
have been directed toward clarifying what the alternatives
might be to traditions that need to be abandoned or radically
altered—such as forms of education that continue to empower individuals and corporations to exploit the environment, and approaches to politics and philosophy that fail to
take account of how humans are dependent upon the viability of the Earth's ecosystems. It would not be unfair to say
that the postmodernists' hostility toward tradition, and their
indifference to the need to discriminate between viable and
destructive traditions, reflect their assumption that out of
the mix of complexity, disorder, and complete freedom of individuals to invent their own lives, the conditions of human
life will advance beyond the limitations of the past. In short,
the postmodernists share the modernists' assumption that
change is progressive—even as they criticize the idea of
progress as groundless.

  The third reason postmodernism should be understood
as representing a continuation rather than a genuine alternative to the modern form of consciousness is that that their
theorizing retains the same anthropocentric perspective
that has dominated Western philosophers since the time of
Plato. Derrida, Foucault, Lyotard, Barthe, and all their followers have, to this point, ignored the relationship between
culture and natural systems. In transforming all aspects of
culture into texts that can be deconstructed in terms of the
hidden constitutive assumptions and contradictions, they
failed to recognize that human ideas and practices are *always* situated within the context of energy and information
exchanges that enable other life systems to survive and

evolve. The obsession with the failures of modern thought limits their analysis to the same artificial bifurcation that modernists took for granted—that is, that the human situation can be understood and advanced in total disregard of how humans impact natural systems. While postmodernist academics indoctrinate the students who will be joining the elite groups that set the agenda for the further globalization of commodity-oriented technologies (which will replace traditional cultures with virtual realities and hyper-space) farmers in the Mid-west are rapidly depleting the Ogallala Aquifer essential to agricultural productivity, and the elites in "developing countries," eager to participate in the global economy, continue to promote the spread of DDT and other deadly chemicals on the land, water, and people—to cite just two ecologically destructive practices that help put in perspective the priorities that characterize the influence of postmodernist thinking within humanities and social science departments.

As cultural studies draws upon many of the European theorists who inspired postmodernism, it is difficult to determine whether it is a separate intellectual movement, or so inclusive that postmodernism should be considered as only one of its forms of expression. Sorting out lineages is not really our purpose here. Rather it is to point out that cultural studies, which its practitioners view as having the political and moral mission of exposing the historical forces that have shaped the current forms of injustice in all areas of social life (political institutions, the arts, beliefs, social practices, etc.), is based on the same deep cultural assumptions that underlie the high-status forms of knowledge that they want to expose and overturn. While the academics engaged in cultural studies view themselves as engaged in a demystification process that will eliminate social injustice (that is, as social interventionists whose achievements will be, in turn, demystified by successive cultural studies), they, like their postmodernist and supposedly more traditionalist colleagues, also ignore the impact of cultural beliefs and practices on natural systems. By ignoring the complex cultural issues surrounding the challenge of reforming those aspects of modern culture that undermine the possibility of long-term ecological sustainability, the academics engaged in cultural studies fail to address the double binds that their own modernist assumptions help to perpetuate. The characteristics of ecologically centered cultures, such as the role of elders in transmitting mythopoetic narratives that frame humans and other forms of life into a seamless moral universe, are not only absent in their writings; they are irreconcilable with their modern assumptions about the nature of change, traditions, authority of critical reflection, and a secular view of the universe.

Any discussion of why environmentalists should be concerned with what now passes as liberal education must also take account of how socal science departments, in particular, strengthen the modern approach to high-status knowledge. Both humanities and the social science departments reinforce the Western patterns of thinking that characterize the modern expert in such fields as economics, politics, medicine, computer technology, urban planning, agriculture, and so forth. These patterns of thinking are based on print-based storage and communication of knowledge (now electronic), rather than on face-to-face communication. Print-based communication and storage, in turn, contribute to expert forms of knowledge that are abstract and thus generalizable across cultural contexts, which lead to undermining local forms of knowledge. Indeed, local knowledge (if it is even recognized) is represented as backward because it is not scientific or part of a literate tradition. Furthermore, students in the social sciences learn to think in terms of organizing reality into self-contained components that can be rationally reconceptualized into new systems and techniques, and to determine the efficacy of the new systems in terms of measurable outcomes. This abstract "systems" approach also leads a continual search for ways of improving the efficiency (output) of the system, and to integrating it (and the host culture) into a larger set of systems.

The education of the modern expert, in effect, reflects the influence that scientific and mathematical models of understanding have had in certain areas of the social sciences, and the lack of understanding of how different cultures have adapted (with varying degrees of success) to local ecosystems. It further reflects how humanities and social science departments have totally disregarded the challenge of reconceptualizing their respective traditions of thought in ways that would contribute to more ecologically sustainable cultures, such as how to live less consumer oriented lifestyles. That some departments now offer a course or two that encourages students to consider social issues and the use of technologies from an ecological perspective does not lessen the need to pressure for radical change in the majority of courses they offer students. Nor should the fact that the more ecologically sensitive experts are now turning their attention to solving social problems resulting from breakdowns in natural systems be allowed to obscure the real issue, which is that these experts have largely been educated by universities to understand ecological problems in ways that do not take account of the deep cultural patterns that are contributing to the degraded environments that experts are attempting to revitalize. Whether these environmental experts now join in the effort to reform what passes as liberal education (which continues to be based on the cultural assumption that gave the Industrial Revolution its energy and sense of direction) will be important in determining whether the greening of this area of the university curriculum will succeed.

Professional Schools of Business and Education

While the humanities and social sciences provide the ability to think more critically and to put issues within complex theoretical frameworks essential for the continual reconceptualization processes that characterize modern culture, it is the professional schools that provide direct access to the most change-oriented sectors of modern culture. The inability of journalism graduates to explain how taken-for-granted cultural beliefs and practices are at the root of many of environmental events and issues they report on suggest that schools of journalism are in need of radical reform. Journalists created such misunderstanding among

the public in their reporting of Vice President Al Gore's
views on environmental issues during the 1992 presidential
campaign that he was forced to downplay one of the most
important set of issues facing the nation. Other examples of
journalistic failures to make the connection between consumer oriented culture and environmental issues can easily
be cited. One of the most recent was the statement that appeared in *U.S. News & World Report* that represented the
ideas of mainstream environmental thinkers as "antisociety
and antiscience indictments" and a source of "paranoia"
that encourages extremists (Budiansky, 1996, p. 434). But
here I wish to focus on two other professional schools that
promote complementary cultural agendas that are particularly environmentally destructive. How these two professional schools complement each other has gone largely
unnoticed, even as corporations are increasingly producing
curriculum for schools and promoting a narrow view of
learning that fits the capabilities of computer technology.

Graduates of schools of business administration play
an important role in expanding the world's rate of economic
growth, and thus the spread of the monoculture of consumerism. Graduates of teacher education programs (as
well as teacher educators who have earned a Ph.D. in a college of education) socialize the broader population of youth
to the taken-for-granted patterns of thinking that equate
progress with the continual expansion of technology into
more areas of cultural life, and with continued economic
and consumer "opportunities." That is, the influence of colleges of education can be seen in the fact that generations of
adults who share the common experience of public school
education have been socialized in a way that makes it unnecessary for business and technological elites to explain
how their guiding assumptions about the nature of economic progress can be reconciled with the rapidly degraded
condition of the environment. As Ivan Illich observed in the
early seventies, "if it teaches nothing else, school teaches
the value of escalation" (1971, p. 42).

Of all the professional schools, schools of business administration and education deserve the most careful and immediate scrutiny by environmentalists. In addition to their

influence in perpetuating an uncritical acceptance of the culture of modernity, both have had a important influence on the development of other countries. The worldwide influence of prominent graduate programs can be seen in the growing number of American-educated business and educational leaders in non-European countries. For example, the Harvard Business School reported in 1994 that it had 1,097 alumni in Latin America and the Carribean, 2,402 alumni in Asia, and 955 alumni in Africa and the Middle East (1995, p. 11). The Massachusetts Institute of Technology, Stanford University, the University of Chicago, as well as other equally prestigious business schools can produce similar figures on the worldwide distribution of their graduates. The leading graduate schools of education can also claim to be responsible for equally powerful networks of educational leaders who are promoting the modern (Western) form of knowledge essential to a viable workforce and the mass of uncritical consumers that the technocratic business elites depend upon. Indeed, the symbiotic relationship between educators and the business community is being further strengthened through the current representation of computer-based technology as the primary medium of thought and communication. It might be even more correct to state that the boundaries between the domains of business and education are fast disappearing as the nearly 40,000 networks in 159 countries that now make up the Internet (a figure that will be obsolete by the time this is read) make digitalized information the dominant form of knowledge.

The "Growthmania" Syndrome of Schools
of Business Administration

The term "growthmania" is used by Herman E. Daly in his book, *Steady-State Economic* (1991) to describe the economic orientation of modern cultures. As he states, "economic growth is held to be the cure of poverty, unemployment, debt repayment, inflation, balance of payment deficits, pollution, depletion, the population explosion, crime, divorce, and drug addiction. In short, economic growth is both the panacea and the *summum bonum.*" He further observes that growthmania creates a double bind that few economists and business leaders recognize: namely, that "when we deplete geological capital and ecological life-support systems and count that depletion as net currrent income, then we arrive at our present state of terminal hyper-growthmania" (p. 183). It is a terminal condition because continued economic growth is being achieved by exploiting renewable resources at a rate that now exceeds the self-renewing characteristics of natural systems. In spite of the adverse impact this will have on the prospects of future generations, schools of business administration continue to perpetuate the doctrine of economic colonization that treats both the world's cultures and ecosystems as an increasingly integrated market system. The guiding values and concepts of this doctrine are summed up in the terminology that appears in nearly every description of business school courses: competition, strategy, efficiency, and leadership. The ability to operationalize these terms in the context of business leads, of course, to increased profits— which is the ultimate justification. The profit motive is further insulated from criticism by the argument presented in business schools that the forces of the marketplace provide the most rational basis for making decisions about the sustainable exploitation of natural resources.

Environmentalists might be excused for not recognizing how the sciences have introduced changes into the world's cultures that have put them on the modern pathway of media orchestrated consumerism, and for not challenging the nihilistic intellectual fads that humanities and social science faculty borrow from European intellectuals, but it is difficult to understand why environmentalists have not awakened to the fact that what is taught in schools of business administration massively contributes to the growing list of environmental problems. My experience as a faculty member of a university in the Northwest that has both an above-average number of environmentally oriented faculty in a number of disciplines and a strong school of business administration is typical of the "live and let live" attitude toward the environmental miseducation occuring in such business courses as "International Business Strategy," "International Finance and Investment," "Management of

Technology and Innovation." The basic conflict between the "growthmania" orientation taught in these courses and the deep commitment that many community based environmental groups have to reversing ecologically destructive practices in the Northwest also went unnoticed. By way of contrast, during the anti-war demonstrations of the late sixties and early seventies the ROTC building opposite my office was burned to the ground because it was seen as a symbol of the military establishment's political agenda. More recently, the overt teaching of patriarchal values and interpretative frameworks led to political protests and exposure in the local press. If racist or fascist beliefs were to be presented in a course as one of many intellectual stances that might be legitimately adopted in a free society both students and faculty would engage in forms of protest that would attract immediate media attention. In spite of this continual scrutiny for evidence of reactionary thinking in other departments, the courses in the school of business administration continue to be viewed as a legitimate part of the university's mission to enlighten minds and to improve the prospects of future generations.

One of the ironies of the environmental movement's indifference toward the role that business schools play in transforming the Earth's ecosystems into commodities that fill our shopping malls, and in expanding the domain of economic activity in people's daily lives, is that the pressure to green the curriculum of business schools is coming from corporations that must deal with environmental regulations. The growing awareness that environmental issues are now a fact of business culture—from knowing how to do a cost analysis of different corporate responses to environmental laws to increasing profits through the use of pollution reduction technologies—has led a number of business schools to introduce environmental issues into their curricula. But this slight greening of business schools should not be seen as evidence of any fundamental rethinking of the basic assumptions about the need to make economic growth and profitability the primary focus of business decisions. Even business schools that offer specialized programs with an environmental focus, such as the University of Washington's

Environmental Management Program, the University of Michigan's Corporate Environmental Management Program, and Stanford University's Corporate Environmental Solutions Project, easily reconcile their focus on environmental issues with more traditional assumptions about the need for continuous economic growth. This is achieved by emphasizing successful (i.e., profitable) corporate strategies for dealing with environmental issues.

While it is now estimated that corporate pressure has led nearly one hundred of the nation's seven hundred business schools to introduce problem-solving and profit-maximization approaches to environmental issues into some of their courses, the dominant ethos that should concern environmentalists is reflected in the Harvard Business School's description of the course on "Business, Government, and the International Economy":

> How should the issues confronting the economy of the former Soviet Union be addressed? For those hoping to sell products there, how should its economy be understood? Or the economies of India, Mexico, Brazil, Japan, Canada, or the United States? This course takes an integrated, conceptual approach to the analysis of the international environment and national economic strategies. It provides a management framework and analytical tools for evaluating trends in the economic, political, and social contexts of business throughout the world. Students compare and develop strategies in a variety of nations, consider their influence on business, and assess their impact on managerial decisions and international competitiveness. Monetary policy, national economic performance, trade relations, and industrial policy are discussed, with attention to political concerns. Students analyze the key resource flows that tie nations together—money, oil, trade, and technology—in order to better understand the structure and dynamics of the international economy. Discussions focus on developments in the European Common Market, the opening of markets in Eastern Europe, and emerging trends in Pacific Rim and Latin American markets. The international diversity of each section enriches this learning experience. (1995, p. 22)

As the environment is not directly referred to in this course description, the reader can only assume that it is one of the elements in the "resource flow" that tie nations together. That it is a rapidly diminishing resource does not alter the main focus of the course—which is to identify the optimum economic (i.e., profit-generating) strategy within a given set of variables. Nor does the course address the loss of local economic self-sufficiency, with its supportive cultural traditions, that results from integration into the international technological and economic system. Just how marginal environmental issues are in the MBA programs at the most prestigious universities can be seen in the fact that the Harvard Business School offers only two courses that address issues related to hazardous wastes, resource economics, and sustainable economic growth; and the MIT Sloan School of Management offers only one course in this vital area. Unless students happen incidentally to enroll in one of these courses they could earn their MBA degree without being challenged to reconcile the system of beliefs and values taught in their courses with Herman Daly's observation that "human beings must . . . ultimately live within that constant long-run bio-physical budget" (p. 227). Even for students who enroll in one of these three courses, it is unlikely that they will be challenged to think deeply about the implications of the diverging trendlines that characterize the rising human demand on natural systems now in rapid decline. Deep reflection on the cultural assumptions that were the basis of the Industrial Revolution, and which continue to influence professors in business schools to argue that market forces are the most rational and efficient means for allocating scarce "natural resources," will require a radical shift in cultural paradigms. And this shift will be difficult because it will require changing the conceptual and moral foundations upon which faculty have based their courses and personal careers. However, until environmentalists challenge this sector of the academic business establishment to adapt their courses in ways that take account of the ecological realities that exist today, and which will worsen in the decades ahead, business schools will continue to perpetuate economic and technological practices that undermine the broader and long-term goals of the environmental movement.

How Colleges of Education Package the Myth of Modernity

Professors of education responsible for providing the professional knowledge that public school teachers will use as a basis for making curricular and pedagogical decisions in the classroom, and for guiding the graduate studies of the next generation of teacher educators, have relatively low status within the academic community. Indeed, they are near the bottom. But their contribution to perpetuating the most extreme expressions of modern consciousness, and thus their contribution to raising the next generation of youth who will carry modernity to an even further extreme (with all its consequences for the environment), surpasses that of the more high-status departments known for their scholarly rigor and accomplishments. The academic status system, however, does not take account of the fact that what is taught in education courses, as well as what is ignored in these courses, will exert a powerful influence on young students during their most formative period of intellectual and moral development. The conceptual and ideological framework that public school students acquire through the content of the curriculum, which can be traced back to what their teachers acquired from their professional education classes, lays the groundwork for their receptivity to the mythic dimensions of Western modernism being further elaborated in the courses they will take in departments of philosophy, economics, psychology, history, and so on.

To put this another way, when students enroll in the university they have already acquired the basic conceptual and ideological categories that their university-level classes will build upon. And for public school students who do not go on to some form of higher education, their limited classroom and enlarged television-based education will leave them with the taken-for-granted patterns of thinking that will make them easily influenced by business and technological elites who face the continual challenge of creating consumer demand for the new products essential to growth-mania. As discussed earlier, these conceptual and ideological patterns of thinking include the following: the Western myth of an anthropocentric universe; an individually-centered way of understanding intelligence, creativity, and moral judgment; a view of science and technology as both culturally neutral and as the manifestation of human progress; the experience of time as linear and progressive (thus making the judgment of the individual the primary authority for assessing the relevance and worth of traditions—which are understood in astonishingly simplistic ways); the privileging of literacy-based thought and communication over oral-based forms of cultural storage and renewal; and the continual search for what is new and innovative (often based on the emotive expression of a supposedly autonomous individual or driven by the messianic ideology that equates competitive relationships with the discovery of a higher truth and economic growth). These patterns of thinking, which are essential to the organization of knowledge in most university classes, and to sustaining a taken-for-granted attitude toward the economic and technological agenda of modernity, are learned indirectly (that is, largely unconsicously) as students proceed from the elementary grades through high school. When they arrive on the university campus, or at their first low-paying, low-skill job, they bring with them these deeply held and mostly taken-for-granted patterns of thinking. While other university departments gild the lily, provide the credentials that will enable their technologically oriented graduates access to elite professions, and look upon their colleagues in education departments with disdain, it is these low-status professors of education who are ultimately responsible for the sense of mission and narrowness of vision that accounts for the cultural mediation and consciousness-forming process that occurs in most public school classrooms. In fairness, responsibility for the cultural myths reproduced through the curriculum of the public schools should also be borne by the professors who teach the more "academic" classes required as part of the teacher certification process.

These criticisms do not apply to all public school teachers or, for that matter, to all professors of education. In the use of any powerful generalization, the margins are not as accurately represented as the mainstream. Here we are addressing the modern orthodoxies that serve as the conceptual and ideological framework for the professional educational establishment, which includes graduate schools of education, teacher education programs, professional journals, and the educationally oriented entrepreneurs who promote the latest fads borrowed from scientific research (e.g., brain research) and pop psychology. How some public school teachers resist being swept along in the current of educational fads by quietly and persistently providing the basis for a deep and critical understanding of cultural experience must also be taken into account in any effort to put education on a more ecologically responsive pathway. It is also important to recognize the efforts of the few professors of education who are attempting to introduce into the study of education, and into teacher education programs, an understanding how the classroom can be used to foster understandings and experiences that renew human/environmental relationships. However, working collaboratively with these marginalized educators who are committed to a deep cultural and environmental approach to all areas of education will not bring about changes on the scale that is now required. The basic reality is that their efforts are still marginalized.

To the casual observer, it might appear that teacher education, as well as graduate education programs, are characterized by a diverse number of theoretical frameworks. The increased emphasis on computer-mediated learning appears to be based on a different set of assumptions than approaches to education that promote a more critical and participatory approach to decision-making—such as comes out of the John Dewey and Paulo Freire traditions of educational thought. But an examination of such seemingly diverse approaches as cooperative learning, direct instruction, outcome-based education, assertive discipline, multiple intelligences, and critical literacy, will reveal that the surface diversity is less significant than the deep cultural assumptions shared by all these approaches. That is, each

of the approaches, while representing the process of learning as occurring in different ways, reinforces the modern
view of the individual. And this modern view ignores (as
pointed out earlier) how individuals are cultural beings and
how cultures are dependent upon natural systems. While
differing over how to facilitate change (which they all associate with progress), each approach misrepresents the nature of tradition, and thus the differences in how cultures
recognize and value what has been learned and handed
down over time, as backward and in need of being modern-
ized. The significance of the differences between educators
who associate empowerment with procedural problem-solving, emotive-based judgment, and critical reflection, largely
disappear when we realize that all three approaches reinforce the highly experimental approach to cultural life that
is the hallmark of modernity.

   This experimental orientation, where new ideas, values, and techniques (and technologies) are seen as progressive steps forward, leads to viewing as both irrelevant and
obstructionist the forms of transgenerational communication that characterize ecologically centered cultures. Stated
more succinctly, none of the current approaches to educational reform (with the possible exception of the Foxfire
Curriculum) help to clarify the nature and importance of
transgenerational communication—and how youth play a
necessary part in this vital cultural renewal and ecologically centering process. Lastly, these seemingly diverse
approaches to education, with their equally diverse vocabularies, all reinforce the most extreme expression of Western
anthropocentrism—that is, the individual is represented as
totally separate from the environment. Even the greening of
certain areas of the public school curriculum (which seems
further advanced than what can only be described as the
culturally reactionary position of university level professional education courses) has not led to the recognition that
the core values and assumptions of modernity are themselves ecologically problematic.

   Just as professors of education and classroom teachers
became aware of gender discrimination in the curriculum
and staffing patterns *only* after feminists had made signif-

icant gains in focusing public attention on the problem, professors of educators and classroom teachers are again repeat-
ing this earlier pattern by promoting a taken-for-granted
attitude toward the deep cultural assumptions now being
questioned by the more thoughtful individuals within the environmental movement. But it is more complex than being
trapped in what is now a reactionary pattern of thinking. If
the literature that represents the cutting-edge thinking of
the technocratically oriented educators is considered, it becomes clear that educational reform is being influenced primarily by powerful economic and technological interest
groups. Evidence of this trend can be seen in the number of
states and provinces across North America shifting to what is
called "outcome-based education." The justification for this
approach to educational reform is couched in language that
explains the need to contribute directly to the country's economic and technological competitiveness in an increasingly
globalized economy.

The following explanation of what is termed "transfor-
mational outcome-based education" is important because it
clearly suggests that there is a need for a new form of linkage between the content of the curriculum and life experiences—which educational and political reformers are
interpreting to mean life experiences in a computer-mediated work environment. According to William Sprady, a
leading advocate of educational restructuring,

> transformational OBE (outcome-based education) means
> that curriculum content is no longer the grounding and
> defining element of outcomes. Instead, outcomes are seen
> as culminating Exit role performances that include some-
> times complex arrays of knowledge, competencies, and ori-
> entations and require learning demonstrations in varying
> role contexts. . . . The bottom line of Transformational
> OBE is that students' learning is manifested through their
> ability to carry out performance roles in contexts that at
> least simulate life situations and challenges. (1992, p. 54)

Learning to carry out performance roles that simulate
"life situations" does not include the small-scale commu-
nity-oriented economic and technological practices that ful-

fill local needs. Nor does it involve learning to participate in renewing and carrying forward local traditions not dependent upon consumer and work-oriented relationships. Rather, when educational reformers think of performance outcomes that take account of the challenges that lie ahead, they have in mind the need to contribute to the development and use of the new computer-driven technologies that will keep the economy expanding and the local work force fully employed. What is not being considered is the connection between the globalizing of the technologically based economic system that educational restructuring is helping to further and the ecological crisis. Nor do educational reformers recognize that computer-based thinking and communicating threaten the stability of local economies and help create what Barbara Garson has called the "electronic sweatshop".

The varied concerns of environmentalists are also being ignored by educational reformers who identify themselves with the emancipatory, consciousness-raising tradition of liberal education. These reformers write a great deal about the need to use the classroom to foster critical thinking, to instill in students a sense of social justice that will lead them to work for the elimination of all forms of social oppression, and, in the name of democracy, to celebrate cultural differences while continually renegotiating the basis of relationships that govern everyday life. Using the language of postmodernism that represents every aspect of culture as a text, and critical literacy as the ability to deconstruct the forms of domination encoded in the texts (language systems of a culture), Peter McLaren and Colin Lankshear summarize what is seen by radical educators as the democratic alternative to the direction mainstream educational reform is moving in. As they state it,

> *critical literacy*, as we are using it here, becomes the interpretation of the social present for the purpose of transforming the cultural life of certain groups, for questioning tacit assumptions and unarticulated presuppositions of current cultural and social formations and the subjectivities and capacities for agenthood that they foster. It aims

at understanding the ongoing social stuggles over the signs of culture and over the definition of social reality— over what is considered legitimate and preferred meaning at any given historical period. (1993, p. 413)

This statement, which is representative of the thinking of radical educational reformers, also reveals why environmentalists should not be optimistic about finding allies within this group. While borrowing variously from pre-ecological thinkers such as Marx, Dewey, Freire, and now the deconstruction tradition of postmodern European intellectuals, they have retained as the basis of their vision of educational emancipation the most nihilistic elements of the modern mind set. By identifying the critical reflection of the individual as the sole source of authority for all forms of judgments, including moral judgments, their approach to education reinforces all the assumptions of modernity identified earlier: an extreme form of individualism supposedly free of all cultural influence, change as the expression of progress, anthropocentrism, and so forth. If these radical educational theorists were to address specific forms of social injustice, recognize that the modern nihilistic way of thinking they uphold as a universal human need is actually a culturally specific way of thinking, and take seriously the possibility that the conceptual and moral foundations of their view of emancipation have been turned into a reactionary position by the ecological crisis, environmentalists might then be able to establish a working relationship with them. Instead, this group of reformers continues to think in the context-free metaphors of freedom and equality, without considering the fundamental differences that exist between cultures and how these differences represent alternative pathways to living in relative balance with local natural systems.

Recent efforts to think about curriculum reform have also ignored the connections between the cultural patterns reinforced through education and the growing evidence that humans are altering both the micro- and macro-patterns of life in the Earth's ecosystems. Curriculum reform within the educational mainstream is increasingly being influenced by developments in the area of computer-based technologies—

with more of the curriculum reflecting the shift from books to interactive software programs. Changes in curriclum are also being influenced by professors of education who promote the modern idea that knowledge is constructed through the creative insight of the individuals, and through participatory decision making within the same age group. Even among the curriculum theorists who see themselves as extrapolating from postmodern thinking, and the principles of quantum physics, the form of curriculum that will enable people to live meaningful lives in the next century cannot escape the problem of using the vocabulary that privileges the reactionary beliefs and values of modernity. But it is a vocabulary that will make sense only to those teachers who already assume that everything is relative, and that what is immediately meaningful to the student should be the primary concern of the educator. Witness the concluding statement by Jacques Daignault, who is described by another leading curriculum theorist as the "major post-structuralist theoretician in curriculum studies":

> Hence learning is relevant to a logic of the signified; and teaching, to a logic of the signifier. And everybody repeats: the teacher, his analogies; the learner, his errors. So that the play of the repetition and the difference digs an abyss in the core of the teaching-learning process. Now, there is a paradoxical instance that circulates in the difference of the teaching-learning process: the 'nonsense' of the differential repetition of analogies to themselves. And this *sui-reference* of analogies is itself a function of the differences put forth for the joy of teaching. (1992, pp. 212–213)

And from a philosopher turned curriculum theorist, we learn that quantum physics and chaos theory have revolutionary implications for organizing school knowledge in ways that will foster a form of consciousness more in harmony with the ongoing process of becoming. Wayne B. Hamilton describes this new "holographic curriculum" in the following way:

> By exposing our students to the holographic core curriculum, we may affect their entire thought process. Thought

now has totality as its content. As such, it is more like an
art form than definite knowledge about how things are; its
function, like that of all metaphorical thinking, is to give
rise to a *new* perception, to *new* ways of looking at the
whole. Knowledge and thinking are thus related to the
ever-changing flux, the dynamic character of reality and
knowledge. (italics added, 1994, p. 19)

The thinking of Daignault and Hamilton may appear extreme to readers who are unfamiliar with educational literature. But it is not fundamentally at odds with the
"anti-tradition tradition" of thinking that underlies the
process-oriented followers of Freire and Dewey. Nor is it at
odds with the view of knowledge being promoted by the computer industry. CD-ROMs that enable students to "navigate"
through stored images and data in route to constructing their
own interpretations and narratives (indeed, their own sense
of history), and the prospects of entering virtual realities as a
way of escaping the limitations of their cultural embeddedness, are simply a more technologically based expression of
the same anthropocentric, change-oriented, individually centered form of modernism. But these expressions of modernism have a particularly ironic consequence: namely, the
more extreme the form of individualism, the more the individual is vulnerable to being manipulated by elite groups
who have an economic interest in representing "progress" in
terms of the latest technological innovations. Alasdair Mac-
Intyre's observation that self-identity is constituted within
the context of a particular set of cultural narratives seems
particularly relevant here. He notes that the individual

> can only answer the question 'What am I to do?" if
> (she/he) can answer the prior question "Of what story or
> stories do I find myself a part?" We enter human society,
> that is, with one or more imputed characters—roles into
> which we have been drafted—and we have to learn what
> they are in order to be able to understand how others re-
> spond to us and how our responses to them are apt to be
> understood. (1984, p. 216)

If the stories are about communication over the Internet,
the continuous changes in computer technology and navi-

gating through the storehouse of digitalized cultural artifacts, a corresponding form of subjectivity will emerge. Similarly, if the stories are about deconstructing all cultural
texts and creating one's own ideas and values, the individual's self-identity and sense of moral responsibility will be
equally limited. But these will not be forms of individualism
that take for granted a sense of moral connectedness to the
life forms that constitute the non-human environment. Nor
do they represent forms of individualism that will experience a sense of responsibility to carry forward and renew
the culture's wisdom and practical knowledge of how to live
within the limits of the environment—which is essential to
ensuring that the prospects of future generations are not
diminished.

As these brief observations about the modernizing orientation of public schools and universities suggest, radical
reform is urgently needed. But it will be difficult to achieve,
partly because the culture of modernism is also the basis of
progressive thinking so highly valued at all levels of education. The various professional languages, regardless of
whether they are technological or emancipatory in orientation, continue to reinforce the educator's natural attitude
toward the moral and intellectual certainties of modern consciousness. But the challenge of initiating fundamental reform will be no more difficult (or should we say at least as
difficult?) than getting scientists to recognize (and to take
responsibility for) changes they introduce into the world's
cultures, and in getting humanists and social scientists to
recognize the importance of learning from more ecologically
centered cultures. However, before discussing the specific
strategies that might serve as starting points for greening
the curricula of universities and public schools, it will first
be necessary to identify some of the characteristics of culture that are compatible with long-term sustainability.
Without these reference points it will be difficult to determine whether the reforms are part of the solution or are
helping to perpetuate the problem. It is also important to
recognize that some of the characteristics of ecologically
sustainable cultures I will identify in the next chapter
should themselves become the focal point for further discussion by environmentalists and the larger public.

Chapter 3

RETHINKING THE IDEOLOGICAL
FOUNDATIONS OF AN
EDUCATIONAL STRATEGY

In 1971, Ivan Illich observed that the "paradox of the school is evident: increased expenditure escalates their destructiveness at home and abroad" (p. 9). In terms of our discussion of how public schools and universities promote the culture of modernism, it would be appropriate to include them as part of the paradox—or as I have suggested, as part of the double bind that undermines environmentalists' efforts to halt the degradation of the environment. Illich clearly articulated the connection between high-status forms of knowledge promoted in public schools and universities and the worldwide expansion of a technologically driven approach to consumerism, but the message of his book, *Deschooling Society*, made little sense to most modern readers. To the more receptive readers, it suggested a return to a form of cultural behavior that few had experienced directly. The proposal to deschool society also seemed too extreme, particularly in a decade when radical educators were becoming preoccupied with theoretical issues surrounding the use of the schools to achieve Marx's vision of a classless society. As this vision of a nonexploitive society was predicated on the modern myth that science and technology provide the most advanced means of exploiting the environment for the good of all humanity, Illich's ideas were of little interest to these educational theorists. Nor was Illich's warning about the dangers of associating progress with the commodification of every aspect of cultural life, from the arts to the genetic commons (which is

the latest frontier of commodification) understood in relation to the emerging awareness of an ecological crisis.

With today's fuller understanding of the many ways in
which the biotic community is being threatened, Illich's critique of public schools and universities takes on greater relevance. Reading his analysis today, I find it increasingly
difficult to disagree with his observation about the role of
formal education in North America (and in other parts of
the world that use the Western model of education). As he
put it,

> the school system today performs the threefold function
> common to powerful churches throughout history. It is si-
> multaneously the repository of society's myth, the institu-
> tionalization of the myth's contradictions, and the locus of
> the ritual which reproduces and veils the disparities be-
> tween myth and reality. . . . The American university has
> become the final stage of the most all-encompassing initi-
> ation rite the world has ever known. (pp. 37–38.)

His pessimistic conclusion is that "we cannot go beyond the
consumer society unless we first understand that obligatory
public schools (and universities) inevitably reproduce such
a society, no matter what is taught in them" (p. 38). But I
find that I cannot make the leap to a deschooled culture
when thinking about educational reform—even when reform appears increasingly urgent.

Western style public schools and universities, for all
their recognized faults, are still spreading throughout the
world. And while many of the educational activities they
once had exclusive control over are increasingly being "de-
livered" through computers in ways that further limit critical reflection on what is being learned, I still find myself
confronted with the reality that the educational reforms essential to long-term ecological survival must start within
the context of existing educational institutions. Overcoming
the contradictions that Illich viewed as inherent in modern
educational institutions may lead to drastic changes in the
years ahead. But the process of reform must begin at those
leverage points within the existing educational system that

can best facilitate radical change. Educational reform must also be directed by a level of consensus about the general characteristics of ecologically sustainable cultures and, even more importantly, by an understanding of how specific educational reforms relate to these characteristics. As modern and largely urbanized cultures have evolved few patterns that are ecologically sustainable, my suggestions about both the characteristics of ecologically sustainable cultures and the curricular reforms that will help foster these characteristics should be seen as helping to frame the dialogue about the connections between education, culture, and ecosystems that the various groups that make up the environmental movement need to initiate and model for the public at large.

Two questions now need to be asked: "Which cultural patterns perpetuated by public schools and universities are ecologically sustainable?" and "Which patterns are based on cultural assumptions that do not take account of how humans are dependent upon the viability of natural systems?" We are just beginning to understand the complexity of indigenous peoples' ecological knowledge. Because our modern conceptual categories are based on deeply held assumptions about what separates progressive, enlightened cultures from traditional, backward cultures, it has been difficult to recognize that the traditional knowledge (including technologies) of indigenous peoples is location-specific and, as R. Norgaard observed, is accumulated and refined "through a unique co-evolution between specific social and ecological systems" (1985, p. 876). Indeed, our modern biases have made it difficult to recognize the significance of context specific knowledge. The dominance of economic and technological values in the thinking of modern observers has also made it difficult to understand cultural groups that have organized themselves on the basis of mythopoetic narratives which privilege other values as the basis for understanding essential relationships and give a sense of purpose to their lives. Generally, indigenous cultures that are centered on communal ceremonies, and that limit their economic and technological development by strict adherence to the principles of *reciprocity* in human/

nature relationships and redistribution in their human relationships, have been viewed as representing an earlier
stage in the process of human evolution—and thus as
anachronisms that have no relevance to modern people.
The writings of Marshall Sahlins, Stephen Lansing,
Helena Norberg-Hodge, and R. Norgaard, among others,
are helping us recognize the wisdom of the ecological practices of many indigenous cultures. But this revised way of
understanding cultural groups that are still threatened by
powerful interests who seek to modernize them does not directly answer the question about which of our own cultural
practices will contribute to a viable future for the biotic
community as a whole. Understanding the complexity of
local knowledge, as well as the ability of indigenous cultures to avoid the modern mistake of commodifying nature
and naturalizing the scientific approaches that will attempt
to bring every aspect of life under the control of experts, provides an important vantage point for recognizing the aspects of modern consciousness that are largely taken for
granted. This is important, but it still leaves us with the
problem of coming to terms with the challenge of evolving
our own ecologically sustainable cultural patterns—a challenge made even more difficult by our being a culturally diverse and largely urbanized society. Furthermore, while we
can learn from traditional ecologically centered cultures, we
cannot base changes in our own culture on their metanarratives and sacred ceremonies—which is the mistake of
some New Age thinkers. Radical reform of modernist assumptions requires, instead, that we address the problematic nature of our own tradition of distrusting traditions,
and thus find our own pathway to a less ecologically destructive form of existence.

Rectifying Our Political Vocabulary:
Confucius and Berry

As pointed out earlier, we use the languages of our culture (spoken, written, kinesic, architectural, legal, and so
forth) to communicate about relationships. At the same

time, these languages act on our thought processes and behavior by privileging the schemata of understanding encoded from past culturally mediated experiences. These
schemata for organizing, understanding, and valuing experience in culturally congruent ways are acquired as we
learn to think within the languages of our cultural group.
The cultural schemata stored and reproduced with only
minor variations in most instances of daily experience thus
serve to "normalize" how we understand the world. In addition, the relationships that language helps us understand
and negotiate *always* have a moral dimension to them. This
can be seen in the connection between moral behavior and
the way language represents the cultural group's understanding of relationships—such as in gendered language,
anthropocentric language that represents the environment
as natural resources, and so forth. The connection between
the cognitive schemata created through language and how
the schemata influence how we understand relationships
and of what constitutes appropriate moral behavior within
these culturally specific relationships can be seen even
more clearly in how people are now being identified as possessing genetic characteristics that predispose them to certain psychological and physical diseases. At the present, the
old moral codes still govern our relationships with these
people, but as economic forces become an even more dominant factor in how relationships are understood, the moral
codes that govern relationships with this group of people
will be dictated by the new "reality" that they are an "un-
touchable class."

To summarize this vital point, we use the languages of
our culture to communicate about relationships, and these
languages reproduce the culture's moral codes of how we
are to act in terms of these relationships. In recent years we
have witnessed how some individuals have remetaphorized
words in ways that lead to new understandings of previously taken-for-granted relationships, and thus to new expressions of moral behavior.

Over centuries of cultural practices and reinterpre-
tations, Confucian thought has helped clarify our understanding of the connections between language, relationships,

and the moral ecology of a sustainable society. Although it can be argued that Confucius was primarily concerned with human relationships, rather than with the relationships between humans and nature, the following passage from Ezra Pound's translation of Confucius' "Great Digest" seems relevant to understanding the importance of rectifying our use of language—especially if we are to become aware of how language can normalize our relationship with the environment in ways that reproduce past misunderstandings. According to what has come down to us over centuries of reinterpretation (including Pound's own translation), Confucius is purported to have written:

> The men of old wanting to clarify and diffuse throughout the empire that light which comes from looking straight into the heart and then acting, first set up good government in their own states; wanting good government in their states, they first established order in their own families; wanting order in the home, they first disciplined themselves; desiring self-discipline, they rectified their own hearts; and wanting to rectify their own hearts, they sought precise verbal definitions of their inarticulate thoughts (the tones given off by the heart); wishing to attain precise verbal definitions, they set to extend their knowledge to the utmost. This completion of knowledge is rooted in sorting things into their organic categories. (Pound, 1950, pp. 29–30)

As one of the main insights in this passage might be obscured by arguments over its failure to represent how difficult the rectification of language is when the connections between culture, language, and the taken-for-granted attitude of the individual are fully understood, I would like to bring into the discussion Wendell Berry's observation relating to the misuse of language to what he sees as the growing sense of disorder both in our communities and our relationships with nature.

In the essay, "Standing By Words," Berry suggests that accountability in the use of language involves representing clearly and accurately what is going on inside the individual, as well as the nature of her or his external relationships (1983, p. 24). That is, language should be used in ways that rectify the culturally derived conceptual and moral categories that govern the individual's inner world of meaning, identity, and self-direction. The language should also represent clearly and accurately how culture is nested in the autopoietic systems that make up the natural world. In many ways, Berry is giving us a modern rendering of the Confucian insight that if we want to rectify our relationships with each other, and with our environment, we must first rectify our use of language.

Berry further suggests accountability in the use of language must meet the following three conditions:

1. It must designate its object precisely.

2. Its speaker must stand by it: must believe it, be accountable for it, be willing to act on it.

3. This relation of speaker, word, and object must be conventional; the community must know what it is. (p. 24)

I would add that accountability also requires a greater awareness of the cultural and historical origins of the language being used to "designate its object precisely." For example, when environmental reformers today use a metaphorical language that was the basis of a cultural era that put us on our current ecologically destructive pathway, they are being trapped in a linguistic double bind that contributes to confusion about what the priorities of the community should be. Berry's second condition, that there should not be a discrepancy between the speaker's language and personal life, seems clear enough. But it should be recognized that without an ecologically centered cultural support network it is difficult for environmental reformers to live what they advocate—in the same way that other reformers were unable to escape entirely the contradictions of their times. Berry's third condition should be expanded to read, " the community must know what it is in the context of the traditions that have co-evolved in response to changes in local ecosystems." Without this qualification, the community could be based on a form of economy that is environmentally destructive. It could even be xenophobic, or exploitative of other people.

Toward an Ecologically Centered Ideology

Of all the discussions of ideology I have read over the years, Clifford Geertz's description seems the most adequate for clarifying how language frames our way of understanding relationships—and our moral responsibilities within the culturally defined web of relationships between humans and their environment. According to Geertz,

> Cultural patterns—religious, philosophical, aesthetic, scientific, ideological—are "programs"; they provide a template or blueprint for the organization of social and psychological processes, much as a genetic system provides such a template for the organization of organic processes. (1973, p. 216)

As these cultural patterns are communicated and reenacted through the language processes of everyday life, they are expressions of a living ideology, or worldview. In terms of Western cultures, however, one of our patterns that goes back to the origins of print-based thought and communication is to view abstractly formulated ideas as a progressive basis for directing the course of social change. Thus, on one level our everyday lives, enmeshed in cultural patterns we take for granted, are guided by the deep ideological orientation Geertz describes. And at the same time, different interest groups are competing to win suppport from society for using their more abstract ideas and values as the basis for social reform. Ironically, these ideologues live their everyday lives in accordance with the cultural patterns they want to change. This separation of abstract ideas about improving the future from the reformer's everyday life has also become an accepted cultural pattern. But we now need a new standard against which to judge the merits of these abstract ideologies. A reformist ideology has most often been judged in terms of how it addressed social justice issues, but this standard overlooked the way in which the ideology based the vision of a better human future on an anthropocentric understanding of the environment as a human resource, and on the need to use science and technology for the purpose of expanding society's material well-being. Given our increased understanding of the dangers of anthropocentric thinking, especially when it is based on the assumption that change is inherently progressive in nature, we can now recognize that a reform-oriented ideology must be ecologically centered. That is, it must reflect an awareness that individual thought and behavior cannot be separated from the complex language processes that characterize a living culture, and that cultural patterns cannot be separated from the natural systems that are the basis of physical and symbolic life.

Over the last three hundred or so years, there have been a number of theoretically based ideologies intended to promote modernization in one form or another; the various expressions of Marxism and liberal capitalism are the most obvious examples. Indeed, the influence of these ideologies can be seen in how many of our cultural patterns that are taken for granted now conform to these originally abstract schemata: for example, how we consider ourselves as separate from what we observe and think about, our proclivity to identify new technologies with progress (even when the technologies de-skill workers and diminish work opportunities), and our tendency to limit our sense of responsibility to what can be immediately experienced, rather than to consider our responsibility to traditions and to the needs of unborn generations. But when we recognize the connections between these modernizing ideologies and the often wasteful human demands that are now overwhelming the sustaining capacity of natural systems, it becomes obvious that we need to change the conceptual and moral foundations of the ideas and values that are to guide us into a sustainable future. Furthermore, as ideological orientations are encoded and reproduced in the language patterns of everyday life, this means we must also become more aware of the nature of relationships affected by our language. That is, as we have a clearer understanding of the nature of an ecologically centered ideology, we will also use language in a more accountable way. And this change in language will lead, in turn, to changes in our moral relationships.

To summarize the above discussion, an ideological framework influences not only what we are aware of, but also how we understand basic relationships—including our sense of time, and how we are connected to both human and nonhuman communities. An ideology also influences what we will ignore, and what we will understand in ways that reproduce past biases and misconceptions. A modernizing ideology, in effect, influences people to be aware only of the patterns that are expressions of modernity, and to be less able to recognize or value cultural patterns based on more traditionally oriented metanarratives. For example, in writing about the impact of modern tourists on the Ladakh culture wedged between China and India, Helena Norberg-Hodge observed that "tourists can only see the material side of the culture—the worn-out robes, the dzo pulling the plow, the barren land. They cannot see peace of mind or the quality of family and community relations. They cannot see the psychological, social, and spiritual wealth of the Ladakhis" (1991, p. 95). A modernizing ideology also limits people's ability to recognize patterns in both the mainstream and minority cultures that should be valued because they are ecologically sustainable.

The connection between ideology and what we are aware of and value makes it essential that the reform of public schools and universities be based on an understanding of how a guiding ideology must reflect the characteristics that our mainstream culture will need to adopt if it is going to be ecologically sustainable. It is also essential for environmentally oriented reformers to be aware of the characteristics of modernizing ideologies that contribute to the destruction of the environment. As many of our progressive ideals are grounded in these modern ideologies, this process of thinking against the grain is very difficult indeed. This process of rectifying our political language, in turn, will help environmentalists recognize why different cultural expressions of cultural/bio-conservatism, rather than modern liberalism, are ecologically accountable.

Influence of Liberal Ideologies on Education

In recent decades two forms of liberalism have alternately guided educational reform at both the public school and university levels: emancipatory liberalism and technocratic liberalism. The third distinct expression of liberalism, neo-Romantic liberalism, has been largely limited to reform efforts in the early grades of public and private schools. However, a strong case can now be made that the view of the individual as the constructor of knowledge that was the hallmark of this strand of liberalism is increasingly being embraced by technocratic liberals who are promoting the use of computers at all levels of the educational process. While I shall discuss separately how each form of liberalism emphasizes different aspects of modernity and thus contributes to the moral framework of a consumer oriented culture, it should be kept in mind that they share a common set of assumptions that serve as the core conceptual and moral underpinnings of modern culture. These shared assumptions lead to the following attitudes: (1) thinking of change (in ideas, values, technologies, etc.) as expressions of social progress; (2) viewing the environment from a human perspective (indeed, the environment has been entirely ignored in most discussions of educational reform); (3) representing the individual as the basic social unit responsible for establishing the authority of ideas and values; and (4) promoting the over-turning of tradition in all areas of cultural life. While the following discussion will focus on the assumptions and values foregrounded by each form of liberalism, it should be kept in mind that they all share a common geneology that can be traced back to the founding "fathers" of our modern scientific and technologically based culture: René Descartes, John Locke, Francis Bacon, and Thomas Hobbes, among others.

Connections Between Neo-Romantic Liberalism and Constructivism

The roots of this tradition of liberalism in education can be traced back to Locke, but its distinctive orientation was more directly influenced by the ideas of Jean Jacques

Rousseau, Sigmund Freud, the followers of John Dewey who took seriously only part of his educational theory, and such recent advocates of reform as A. S. Neill and Carl Rogers. Their emphasis on the freedom and inherent goodness of the child led to creating educational settings where students could use their curiosity and free imagination to create their own ideas, values, and understanding of relationships. Adults were to play the role of facilitators by helping to organize stimulating environments for youthful learners. They were not to pass on any knowledge gained from their own experience, as it would inhibit the students' own processes of self-discovery. Centering the educational process on the freedom of students to learn for themselves led to viewing immediate experience as the only valid time frame for "authentic" learning. Thus, learning about the connections between past, present, and future was viewed either as oppressive or irrelevant. Similarly, learning how their own subjectively constructed ideas, values, identities, sense of meaning, and so forth, were expressions of deeply held cultural patterns, and how these patterns were altering local ecosystems, was also considered irrelevant. The anthropocentrism of this stream of liberalism was so strong that the environment was viewed as the physical context for the students' free and playful explorations—in effect, it was the giant sandbox within which the students' self-discovery took place.

Since the 1900s, this form of educational liberalism has appeared twice as short-lived educational reform: in the first decades of the nineteenth century, and in the late sixties and early seventies. In both instances it was partly a reaction against what was perceived as the stultifying effects of forcing education to fit the regimented and competitive demands of the workplace. It also expressed a genuine desire (mostly on the part of middle class parents and educational theorists) to provide a form of education that would let children be natural, creative, and playful. But in recent years, the distinctive view of learning that characterized this ideologically driven view of the child has become more widely adopted in institutions responsible for the professional education of teachers, and, more importantly, by developers of educational computer software. In colleges of education across the country students taking professional education courses are told that individuals, either by themselves or in cooperative learning situations, construct their own knowledge. This neo-Romantic view of the autonomous learner is now spreading through higher education as computers become more widely adopted.

The sandbox, which is an appropriate metaphor for the earlier expressions of neo-Romantic approaches to elementary education, is now being replaced by the Internet, which allows students and professors to "surf" as their intellectual curiosity dictates. The assumption about learning now shared by advocates of the "open classroom," constructivist professors of education, and developers of software for classrooms is that individuals should use their own direct experience as the basis for constructing their own ideas and theories. The influence of culture, particularly the role of language in providing the schemata that contributes to thinking in conceptual and moral categories of the language community, is totally ignored. One of the great ironies of recent years is that, with the rapid growth of educational computing, one of the main conceptual underpinnings of neo-Romantic liberalism is now being incorporated into the thinking of technocratic liberals promoting the use of computers by children. What began as an educational reform effort to protect the early years of learning from the distortions of materialistic and power-oriented adults has now become the central underpinning for making technology the basis of learning at all levels of the educational process—from pre-school through graduate school. The over five hundred software programs now being marketed to children from three to five years old may appear benign to many parents, but as children abandon the sandbox for the computer keyboard that controls the seemingly amazing animations on the screen, they are being indoctrinated with a subtle yet destructive form of environmental education. And graduate students who are now being technologically conditioned to accept the neo-Romantic view of themselves as constructivist learners will have even more difficulty recognizing how cultural patterns that they take for granted contribute to the ecological crisis. In addition to reinforcing the modern cultural assumptions about change, anthropocentrism, and so forth, computer-mediated thinking and communication reproduces the same Cartesian way of thinking that ignores the shaping influence of such cultural patterns, and their historical continuities.

Technocratic Liberalism and the Commoditization of Knowledge

While neo-Romantic liberalism has been primarily associated with the education of young children, technocratic liberalism has its roots in the early epistemological traditions that were the basis of modern science. Technocratic liberalism also has deep roots in Classical Liberal thinking about the efficacious connections between economic competition, the quest for greater technological efficiency, and the need to incorporate more aspects of cultural life into the marketplace. The influence of technocratic liberalism on education can be seen in educational reforms that still mirror the changes that took place in the Industrial Revolution, and now in the Age of Information. Initially, classrooms were modeled on the early factory system, and later on the principles of scientific management that have undergone their own evolutionary process. Even the language used today for understanding student/teacher relationships, as well as the purpose of education itself, reflect the continuing influence of technocratic liberalism. The emphasis on efficiency, measurable outcomes, and "products" of effective classroom management that were so popular just over a decade ago, have now been replaced by the need to adapt schools and universities to the requirements of the new technology and to the process of "restructuring"—which is the new buzzword among educators. Indeed, the publications of both the computer industry and the educational establishment now agree that the single most important skill in the 21st Century will be the ability to manage information.

Technocratic liberalism has marginalized the potential of the critical stance inherent in the neo-Romantic emphasis on discovery-based learning by adopting their constructivist view of learning. They have also succeeded in indoc-trinating the middle class with the idea that computer-based education is the best defense against the growing specter of unemployment. With so many trendsetting groups embracing the technocrats' vision of progress, it is important to have a clear understanding of why this latest expression of technocratic liberalism should be challenged by environmentalists—whether concerned directly with ed-ucational reform or not. Because the focus here is on the need for radical educational reform, I shall frame the eco-logically problematic nature of technocratic liberalism in terms of educational issues.

Many environmentalists find computers indispensable for modeling the complex changes occurring in ecosystems. Computers are also being used constructively in a variety of other work and educational settings. It is important to ac-knowledge this in order to avoid the impression that I am suggesting we should turn our backs entirely on computer-based technology. This would be an impossibility, even if co-gent arguments could be articulated. But it is absolutely essential that we do not get caught in the cultural myth, and impose it on other cultures, that computers represent a superior form of intelligence, and that expert systems should take over more areas of individual and cultural life. Not getting caught in this new version of the technological determinism myth requires being able to put computers, and the underlying ideology of technological liberalism, in a more balanced perspective.

In terms of the problem of educational reform, this will require having a better understanding of the cultural ori-entations reinforced through the use of computers, particu-larly in educational settings. It also requires a more critical understanding of how these cultural orientations now rep-resent the latest stage in the development of modernity. How a technology amplifies and reduces the cultural and subjective experiences of the individual who is using it, which I explained more fully in the previous chapter, needs to be brought into the discussion of technocratic liberalism. As suggested earlier, computers amplify explicit and digi-talized forms of knowledge, and reduce (put out of focus) tacit and contextual forms of knowledge. That is, computer mediated learning (which involves mostly some form of a problem solving situation) makes it difficult to be aware of the cultural patterns that are an integral aspect of all human experience. These cultural patterns may be at the deep level of assumptions and mythopoetically grounded schemata that influence how we "interpret and process the data"—to use the current technocratic metaphors for representing human thought. To put this another way, computers are unable to amplify or bring into the data manipulation process the deeper levels of a culture's symbolic system partly because the people who design the technology, including the software programs, do not understand the deep metaphorical foundation of their own culture and how it differs from other cultures. In effect, computers amplify a cultural view of learning that represents data as the basis of thought, and puts out of focus how the metaphorical language that appears on the monitor encodes and reproduces a culturally specific form of intelligence. The corresponding inability to represent the epistemic patterns of other groups also makes the computer particularly unsuited for helping students understand in any other way than to project their own patterns of thinking onto these other groups.

As long as culture is not seen as contributing to the ecological crisis, the computer and the liberal ideology that underlies its further technological development will be seen as part of the solution to today's problems. But when it becomes more widely recognized that culture is a powerful and largely unconscious shaper of people's thoughts and behavior, we will then have to ask whether the expansion of computer use in educational settings will enable students and teachers to address the deep cultural roots of the ecological crisis. The educational challenge is made more difficult by the fact that computers hide the cultural assumptions built into their design and software by incorporating them into the process of interacting with the technology. It is a difficult double bind to recognize, much less get free of, particularly when university professors and classroom teachers continue to ignore that the ecological crisis must be addressed at the level of culturally influenced values and perceptions of reality. The specific cultural assumptions reinforced through the use of computers include the following: that data/information is the basis of thought; that thought is an individually centered process; that the external world is understood and manipulated in terms of human thought and values; and that the simulations, problem solving, and everything else done with computers is an expression of progress. These are all elements of the anthropocentric and experimentally oriented culture discussed earlier. They also contribute to undermining the authority of local traditions that otherwise would inhibit the spread of consumerism.

What has not been mentioned before is that technocratic liberalism (including computers) reinforces a pattern of thinking that contributes to the increasing power of experts to legitimate the forms of knowledge and values that are to guide human practices. These forms of knowledge, in turn, serve further to strengthen the perception that experts are the best qualified both to identify the problem (regardless of where in the world it is) and to provide the technologically and scientifically based solution. In effect, the increasing dominance of this form of knowledge represents the primary basis of authority for Western educated elite groups who are now promoting the globalization of modern culture.

These privileged forms of knowledge reflect the distinct characteristics of what has been referred to as a technological form of consciousness (Berger, Berger, Kneller, 1974, pp. 23–40). In addition to creating a hierarchy of experts who possess increasingly specialized knowledge, the technological form of consciousness now being promoted as the highest achievement of modernity involves making sense of the world in a very special way. According to Peter Berger, Brigitte Berger, and Hansfried Kneller, the co-authors of *The Homeless Mind: Modernization and Consciousness*, the most basic characteristic of this form of consciousness is the taken-for-granted pattern of reducing experience to self-contained units—that is, the component parts of experience. This enables the technocrat to analyze and refigure the component parts of cultural experience into new and more experimental patterns. This process involves a heavy reliance on theoretical thinking. The success of refiguring a new pattern is determined by continual measurement of results that occur when different variables are introduced. The emphasis on measurement, in turn, leads to equating efficiency with what is the best solution—that is, what should be most highly valued.

The cognitive style of the technological expert, with its proclivity for constructing more efficient and theoretically based solutions, is further buttressed by the assumption that scientifically based solutions (e.g. mechanical and social techniques, models, procedures, etc.) can be universally applied—regardless of local traditions and unique characteristics of local ecosystems. Norberg-Hodge gives the following account of how the knowledge of Western experts is being universalized:

> The same yardsticks, originally developed for Europeans, are used everywhere. For instance, the indicators that determine how much a baby should weigh at a certain age, what the minimum room temperature should be, and what a healthy diet is, are applied universally. Western experts refer to both the people and animals of Ladakh as 'stunted' because they are smaller than the global standard! The accepted levels of exposure to radiation, which were established for young European males, are applied to all people regardless of age, sex, or size. The narrow and specialized outlook of some experts prevents them from seeing the broad implications of their work and the cultural insensitivity of their universal answers. When asked, at a recent symposium, about the vegetables they used to eat in Africa before we started exporting seeds to them, a Swedish agricultural expert answered, 'They didn't have any. They used to eat weeds.' To him the plants they ate did not have the same status as the plants he was used to calling 'vegetables.' (1992, p. 152)

Other cultural ways of knowing that enfold locally originated techniques within a moral ecology constituted by mythopoetic accounts of the relationship of all forms of life are simply not recognized by the technocrats' reductionist and decontextualized way of thinking. Local traditions, including what is regarded as sacred, are also disregarded by the claims of scientific and technologically based knowledge. While technocrats use the rhetoric of liberalism to represent how their activities are culturally transcendent expressions of human progress and the search for new knowledge, they are, in reality, also motivated by a concern with profits and power.

When students learn to think in the cognitive patterns of the liberal technocrats encoded in the software of computers, they are being indoctrinated into a supposedly culture-free pattern of thought. Indeed, a strong case can be made that any form of literacy-based learning helps reinforce the assumptions that represent the technological cognitive style as the next progressive step in human development. The printed word, whether in a book or on a computer screen, reinforces the sensation of being an individual observer and thinker. Through the printed representation of some aspect of the experiential world, print helps to create an inversion where the abstract word becomes more real than what is directly experienced. Print also provides the basis for transforming the flow of experience into fixed entities and events that allow the supposedly objective observer to make analytical and comparative judgments. The participatory nature of face-to-face communication, in addition to reliance on the multiple sources of information from the use of all the senses, tends not to reinforce the cultural notion of an observer and thinker who is analyzing the "objective" reality represented in print. In effect, oral-based cultures are less likely to evolve along the same technological pathway taken by Western cultures already grounded in anthropocentric metanarratives.

*Merging of Emancipatory Liberalism
and Cognitive Science*

The tradition of liberalism that equates critical reflection with the civic-minded and morally responsible individual goes back to Socrates. Since his time, philosophers,

political theorists, and, more recently, educators have justified the importance of critical reflection on a variety of
grounds. But their justifications for what some thinkers
have associated with the essence of being human, when distilled down to the basic issue, are based on the assumption
that critical reflection is essential to human progress. While
this tradition has led to important contributions to improving the human condition, particularly in the area of social
justice, it has also contributed to the nihilistic orientation of
modern culture where cultural norms and values are being
relativized by the subjective judgment of the "autonomous"
individual. The current emphasis on individuals giving
meaning to their "own" experience, to creating their own
"authentic" ideas and values, and to judging whether traditions have any personal relevance, are now based less on the
individual's powers of critical reflection than the advocates
of this tradition of liberalism would like to think. The tradition of critical reflection, by placing authority in the judgment of the individual, opened the door to placing authority
in other areas of individual experience—emotions, intuition,
feelings of group solidarity, and so forth. Ironically, this conceptual and moral underpinning of our modern and increasingly individual-centered culture is not found in ecologically
centered cultures. Nor did it achieve widespread acceptance
in mainstream Western culture until the myth of progress
had also become an assumption taken for granted by the rising business oriented middle class.

In recent decades, emancipatory liberals have often
viewed technocratic liberals as their main enemy. By mislabeling them as "conservatives," recent emancipatory liberals, following in the tradition of Paulo Freire, failed to
recognize that they were part of a different anti-tradition
tradition than that of the technocrats. The anti-tradition orientation of technocratic liberals led to undermining craft
and other forms of folk knowledge that had been passed on
through the generations, and to elevating the authority of
scientifically based experts who were attempting to create
economic markets through the commoditization of every aspect of life. The emancipatory liberals' tradition of being
against all traditional forms of knowledge and practices, on

the other hand, had the effect of undermining the community of memory that could have served as a source of resistance to the modernizing efforts of the technocratic liberals. While emancipatory liberals were correct in recognizing that technocratic liberals were changing the cultural dynamics that favored elite groups, they failed to recognize that they both shared the core assumptions of modern culture: the progressive nature of change, an anthropocentric view of nature, the secular and reductionist interpretation of life given legitimacy by Western science, and the view of the individual as the basic social unit. They also shared with technocratic liberals the assumption that individual judgment is the final source of authority, but they interpreted this assumption in a radically different way. Emancipatory liberals viewed it as a potential of every individual that could be realized only through the development of critical reflection, while the technocratic liberals understood the rational process in more Cartesian terms. That is, the rational process for the latter involves procedural problem solving approaches to thinking that can only be carried out by the people who possess the mathematical and scientific knowledge necessary for using data to improve the efficiency and predictability of techniques. They view technical expertise as a goal of education, whereas the emancipatory liberals argue that critical reflection is essential to a participatory democracy and to achieving a more egalitarian society.

The assumptions that Gouldner identified as basic to the culture of critical discourse, which was discussed in the last chapter, are also shared by emancipatory and technocratic liberals. That is, both take for granted the assumption that ideas and values should be determined in a competitive setting where everybody is free to make up their own minds about the meaning of the evidence. Stated somewhat differently, neither group recognizes the authority of various forms of communal traditions—including the authority of elders. The difference between the two groups is that technocratic liberals require what amounts to evidence of scientific and technological competence as a precondition to participation in the culture of critical discourse. Furthermore, both forms of liberalism share the modern proclivity to claim that their ideas, technologies, and values have universal applicability.

An observation that Gouldner makes about rules of the culture of critical discourse shared by both emancipatory and technocratic liberals helps put in focus another issue that is particularly critical to any discussion of why some traditional cultures are able to live within the limits of local ecosystems while modern cultures are not. Gouldner notes that adherents to the rules of critical discourse de-authorize "all speech grounded in traditional societal authority, while it authorizes itself . . . as the standard of *all* 'serious' speech" (1979, p. 29). This means that sacred texts, use of narratives and ceremony as a form of cultural storage and renewal, knowledge of elders, and so forth, should be disregarded in favor of knowledge that has met only the test of critical (competitive) discourse. Ironically, the free marketplace of ideas has its corollary in the free market that is used to determine both what should be produced and how it should be priced. The marketplace of ideas, like the free marketplace that is supposed to govern economic activity, is predicated on the modern assumption that all forms of change, over time, lead to human progress. That is, neither is judged in terms of how they contribute to the cultural group's ability to sustain itself in an environment where the margins of survival are constantly changing.

In addition to these shared assumptions, both forms of liberalism also share a distorted understanding of the nature of tradition and community. As I shall discuss the connections between these two fundamental aspects of human existence within the context of cultural/bio-conservatism, the treatment here will be limited to examining why emancipatory and technocratic liberals either take an oppositional stance toward both the authority of tradition and community, or omit any reference to either of them. Their misunderstanding of these two aspects of human experience is partly a result of the problem discussed in the previous chapter: that is, the explanatory frameworks acquired as part of their university education were not based on a deep understanding of the nature of culture. Both groups of liberals acquired the language that foregrounds change as progressive in nature, but they did not encounter coherent explanations of how the historical aspects of culture (that is, all the patterns and technologies handed down from the past) can be understood as tradition. Some of the traditions, such as how the relationships of humans with the biotic community continue to be understood in narrow economic terms or the use of technologies that encode assumptions about the plenitude of "natural resources," need to be radically altered. But many traditions handed down from the past and renewed over generations are sources of empowerment and contribute to the quality of individual and community life: civil liberties, print technologies, food preservation technologies, ceremonies that renew awareness of fundamental relationships, and so forth. The blanket rejection of tradition inherent in the emancipatory liberal's appeal to the individual's critical reflection as the final source of authority and in the technocratic liberal's proclivity to use the values of efficiency and profitability as the primary criteria for determining which traditions are to be replaced by more experimental technologies, suggests a basic ignorance of how human experience, even in modern cultures, is dependent upon the past.

The other reason for their respective ways of rejecting tradition can be found in how certain key aspects of their ideology are understood. Their view of time as a linear unfolding and improvement in human possibilities makes it difficult to acknowledge that most of what is viewed as today's innovations involve building upon what has come down to us over time. Recognizing the destructiveness and disorienting nature of some traditions, such as technologies that enable us to build nuclear bombs and art forms that celebrate nihilism, might lead to the awareness that some of today's achievements are as equally misguided as holding on to outworn traditions. When personal gain is achieved through the introduction of new technologies it is even more difficult to be cautious about equating innovations with progress. The other aspect of their ideology that makes it difficult to acknowledge the complexity of cultural continuities (traditions) is the central role they ascribe to the individual. The metaphor of the individual nested in culture,

and culture nested in ecosystems simply cannot be accommodated by their ideologically based way of understanding
the individual. The following statements suggest the difficulty of reconciling the abstract idea of an autonomous individual with how we are actually embedded in diverse
cultures and ecosystems. Freire's statement is particularly
interesting because educators around the world embraced
his ideas as the basis for decolonizing human consciousness
without realizing that Freire's own view of time, individualism, and the power of critical reflection made him an apos-
tle of Western modernity. In his world famous book,
Pedagogy of the Oppressed he writes:

> Human existence cannot be silent, nor can it be nourished
> by false words, but only by true words, with which men
> transform the world. To exist humanly, is to *name* the
> world, to change it. Once named, the world in its turn
> reappears to the namers as a problem and requires of
> them a new *naming*. Men are not built in silence, but in
> word, in work, in action-reflection. (1974 edition, p. 76)

This liberal view of the autonomous individual is being
further strengthened by scientists who continue to ignore
the influence of culture in their attempts to explain the nature of consciousness and the basis of language—two aspects of human life that are in particular need of being
understood in a culturally comparative way. For example,
David J. Chalmer's explanation of how the scientific study
of the brain has not yet led to an adequate understanding of
consciousness is typical of how culture, both as a source of
tacit meaning and categories of understanding, is being
ignored.

> From an objective viewpoint, the brain is relatively com-
> prehensible. When you look at this page, there is a whir of
> processing: photons strike your retina, electrical signals
> are passed up your optic nerve and between different
> areas of your brain. . . . But there is also a subjective as-
> pect. When you look at the page you are conscious of it, di-
> rectly experiencing the images and words as part of your
> *private, mental life*. . . . Together such experiences make

up consciousness: the *subjective, inner life of the mind.*
(italics added, 1995, p. 80)

The autonomy of the individual is further supported by
Steven Pinker, who is the director of the Center for Cognitive
Neuroscience at the Massachusetts Institute of Technology.
In making the case that language is not "an insidious shaper
of thought," but rather a "biological adaption to communicate
information," Pinker restates what has become a scientific orthodoxy: namely, that "the computations underlying mental
life are caused by the wiring of the intricate networks that
make up the cortex, networks with millions of neurons, each
neuron connected to thousands of others, operating in thousands of a second" (1993, pp. 19, 317). A third example of how
scientists are buttressing the conceptual and moral foundations of liberalism at the very time that the ecological crisis is
signalling its failure can be seen in the keynote address given
by Robert Haynes to the 16th Congress on Genetics. While
the following statement indicates that the liberal assumptions about the nature of progressive change and the ability
of rational thought to far surpass nature's design are still
basic to how the promise of science is now being understood,
the statement also serves to legitimate the autonomous individual who is free of all moral responsibility. Indeed, if the following statement by Haynes were to be taken seriously, a
totally individualistic and nihilistic lifestyle could be justified
on the grounds that regardless of the behaviors of individuals
progress will still be guaranteed by the scientists' technical
knowledge of the genetic basis of life.

> What the ability to manipulate genes should indicate to
> people is the very deep extent to which we are biological
> machines. The traditional view is built on the foundation
> that life is sacred . . . Well, not anymore. It's no longer pos-
> sible to live by the idea that there is something special,
> unique, even sacred, about living organisms. (quoted in
> Kimbrell, 1992, p. 17)

By framing the nature of the autonomous individual in a
way that requires experts to play a guiding role, liberal sci-

entists are able to ignore the importance of cultural traditions in shaping the attitudes of the individual—even the taken-for-granted attitude toward thinking of humans as machines that can be further engineered.

All forms of liberalism have had difficulty reconciling the moral responsibility of humans with the larger biotic community because of their emphasis on individual freedom, the emancipatory power of critical reflection and instrumental rationalism, and the expectation that change represents a continual expansion of human possibilities. The emancipatory and technocratic liberals have largely gotten around this difficulty by focusing on the socially ameliorative qualities of critical reflection and the steady advances of scientific technological expertise. The two most prominent emancipatory liberals, John Dewey and Paulo Freire, have directly written about how individuals are to be involved in the reform process of community life. However, both demonstrated a limited understanding of communities where the distinctive cultural patterns that connect the past with the present and future are visible—as in many ethnic communities. This disregard for the distinctiveness of cultural traditions in language and thought processes, to cite one of the more critical aspects that separate cultural groups, enabled Dewey to argue for a form of ongoing community renewal based on the group's use of the scientific method to make collective decisions. Freire continues to view the process of community renewal in terms of consciousness raising where each critically reflective individual enters into dialogue with others, including the privileged classes, about the oppressiveness of all cultural patterns. In effect, both assume that healthy communities are characterized by continual reflection and ongoing negotiation of what should be the basis of community life. That is, both understand community within the liberal framework that bases continual cultural change and experimentation on the limited perspective (and experience) of critically reflective individuals.

Technocratic liberals such as Frederick W. Taylor, B. F. Skinner and current promoters of computer-based learning have also understood community as inherently backward and limiting. Their approach to improving the productivity of community members involved marginalizing people's own skills by elevating the role of experts, and undermining other forms of local knowledge by using the scientific method as a basis for finding more efficient and profitable corporate approaches to commodifying human needs—including farming, manufacturing, education, and communication. The main point here is that technocratic liberals indirectly communicated their understanding of community through their continual efforts to bring all aspects of everyday life under the control of scientifically based technologies. Like the emancipatory liberals, they continue to understand community as part of the project of progressive modernism, and they ignore the fact that their messianic vision of bringing the same form of modernism to every city and village in the world represents an even more destructive form of colonialism. As many environmentalists now recognize, it is a form of colonialism that undermines the ability of local communities around the world to live less destructively in their relationship with local ecosystems.

The major reason that the theory and practices of both forms of liberalism lead to undermining the ecology of morally coherent communities is that the basic nature of community has not been understood. The emphasis on emancipating individuals and finding more efficient techniques, which represents the primary goals of these two traditions of educational liberalism, is based on a misconception of a basic reality of all communities—namely, that they are conservative in nature. This conservative quality can be seen in how both Wendell Berry and Robert Bellah describe the nature of a healthy community. According to Berry,

A healthy culture [community] is a communal order of memory, insight, value, work, conviviality, reverance, inspiration. It reveals the human necessities and the human limits. It clarifies our inescapable bonds to the earth and to each other. It assures that the necessary restraints are observed, that the necessary work is done, and that it is done well. (1986, p. 43)

These qualities, as expressed by cultural groups still under the influence of mythopoetic metaphors that represent all live forms as interdependent, are carried forward and renewed by each generation. It is a conserving process that builds on traditions, rather than an experimental effort of each generation to free itself from traditions.

The view of community that Robert Bellah and his co-authors present in *Habits of the Heart: Individualism and Commitment in American Life* (1985) represents even more clearly the conservative orientation of communities—even communities that are now conserving the traditions of technological innovation that will make them more dependent upon an increasingly privileged class of scientific and technocratic experts. In their attempt to articulate the limitations of expressive and utilitarian forms of individualism, the authors represent community in the following way:

> Communities, in the sense in which we are using the term, have a history—in an important sense they are constituted by their past—and for this reason we can speak of a real community as a 'community of memory,' one that does not forget its past. In order to not forget that past, a community is involved in retelling its story, its consititutive narrative, and in so doing, it offers examples of men and women who have embodied and exemplified the meaning of community. . . . The stories that make up a tradition contain conceptions of character, of what a good person is like, and of the virtues that define such character. But the stories are not all exemplary, not all about successes and achievements . . . And if the community is completely honest, it will remember stories not only of suffering received but of suffering inflicted—dangerous memories, for they call the community to alter ancient evils. The communities of memory that tie us to the past also turn us toward the future as communities of hope. They carry a context of meaning that can allow us to connect our aspirations for ourselves and those closest to us with the aspirations of a larger whole and see our own efforts as being, in part, contributions to the common good. (p. 153)

Both accounts of community are based on an understanding of continuities and interdependencies of generations that match up with anthropological studies of real communities in ways that the liberal view of community does not. Furthermore, understanding "our inescapable bonds to the earth" and participating in a community of memory that frames a common vision of the future are dependent upon a process of transgenerational communication where both elders and the new generation understand the importance of their respective responsibilities in terms of the needs of the community—rather than from the perspective of the autonomous individual or the expert who wants to introduce a new technology.

Further issues surrounding the nature of tradition and community will be taken up later as part of the discussion of cultural/bio-conservatism and the characteristics of ecologically centered cultures. For now, it is important to conclude the discussion of emancipatory liberalism with several observations about its actual influence on the educational process, and about why this group of educational reformers has failed to provide a conceptual and moral basis for addressing the cultural aspects of the ecological crisis.

It is difficult to assess accurately the influence of this tradition of liberalism on public schools and universities. The idea that education should contribute to a more critically reflective individual has been a long-time goal of liberal education, but before the influence of Dewey and Freire became dominant, the source of empowerment was to be derived from a systematic study of the Western philosophical canon. Robert M. Hutchins and, more recently, Allan Bloom were advocates of this tradition of educational emancipation. The emphasis Dewey and Freire gave to critical reflection, which was based on humanizing change as a progressive process, leads to a radically different interpretation of critical reflection. The older emancipatory tradition viewed critical reflection as providing a basis for knowing which traditions should be conserved and why, as well as which traditions were in need of modification or complete abandonment. Critical reflection for Dewey, Freire, and the more recent advocates of emancipation, who now use the deconstructive language of postmodernism, is understood as the educational engine of modernization. That is, one of

the goals of critical reflection is to understand how traditions inhibit the freedom of the individual or members of
the same age group. The advocates of critical reflection
want to make the student's own experience of traditions the
basis for overturning them. What has changed is the way in
which the past is viewed. The earlier advocates of critical
reflection assumed that students would find in the analogues of the past a basis for understanding the present.
The current generation of emancipatory liberals view education as a process of learning about what now is experienced by individuals and groups as oppressive, and the
historical perspective, as well as the radical idea of being responsible for the seventh unborn generation (as some indigenous cultures view it) is totally irrelevant. The more
careful readers of Dewey will dissent from the extreme nihilism of current advocates of emancipation by claiming
that Dewey viewed the past as instrumentally useful in re-
constructing the problematic experience of the community.

Educators at all levels of formal education use the
vocabulary of emancipatory liberalism to justify their curriculum and style of teaching. Even advocates of using computers in all areas of education justify their radical cultural
experiment with the argument that it enables students to
become more critical thinkers. It is difficult to answer with
any certainty the twin questions: "How often is the current
rhetoric a reflection of teachers' and professors' encultura-
tion to the core assumptions of modernity?" and "How often
is it a reflection of having read the writings of liberal educational theorists?"

Determining their influence on the curriculum is also
difficult. Where the public school curriculum is not man-
dated at the district or state level, teachers largely decide
what is to be learned in terms of problem-solving situations,
and in terms of what fits their own sense of relevance—
which is often influenced by what they judge to be the students' sense of relevance. This is not what Dewey advocated.
But the influence of a more popularized interpretation of his
ideas can be seen merging with the modern ethos that celebrates all forms of change as expressions of progress, thus
leading to the view that everybody's experience and perspec-

tive are equally educational. And within the Deweyian tradition of viewing all experience as growth, it is impossible to claim that certain forms of knowledge are more important than others—indeed, it is all relative to the judgment of the individual or group.

But what can be said with certainty about the influence of the emancipatory liberals is that they have failed to recognize that the core assumptions underlying modern culture are contributing to the disintegration of ethnic communities, of what remains of community within mainstream culture, and of traditional cultures that are now coming under linguistic, economic, political, and military pressure to integrate themselves into the emerging worldwide monoculture. It is also clear that emancipatory liberals have not taken seriously the educational implications of the ecological crisis. Indeed, the writings of emancipatory liberals who became prominent during the rise of environmental awareness (e.g., Freire, Giroux, McLaren) do not even acknowledge that there is an ecological crisis. While they often identify themselves with oppressed cultural groups (in a highly abstract way that does not take account of specific cultural patterns), their modernist assumptions about the progressive nature of change, viewing critical reflection as the only basis of knowledge and moral judgment, and an anthropocentric worldview, put them in a conceptual and moral double bind that seems beyond their grasp. In order to maintain their image of being on the cutting edge of radical thinking, they now use the language of Derrida and other postmodern thinkers—who represent the latest and most nihilistic expression of modernity.

One of the ironies today is that environmentally oriented science educators in public schools are beginning to discover the writings of these emancipatory liberals. Since few science or science education classes address the complex nature of culture, much less provide students with an opportunity to examine the differences between modern and more ecologically centered cultures, these science educators have no conceptual basis for recognizing that an emphasis on critical reflection leads to a form of relativism that requires the acceptance of the other major tenets of modernism in order to appear socially ameliorative. What is not recognized by science educators now embracing the goal of emancipation is that critical reflection is only one aspect of an educational process that contributes to an ecologically sustainable culture. Being able to recognize the existing cultural patterns that contribute to an everyday life that do not degrade the environment is equally important to the curriculum and classroom discourse. A clear understanding of the relations between individuals, cultures, and ecosystems, in turn, requires a broad knowledge of cultural groups that have succeeded in evolving complex symbolic ways of understanding and celebrating relationships between humans and their environment. Unfortunately, neither the science courses nor the emancipatory theorists are able to break with the modern mind-set that continues to represent the ecological wisdom of these cultures as backward and primitive. For all their good intentions and scientific knowledge of local ecosystems, these teachers are a manifestation of the problem that occurs when the cultural patterns that have contributed so greatly to the degradation of the environment are used as the basis of reform.

Rectifying the Language of Conservatism

As the previous discussion indicates, the vocabularies of liberalism foreground relationships that contribute to the modern understanding of progress. These vocabularies, when used to guide political, technological, and educational practices, have made important contributions to overcoming many destructive forms of prejudice and physical scarcities. But the forms of relationships valued in modern culture have become distorted and even made destructive by the failure of the languages of liberalism to give legitimacy to the more fundamental relationships that characterize the human role in viable biotic communities. Rectifying these relationships can be facilitated by sorting out the political vocabulary of conservatism. The words "liberal" and "conservative" are often used in the media and even in scholarly writings in an historically inaccurate manner. As a result the words often hide more than they il-luminate. Their increasing use as pejorative terms that are intended to stigmatize the opposition further closes off op-portunities to find common ground and to clarify the rea-sons for basic differences.

In rectifying the languages for designating the different forms of conservatism, I am acutely aware that Geertz's de-finition of ideology as lived cultural patterns can be more accurately understood in terms of the different forms of con-servatism. I am also aware that the study of any ecologi-cally centered culture will disclose that the members are focused on *conserving* and *renewing* sustainable communal beliefs and practices (including technologies)—that is, until they succumb to the false promises of modernism. The lan-guages and thus conceptual categories of liberalism are to-tally inadequate for understanding how these cultures are able to survive within the limits of their bioregions when modern cultures are dependent for their survival on the technological ability to exploit the bioregions of other cul-tures. Thus, I must acknowledge at this point my increas-ingly strong belief that the ideological alternative to the growthmania of modernization will be found in the concep-tual and moral categories and vocabularies of conservatism. And as we sort out the different forms of conservatism, we will see more clearly how to redirect the educational process in ways that conserve human relationships that are more in balance with the larger biotic community—if that is now possible given the recent rapid growth in human population and the destruction (in the name of progress) of the ecologi-cal wisdom of indigenous cultures.

Temperamental Conservatism

One of the most basic relationships we have with our-selves—our sense of continuity with our past experiences—is fundamentally conservative in nature. That is, we tend to repeat (conserve) the patterns of food, conversation, music, work routines, leisure activities, spiritual practices, and so forth, that mesh with our comfort zone and fit our sense of identity. Even people who advocate extreme forms of social change, or expressions of creativity, are temperamental conservatives. Furthermore, cultural patterns such as nonverbal communication, writing from left to right, and speaking in the subject-verb-object pattern of the English language (if that is our primary language), become part of our world that is taken for granted. And what is taken for granted tends to be reenacted, or conserved. To put this another way, most aspects of our cultural life are inherently conservative—with the search for excitement, innovation, or a more satisfying sense of personal identity representing a reconstitution of the core patterns embedded in our sense of self.

Because of the modern cultural pattern of representing abstract ideas as more real than our experience of being embedded in the routines and patterns of everyday life, we have in recent years failed to take account of the ideological orientation of human temperament—our own and that of the people who are being urged to change their lives on the basis of an abstract set of ideological guidelines. Temperamental conservatism, unlike ideologies that are intended to change the direction of people's lives, is not aligned with any specific set of beliefs about how society should be perfected. As temperament, identity, and taken-for-granted cultural patterns are an aspect of everybody's experience, this form of conservatism underlies every possible lifestyle: from the person who makes a killing playing the stock market and then declares himself to be an advocate of wilderness protection, to the person who makes his living creating video games that teach children that killing makes a game more exciting. Marx, Dewey, Berry, Mother Theresa, Gandhi, Black Elk, and people who live more routine lives are all examples of temperamental conservatives.

The acknowledgement that we are all, to some degree, temperamental conservatives helps to overcome the increasingly polarized approach to political discourse where one is categorized either as a liberal or conservative. For more formulaic-thinking liberals who automatically associate conservatism with being economically and socially privileged, and now with extremist political agendas, the awareness that the word conservatism best describes the continuities of their own lives may make it easier to participate in the discourse on how to evolve a more ecologically centered culture—which will be, in part, a discourse about how to "conserve" ecologically viable cultural patterns.

Cultural Conservatism

Cultural conservatism may take as many forms of expression as there are cultural groups. Thus, it cannot be judged in the abstract as desirable or not. It is simply an inherent aspect of the language processes used by cultural groups to sustain their daily routines. To put this another way, if people speak and think within the language of a cultural group they are reenacting the most basic patterns of the culture. This process of reenactment is conservative in nature. Even modern cultures, with their emphasis on continual change and the value of subjective judgments, are conserving culturally specific ideas, values, and approaches to technology. That these traditions equate nihilistic forms of technology and celebrate anomic individualism does not alter the fact that the cultural languages that encode and reproduce these traditions represent a conserving process.

Like temperamental conservatism, cultural conservatism cannot be judged as good or bad in the abstract. The judgment has to be contextualized. For example, Sweden is a culturally conservative society that pursues policies that ensure a high degree of economic security for all of its members. Its approach to social equity involves conserving its core cultural values and traditions. Japanese culture represents another form of cultural conservatism that has contributed to the destruction of old growth forests around the Pacific Rim. As the last example suggests, assessing the different expressions of cultural conservatism should not only take account of social justice issues but also how the environment is affected.

Economic Conservatism

Liberals often identify powerful individuals and corporations who seek to protect their economic interests as conservatives. Indeed, this mislabeling is so common that both the general public and groups who are being mislabeled have come to view themselves as conservatives. As a result, corporations that destroy the economic basis of communities by shifting their factories overseas, and by downsizing the workforce by automating the work process, are seen as examples of conservatives. The label was even misapplied to James Watt, the former Secretary of Interior, who wanted to open the National Park system to private enterprise. At first glance, the arguments advanced by such powerful individuals as Rush Limbaugh and Newt Gingrich about the need to reduce the role of government have a certain Burkean ring to them. And when the argument is made by these "conservatives" that freedom to make decisions at the local community (and boardroom) level leads to a greater sense of community responsibility and self-direction, it even begins to sound similar to the social ecologists' vision of small scale participatory democracy. But if we return to Confucius' insight that languages are about relationships by asking what relationships are being promoted by this form of conservatism, we find that the mislabeling hides the Classical Liberal orientation of this group of "conservatives." The well-established tradition in the United States of associating the word "conservatism" with the advocates of organizing everyday life in terms of the market forces of supply and demand, the right of every individual and corporation to pursue their economic self-interest, and technological practices that degrade the environment in the name of progress, is one of the reasons liberals have difficulty recognizing that an ecologically sustainable culture has a conservative rather than an experimental and progressive orientation. The confusion resulting from the misuse of language, in turn, makes more difficult the rectification of the most basic human relationships.

If we ask the question, "What patterns and relationships do these 'conservatives' want to conserve?" we find them upholding the ideas, values, patterns, and relationships that are the core of modern culture. These include the assumption that scientific and technologically based changes are inherently progressive in nature. These core beliefs also include framing the nature of human freedom in terms of the right to introduce new ideas and technology into the educational and economic marketplace, where the invisible hand of competitive forces is supposed to insure the survival of the fittest. This aspect of the modern mind-set can be traced directly back to Adam Smith's faulty observation about "man's *natural* propensity to barter, truck, and to exchange one thing for another" (italic added). This association of freedom with competition between ideas and economic forces, which is the linchpin that ties together Classical Liberal thinkers and today's prominent individuals and groups who have claimed the right to speak on behalf of all conservatives, has led to undermining other cultural beliefs and values that stand in the way of commodifying every aspect of daily life. For these "conservatives," in order to expand economic opportunities it is first necessary to transform all forms of knowledge, communication, health and spiritual practices, leisure activities, and the arts into commodities that can be scientifically marketed. The comment by a major league baseball player that the prolonged strike made it all the more necessary to put a "good product" on the field if the fans were to be won back is evidence of how far this commodification process has gone. Even educators now refer to the outcome of learning as a "product." Furthermore, these "conservatives" argue that no other forms of cultural authority (i.e., traditions, wisdom of elders, spiritual beliefs and practices) should be allowed to impede the introduction of scientifically based technologies into society and natural systems. That is, morally grounded forms of conservatism, as well as the expressions of conservatism that are based on generations of experience, are to be set aside in favor of scientific and technological criteria—with profits being the bottom line.

As suggested earlier, every group's cultural patterns and beliefs are conserved through their language systems. But what is being conserved in the case of these Classical Liberal beliefs and practices is a culture that is oriented toward experimental change in all areas of life, and in cultures around the world. These "conservatives" are quite candid about the connections between the need to exploit markets today on a worldwide scale in order to have the

capital necessary to support future generations of technological development. The relativizing of cultural traditions
that do not fit the imperatives of the Classical Liberal mind-
set, now buttressed by the increasing authority of science in
all areas of human experience, can also be understood as
contributing to the spread of nihilism—a word that stands
for just the opposite of what characterizes the forms of conservatism of more ecologically centered cultures.

Religious Conservatism

As a large percentage of Americans have some form of
religious affiliation, and in light of the increasing power of
religious coalitions to influence the course of political decisions on the national level, it would be totally wrong to ignore religious-based expressions of conservatism. Because
this category of conservatism covers such a wide range of
spiritual beliefs it would be impossible to clarify how different expressions of conservatism reflect differences in religious beliefs and practices. However, it is appropriate to
suggest that this category of conservatism needs to be more
fully understood in terms of how various religious traditions
contribute to or resist the nihilistic beliefs and values of
modern culture. The ways in which different religious traditions establish the boundaries between the spiritual and
secular domains of life also need to be understood. As Charlene Spretnak and other writers on the spiritual nature of
the ecological crisis have articulated so clearly, the "ecolo-
gizing of consciousness" will require a radical break with
the reductionism and materialism of modern culture. In
States of Grace, Spretnak further observes that:

> no political model will win popular support if it aims to
> shape a brave new world by dragging along all the broken
> processes rent by the cult of modernity—ecology, spiritual-
> ity, community, family, and self-in-nature—to fit in as best
> they can. A new politics, economics, education, medicine,
> and culture that are responsive to the healing and empow-
> ering ecospiritual awakening will be integral with it.
> (1991, p. 229)

As it can be argued that the politics of modernization also have a religious foundation, both within the Judeo-Christian tradition and in the secular religion that has resulted from the fusing of the myth of progress with the increasing dominance of scientific explanations, it becomes all the more imperative that the cultural and environmental relationships fostered by different religious beliefs be understood. Religious traditions that have resisted certain aspects of modernization, and that have been denigrated for holding to their seemingly premodern spiritual convictions, may represent examples of how to live more spiritually centered lives rather than lives based on consumption and technology.

Philosophical Conservatism

This Western tradition of reflective conservatism goes back at least to Edmund Burke, who wrote about the contract between generations. Its distinctive mode of thinking can be seen in the writings of social observers and critics from across the political spectrum—from self-acknowledged conservatives like Clinton Rossiter, Peter Viereck, and Michael Oakeshott to liberals and even marxists and socialists, such as Robert Heilbroner and Peter Clecak. What is distinctive about this form of conservatism, beyond its deeply reflective nature, is that it involves a dialectic way of thinking. But it is not the dialectic of liberal theorists where the truth of critical reflection is guaranteed by the progressive nature of change. Rather, it is a form of dialectical thinking where tensions and contradictions within specific social contexts need to be clarified, and values rectified in a way that restores a sense of balance in individual and communal relationships. What prompts the philosophical conservative to action is any number of forms of extremism: too much emphasis on the rights and freedom of the individual; community orthodoxies that are supposed to be embraced without question; an emphasis on change at any cost; community unwillingness to abandon outmoded traditions; use of abstract theory as the basis of changing society; and so forth. When individualism is carried too far the philosophical conservative attempts to clarify how this threatens the viability of community—as Robert Bellah and his co-authors did in *Habits of the Heart: Individualism and Commitment in American Life*. And when community norms or the centralized power of the state begin to overwhelm the rights of the individual, they will come to the defense of the individual—as Robert Heilbroner did in his important and timely 1972 essay, "A Radical View of Socialism." The opening essay of Michael Oakeshott's *The Politics of Rationalism* warns of the dangers of ideologically driven developments in technology, including the loss of the special form of learning that occurs in mentor relationships. Philosophical conservatives also have a more complex view of human nature. For example, writers such as Russell Kirk and William Golding use religious cosmologies as the basis for accounting for the human propensities for good and evil. Other philosophical conservatives, such as Christina Hoff Sommers, point to the historical record of humankind's moral variability. Unlike Deweyian-type liberals who think that when individuals rely upon a certain form of rational thought they will always act in communally constructive ways, the more mixed view of human nature held by philosophical conservatives leads them to argue for checks and balances—such as in the American system of separate and supposedly equal powers. In the area of education, philosophical conservatives do not accept the liberal assumption that students learn best when left to construct their own ideas and values—even if this were a real possibility. As Mortimer Adler argued in *The Paideia Proposal* (1982), knowledge of past cultural achievements needs to be balanced with the development of the student's own powers of reflective judgment.

While the philosophical conservatives' ability to clarify the values being threatened by various forms of extremism makes them refreshingly non-doctrinaire, they nevertheless share a serious weakness. If we examine the writings of T. S. Eliot, Robert Bellah, Hannah Arendt, or Alasdair MacIntyre (who thinks like a philosophical conservative but objects to being so identified), we find that none of them include the environment in their efforts to keep in balance the basic human relationships. They are, in effect, anthropocentric in their understanding of relationships. While philosophical conservatives often represent within mainstream culture what comes closest to a tradition of elders, they fail to take account of the biological legacy that most needs to be conserved.

Cultural / bio-conservatism

This somewhat awkward phrase has the virture of representing the beliefs, values, and other patterns of cultures that recognize their dependence on the forms of life in their bioregion, and have co-evolved accordingly. Before the impact of Western modernization, the Balinese, Hopi, Koyukon, Ladakh, and hundreds of other indigenous cultural groups demonstrated that conserving local biodiversity is essential to long term survival. Even the disruptive influence of modernization has not entirely destroyed the ecological grounding of these traditional cultures. Thus, the cultural orientation of cultural/bio-conservatism can be seen as already having a long and proven history.

Within the context of modern, experimentally oriented cultures such as ours, this form of conservatism must be viewed as an ideology: that is, a set of guiding principles and values for evolving along a more sustainable pathway. But unlike the guiding principles of the different forms of liberalism, which were based on abstract theory that was then treated as universally applicable to all cultures, the characteristics of cultural/bio-conservatism take account of our unique histories and environmental contexts. It takes account as well of people in rural and urban areas who already live in ecologically responsible ways. The guiding principles can also be derived from the writings that reflect different perspectives within the environmental movement. Gary Snyder's deep understanding of place so beautifully and clearly articulated in *The Practice of the Wild* (1990) reflects a concern with recovering an attitude toward the commons that recognizes "both specific land *and* the traditional community institution that determines the carrying capacity for its various subunits and defines the rights and obligations of those who use it "(p. 30). Wes Jackson's research and writings on the need to restore the species diversity of the prairie grasslands would lead, if taken seriously, to equally radical changes in cultural practices—including the recognition of the need for ecological atonement for the deliberate destruction of local knowledge that was attuned to the rhythms of land, plants, animals, and other natural systems. The ecological atonement he calls for can also be understood as rectifying modern culture's replacement of a conservative orientation toward the complexity of the natural world with exploitative and experimental forms of cultural knowledge.

If we attend carefully to the ideological orientation that underlies Aldo Leopold's land ethic, we can see that the basic orientation of the culture is to be judged in terms of its impact on the health of the environment. The ultimate basis for judging the wisdom of a cultural group's beliefs and practices, as the following quotation makes clear, is the larger community of interdependent life forms. As Leopold states what could be taken as a fundamental principle of all forms of cultural/bio-conservativism, "a thing is right when it tends to preserve the integrity, stability, and beauty of the biotic community. It is wrong when it tends otherwise" (p. 262). Writers such as E F. Schumacher, Wendell Berry, Charlene Spretnak, Dolores LaChapelle, George Sessions, and many other environmental thinkers also frame their criticisms of the destructive characteristics of modernity in terms of whether cultural patterns contribute to the viability of natural systems. What is conserved and renewed through successive generations must conserve the biological basis of life—which means conserving cultural traditions that are attuned to the characteristics of a particular bioregion. Thus, discussions about the importance of local knowledge, of ceremonies that celebrate the interdependence of life processes, and of appropriate technologies and economic practices, are all expressions of the varied discourses encompassed by a cultural/bio-conservative ideological orientation.

Using Cultural/Bio-Conservatism as a Guide to Educational Reform

As the sorting out of the various expressions of liberalism and conservatism suggests, the differences are not as rigid and categorical as popular thinking suggests. Various types of liberals (and I would place socialism and marxism on the extreme end of the liberal continuum anchored in Enlightenment assumptions and misunderstandings about the nature of relations between culture and ecosystems) differentiate themselves by foregrounding certain political goals, such as freedom, equality, rational management of systems, etc. However, they are in their personal lives both temperamental and cultural conservatives. They have identity investments in the conveniences of a modern lifestyle, and even though their personal lifestyles, including their theoretical proclivities, are oriented toward change, the cultural languages they use to interact with others conserve the core beliefs of modernity. The various expressions of conservatism must also be seen in a more contextual way: that is, as situated in and thus influenced by the language processes that sustain the dominant culture of modernism. Again, it is the degree of emphasis as well as differences over the nature of several key relationships (e.g., how community, temporality, and knowledge are understood) that separate the various expressions of conservatism from liberalism, and from each other. Economic conservatives embrace the most extreme tenets of Classical Liberal thinking, and the other forms of conservatism (temperamental and philosophical) involve a number of accommodations with the technological, conceptual, and moral orientations of modern culture.

Cultural/bio-conservatism must also be understood as an ideological orientation that is not categorically unresponsive to many of the concerns of liberals. However, they would support the philosophical conservatives' argument that only communities that have attained the necessary balance for ensuring justice for all its members can nurture the healthy and responsible individual. That is, cultural/bio-conservatives would strongly challenge the liberal claim that philosophical conservatives are reactionary, motivated by a basic selfishness, and indifference toward the plight of the disadvantaged. This criticism can be leveled at economic conservatives—but they are mislabeled Classical Liberals who share more in common with liberal critics who lump together all forms of conservatism into an easily criticized caricature.

Cultural/bio-conservatism would be expressed in terms of a distinctively recognizable form of temperamental and cultural conservatism if people would avoid basing their thought and behavior on the root metaphors that were the basis of the Industrial Revolution. Aside from the anthropocentrism of the philosophical conservative, the cultural/bio-conservative would feel quite at home with the continual need to balance the interests of the individual with the needs of community; the knowledge acquired and refined over generations of collective experience with the need for critical reflection and scientific ways of understanding; and the authority of substantive traditions with the need to renew and innovate in areas of the culture that have stagnated. Indeed, the cultural/bio-conservative would argue that the dialectical way of thinking, where the balancing of potential sources of tension in individual and communal life must be an ongoing concern, is essential to assessing the worth of any educational reform.

But unlike the philosophical conservatives whose thinking is based on the humanistic tradition that goes back to Plato, cultural/bio-conservatives draw upon the experiences of traditional cultures that have evolved within the limits of their bioregions, as well as cultural groups within our own society that have avoided, either out of moral choice or political necessity, the growing consumerism and technological dependence of the dominant culture. While using the traditional Hopi and other indigenious cultures as models may lead to romanticizing them, as well as to losing sight of the basic fact that we cannot graft their cultural traditions onto our tree of traditions, the cultural/bio-conservatives would argue that we can learn from them. Similarly, the cultural/bio-conservatives would argue that we can learn about the cultural characteristics that contribute to long-term ecological survival from Western cultural groups such as the Amish and Mennonites. Even the failed cultural experiment of the Shakers has much to teach us. But learning from them does not mean we have to adopt their specific religious beliefs, technological practices, and rural lifestyle.

At the risk of being criticized for generalizing about radically dissimilar cultural groups, I am going to suggest in the next chapter that in the seeming diversity of ecologically centered cultures can be found characteristics that are shared—and that these characteristics can be used as a starting point for identifying the guidelines for altering the modernizing trajectory that public schools and universities are now on. These shared characteristics can be called common wisdom about fundamental relationships—that is, a form of wisdom derived from experience-based understanding of how humans are nested in cultural communities, and how these cultural communities are nested in ecosystems that are subject to unpredictable changes.

As our educational institutions begin to shift from an emphasis on promoting the forms of knowledge that benefit elite groups bent on pushing the envelope of technological progress to an emphasis on conserving and renewing cultural practices that contribute to long-term sustainability, we will also witness a shift away from the modern emphasis on an approach to politics that privileges individuals and special interest groups. The displacement of folk knowledge and practices in the West, which were once the basis of vital community life, by technologies designed and marketed by experts (a process that can be referred to as the commodification of cultural life) was accompanied by an increasing effort to connect formal education with the goal of enhancing the political empowerment of the individual. Indeed, educating for democracy has been a goal since the rise of public schools and the modern university. The guiding assumption was that education would provide the basis for more rational and autonomous decision-making about both public issues and private interests. Democracy, in turn, was to guide the engine of technology—thus contributing further to ensuring a progressive form of change.

But it has not worked out this way. Political interests competing for the control of public policy were, and continue to be, grossly unequal. Multinational corporations continue to pursue their self-interest at the expense of the human and larger biotic communities. In addition, the increased emphasis on legitimating education as the basis of contributing to a more democratic polity did not take account of the vastly expanded power of the modern state. This is one

of the great ironies of the relationship between modern education and modern politics: the more educational emphasis
on individual autonomy (expressed in the strange mix of
empowerment rhetoric and emphasis on the constructivist
basis of ideas and values) the more power that the state has
been able to exercise—and the more everyday life has become commodified. The process of commodification has now
been extended into all forms of leisure activity, creative
expression, and even into the human reproductive process
itself.

If we take seriously the need to shift from an experimental and consumer-oriented culture to one that is oriented more toward taking responsibility for how cultural
practices impact the increasingly fragile ecosystems, we will
then have to make fundamental changes in the modern idea
of connecting education to a conflict model of democracy,
and to creating a more competitive workforce—which is the
current emphasis. The traditions that are shared by traditional ecologically centered cultures, and by minority
cultures within our own society who have resisted the commodification process of modernization, provide important
clues about the shift in educational priorities that would be
consistent with cultural/bio-conservatism. Cultures based
on mythopoetic narratives that combine an inclusive sense
of moral order (one that includes both humans and the natural world), and a recognition of the importance of transgenerational communication to the survival of future
generations, all have reduced the domain of political decision making. These include groups ranging from indigenous
cultures faced with nurturing life from seemingly inhos-
pitable environments to Amish communities settled on rich
soils with plentiful rainfall. In effect, their approaches to education do not perpetuate the ideology and forms of knowledge that promote autonomous decision making about
micro- and macro-political decisions. While these cultures
have reduced the domain of the political, they have at the
same time provided for involvement in a complex symbolic
world that far exceeds what is experienced in our increasingly individualistic society. That is, instead of viewing the
essential knowledge and values of the culture as being open

to continual politicization in terms of the subjective judgment of the individual, these cultures encode, store, and renew their essential knowledge of relationships in the symbolic and communal languages of music, dance, narrative, and visual arts. These languages represent a different form of cultural coding, one that is highly suited to combining the passing on of a cultural group's wisdom about human and environmental relationships. The sharing of this communal knowledge in participatory ceremonies, mentor relationships, and leisure activities represents one of their primary approaches to education.

These forms of cultural encoding and renewal are undermined by the modern approach to commodifying every aspect of experience, and by the modern proclivity to identify technologically mediated knowledge and communication as having high-status and being more enlightened and progressive than what is known and shared in more predominately oral cultures. They are also undermined by the number of modern orthodoxies that will be examined in the next chapter: specifically, by how intelligence, creativity, moral education, and transgenerational communication are understood by educators, from the elementary grades through graduate classes.

By viewing intelligence, creativity, moral judgment, and experience essentially as attributes of the individual, educators further the modern myth that foregrounds a political process that has, in turn, supported the transformation of life processes into markets that can be technologically and economically exploited. The educators' emphasis on the individual has also led to a reduction in the ability of modern cultures to store and renew a symbolically complex understanding of essential human/nature relationships. The modern paradox of achieving technologically based riches by undermining the viability of the Earth's ecosystems, while at the same time viewing cultures that have evolved complex bodies of ecological wisdom and ceremonies for celebrating healthy human relationships with nature as backward and primitive, can be put in the form of these questions: "What are modern people going to do with their free time when the environment becomes too degraded to support lives dedicated to the work and consumption cycles that are personally and ecologically destructive?" "What are they going to do with their time when computer-based technologies lead to a form of 'restructuring' that leaves them unemployed?"

The following chapter will examine how intelligence, creativity, moral education, and direct experience-based learning can be remetaphorized in ways that will enable educators to recognize the curricular implications of a bio-conservative culture. Why the shift in ideological orientation will become as taken-for-granted by the next generation as the assumptions of modernity are part of the natural attitude of the present generation will also be considered. Like this chapter, the focus will be on important leverage points environmentalists need to take into account as part of an educational strategy.

Chapter 4

AN ECOLOGICAL
REINTERPRETATION
OF MODERN
EDUCATIONAL IDEALS

Recommendations for educational reform usually focus on changes in the content of the curriculum, and on the relation of teacher and student in the learning process. These recommendations have not, in the past, taken account of the role language plays in the very complex process of cultural reproduction, nor have they addressed the deeper cultural assumptions. The result is that reforms are superficial and quickly fade away. Indeed, they are more a matter of changing the outside decor than altering the deep conceptual and moral underpinnings of the culture. For example, Dewey's reform proposals, as well as those of Mortimer Adler (to cite examples of a "progressive" and a "conservative" educational reformer), both were based on the deep cultural assumptions identified in chapter One as the basis of modernism and high-status forms of knowledge. The most recent efforts to reform public education in terms of the workforce needs of the twenty-first century are similarly based.

For environmentalists who take on the challenge of pressuring public schools and universities to reform education in ways that lead to fundamental cultural changes, it will be necessary to understand the mediating role of teachers and professors in the process of cultural reproduction. That is, it will be necessary to understand the dynamics of the process that makes education a form of transgenerational ritual of perpetuating the cultural patterns that are taken for granted. This is an essential aspect of education in ecologically-centered cultures, but this process helps to deepen the crisis when the culture survives largely by degrading the environment. It will also be necessary to understand how the process can be changed in ways that enable students to recognize these patterns that are taken-for-granted patterns (which is the first step toward developing communicative competence), as well as to understand the necessity of reconciling ideas, behaviors, and technologies with the interdependencies that exist within culture, and the dependency of the culture on increasingly fragile ecosystems.

Establishing a basis for understanding the dynamic process of how culture becomes part of the younger generation's natural attitude is absolutely essential to the success of any serious educational reform, and how teachers and professors can change the dynamics of this process will be considered in the next chapter. We shall address here how the deep cultural assumptions ignored by so-called progressive and conservative educational reformers now need to be reconstituted in ways that contribute to a just and sustainable future. Specifically, we shall examine how individualism, intelligence, and creativity (the three guiding concepts of the educational establishment), as well as tradition (which educators at all levels want to overturn and move beyond) take on an entirely different meaning when they are based on the root metaphor of an ecology rather than on the root metaphors of linear and guaranteed progress and a human-centered universe. Environmentalists need to assess educational reforms in terms of whether they continue to perpetuate the deep root metaphors that underlie modern culture, or contribute to more ecologically responsible forms of existence. By explaining how individualism, intelligence, creativity, and tradition can be understood in a radically different way, this chapter will provide environmentalists with a basic set of guidelines for judging the ecological significance of educational reform.

Toward an Ecologically Centered View
of Individualism

The modern cultural invention of the autonomous individual continues to frame how people understand their own
personal sense of centeredness, the basis of their relationships with others, and, in particular, the purpose of formal
education. Even terms like "empowerment," "consciousness
raising," and "economic opportunity," are understood by
modern people as expanding their possibilities as individuals. Environmentalists are not immune from this tendency—which suggests the hold the modern mind-set has
over even the most thoughtful individuals. For example,
Arne Naess's statement that "*you* are not expected to agree
with all its [Ecosophy T's] values and paths of derivation,
but to learn the means of developing *your own* systems or
guides, Ecosophy X, Y, or Z" (italics added, 1989, p. 37), retains this modern view of the self-directing individual even
as he attempts to explain both the unity and diversity of all
forms of life. Aldo Leopold's "land ethic" is also predicated
on the individual's own rational and moral understanding of
how human actions affect the "biotic pyramid" within which
they participate.

Indeed, the modern way of understanding ourselves as
individuals is so deeply held, and influences so many aspects
of modern cultural life, from the legal system to such diverse
areas of cultural life as computer technology, creativity, and
the process of dying itself, that it is nearly impossible to
think in any other way. The result is that reform efforts, including moderate educational reforms, radical economic restructuring proposals, and extremists' efforts to reassert the
primacy of the individual's freedom from governmental in-
terference, continue to reinforce the modern image of the individual as the basic social, psychological, and moral entity.
If environmentalists concerned with how schools can contribute to a basic shift from current forms of consciousness
and behavior ignore the need to rethink the keystone role
that the "autonomous individual" plays in mainstream cul-

tural life, their efforts will only contribute to furthering the double bind of basing educational reform on the cultural ideals that equate progress with exploiting the environment. This double bind can be avoided by framing educational reform in terms of the root metaphor of an ecology. In discussing the need to base educational reform on a different way of understanding individualism, as well as other modern individually-centered ideals, it is necessary to keep in mind that I am addressing only the modern cultural way of understanding. This includes the way educated elites, who are now promoting the globalization of a scientific and technologically based form of consumer lifestyle, understand the individual and the other cultural ideals derived from this form of radical individualism. Thus, my analysis and recommendations for educational reform should not be viewed as addressing how other cultural groups view the nature of individualism, creativity, intelligence, and so forth. I am not discussing American Indian cultures, or other minority cultural groups in North America, nor am I considering cultures in other parts of the world. But my concern about the over emphasis on a particular form of individualism should also be understood as being based on an equal concern about how the mesmerizing effect of modernity is undermining cultural diversity around the world. And in suggesting the need for remetaphorizing how the modern form of individualism is understood, I am also attempting to foreground the importance of taking seriously the ecologically sustainable forms of knowledge, values, technological practices, and sense of community that characterize cultures that have resisted the reductionism and consumer orientation of Western modernity.

There have been many metaphorical images of the individual in the West: the individual as a subject (feudalism), as a citizen (American and French Revolution), as self-expression (German Enlightenment), and as autonomous constructor of ideas and values (contemporary modernism). While many educators continue to look back to Dewey as a means of understanding the nature of the individual in a way that foregrounds interdependency within the social group, I urge environmentalists to use the insights of Gregory Bateson as the starting point for working out an ecologically based image of the individual. Dewey understood the individual in terms of participatory relationships that were always focused on problem-solving situations. But he failed to recognize that the scientific method of problem solving, which was for him the *only* way to grow in the use of social intelligence, is one of the foundations of modernity. In universalizing science as the "method of intelligence," Dewey did not recognize other cultural ways of knowing. Indeed, he would have been particularly opposed to the non-scientific forms of intelligence that indigenous cultures have evolved in response to their need to live within the limits of their bioregions. Dewey's contribution to providing the basis for an ecological approach to education is further undermined by his uncritical acceptance of the Western myth that change is linear and evolves toward greater complexity and order. Given what we now know about the patch dynamics of natural systems and how natural disturbances and heterogeneity bring into question the view of ecosystems as evolving toward a state of equilibrium and cooperative interdependence that held sway in the era of Francis Clements and Eugene Odum, it would be a step backward to use Dewey as the basis of educational reform. Dewey represents the philosophical and educational counterpart to this earlier and more romantic phase of thinking about natural ecologies.

Bateson's Contribution to an Ecological Interpretation of Individualism

Gregory Bateson's understanding of an ecology as a closed and self-correcting system should also be viewed as dated; but his way of understanding the individual as always situated in an ecology of interactive relationships is still sound. More importantly, his way of understanding why the individual responds to certain patterns of interaction and not others, brings culture into the picture in a way that is still ahead of how modern educators (including

Dewey) understand the relationship between individuals and culture. These two aspects of Bateson's understanding of an ecology of mind can easily be reconciled with current thinking that foregrounds the nonequilibrium of biotic assemblages. Perturbations that radically disrupt biotic patterns serve to make the ecology within which individuals are situated less predictable. Thus, the cultural maps that influence at a taken-for-granted level how individuals make sense and respond to changes in human relationships with nature also become less reliable as guides to behavior. Indeed, a strong case can be made that our current understanding of the perturbations that set off changes in unpredictable directions within natural systems makes Bateson's ecological metaphor for understanding the individual all the more relevant.

Like Dewey, Bateson rejected the Cartesian view of the individual as a spectator who observes and acts on an external world. He also rejected another aspect of the Cartesian view of the individual that still survives in the thinking of technocratic and neo-Romantic liberals who argue that individuals, in being free of the influence of cultural traditions, construct their own ideas from data on the computer screen or from direct experience. That is, Bateson's ecological model for representing how individuals are situated in a constantly changing field of relationships takes account of how past forms of cultural coding and storage in the form of metaphorical language continue to influence present and future relationships—including how such catastrophic disturbances as fires and floods are individually and culturally understood.

Bateson used the following example to illuminate how the modern view of the autonomous individual acting on an external and passive world is both overly simplistic and leads to the dangerous myth that the environment can be organized according to the dictates of abstract human reason.

> Consider a man felling a tree with an axe. Each stroke of the axe is modified or corrected, according to the shape of the cut face of the tree left by the previous stroke. This self-correcting (i.e., mental) process is brought about by a

total system, tree-eyes-brain-muscles-axe-stroke-tree; and it is this total system that has the characteristics of immanent mind. More correctly, we should spell the matter out as: (differences in tree)-(differences in retina)-(differences in brain)-(differences in muscles)-differences in movement of axe)-(differences in tree), etc. What is transmitted around the circuit is transforms of differences. And, as noted above, a difference which makes a difference is an *idea* or unit of information. (1972, pp. 317–318)

Earlier disturbances in weather patterns that might have affected the physical characteristics of the tree, or current disturbances such as lightning or a heavy downpour also enter the circuit of "difference which makes a difference."

What Bateson illuminates in this example, which could be repeated in terms of human conversations, driving a car, and every other form of human thought and behavior, is that relationships (i.e., the patterns that connect) are the defining characteristics of being an individual. Unless we are talking about experts who are trained to organize human experience in terms of abstractly formulated plans, most individual experience is not self-constituted and self-directed—although a case can be made that individuals acquire at a level that is taken for granted the modern schemata of understanding that represents this to be the case. In spite of the cultural schemata that leads individuals to believe they are in control when driving the car or cutting down a tree, we still find that differences in movement in the oncoming car leads to differences in how the supposedly autonomous individual responds. The sense of control over what is happening in the relationship (which is the modern misrepresentation) shifts in Bateson's ecological model to a recognition of how we are continually responding to the changes in the interactive patterns—and to the way in which actions are coproduced.

By foregrounding the interactive field of relationships within which the individual is situated, Bateson also avoids the error (and hubris) of identifying intelligence as an exclusive attribute of the individual. To reiterate the critically important point he makes in the previous quotation, "a dif-

ference which makes a difference is an *idea* or unit of information." By identifying "difference" as a form of information
and the basis of an idea, Bateson is able to say that the ecology of mind or intelligence is coterminous with the boundaries of the natural system the individual participates
within. As he puts it,

> The total self-corrective unit which processes information,
> or, as I say 'thinks' and 'acts' and 'decides,' is a system
> whose boundaries do not at all coincide with the bound-
> aries either of the body or of what is popularly called the
> 'self' or 'consciousness'; and it is important to notice that
> there are multiple differences between the thinking sys-
> tem and the 'self' as popularly conceived. (1972, p. 319)

As we have learned from the unanticipated environmental
consequences of humanly engineered environments such as
the Columbia River system of dams or the Mississippi River
system for flood control, Bateson's extrapolation from this
view of the ecology of mind needs to be taken seriously. In
no system, he writes, "which shows mental characteristics
can any part have unilateral control over the whole. In
other words, *the mental characteristics of the system are immanent, not in some part, but in the system as a whole*"
(1972, p. 317).

While emphasizing the "difference" as the basic unit of
information, Bateson recognized (in a way that modern educators who represent intelligence as an attribute of the
individual do not) that culture influences what information
or "difference" the individual will attend to, and the nature
of the individual's response to the information. That is,
Bateson recognized that culture exerts a powerful and generally unrecognized influence over how the individual
makes sense of the act of cutting down the tree, designing
dams along a river, and using chemical fertilizers to increase the economic production of the land, and so forth.
Culture is brought into the picture through the distinction
between map and territory that Bateson borrowed from the
linguist, Alfred Korzybski. The juxtaposition in the metaphor, as we all know from using a map as a guide to un-

familiar territory, reveals that the map only highlights or enables us to recognize what the mapmakers considered to be important features of the territory. If the cultural form of intelligence (beliefs, values, personal experiences, etc.) of the mapmaker is centered on the layout of the highway system in relation to towns and major geographical features, the use of this form of cultural mapping will make it difficult to be aware of the other characteristics of the territory—such as the existence of rare plants and animals, how perturbations have altered the vegetation patterns, and so forth.

The distinction between map and territory takes on special significance when we consider how modern individuals introduce changes into the environment without taking account of (and responsibility for) the subsequent impact on natural systems. The cultural form of intelligence (conceptual maps) originally led individuals to respond to the information circulating through natural systems as a result of the use of DDT by interpreting it as an expression of scientific and technological progress. The disappearance of insects and the increase in crop yields were what they were culturally conditioned to recognize as evidence of the success of their pesticide intervention. At the same time, the cultural maps diverted attention from other "differences" in the patterns of natural systems—such as the changes in bird populations and the toxins in the groundwater. In effect, the cultural maps diverted awareness away from information exchanges (perturbations) set in motion by the use of DDT by putting in focus only the "positive" effect of the pesticide.

The cultural maps, which Bateson also understood as the epistemological orientation of the cultural group, are acquired by individuals as they learn the languages (spoken, written, spatial, temporal, etc.) of their group. That is, the cultural maps that guide individuals to interpret and respond to "differences" in the interactive patterns of a living ecosystem in ways shared by other members of the language community are encoded and reproduced through the use of language. What is encoded are the metaphorically based understandings worked out in an earlier phase of the culture's experience: such as how "wilderness," "private property," "artificial intelligence," "information highways," and so forth, are to be understood. The cultural maps, in effect, serve as the basis of the interpretations that individuals largely take for granted, and they influence which "difference" will be recognized, and which will be ignored. These cultural maps reflect layers of earlier metaphorical constructions that evolved as the root metaphors of the cultural group influenced the earlier processes of analogic thinking. Over time the analogs that prevailed become distilled and encoded in iconic metaphors, which are the non-problematic images or schemata that guide the thought process of later generations (e.g., "data," "creativity," "individual," "Far East," "natural resources," and so forth).

An example of how thought is influenced by the metaphorical constructions of the past, as individuals attempt to articulate their "own" understanding of relationships, was evident in the attempt of an English professor from Princeton University who presented a talk on the "Ecology of the Internet." The generative metaphor (technology is neutral—like a hammer, it depends on the purpose its user gives it) framed his way of understanding computers. The result was that his explanation only dealt with how people are using the computer. The "tool is neutral" image led him to ignore the many ways in which computers mediate different forms of cultural knowledge and communication—that is, how computers privilege certain forms of knowledge (explicit knowledge, a conduit view of language, individualism, anthropocentrism, etc.) and marginalize other forms (tacit and contextual knowledge, transgenerational communication, the metaphorical nature of language and thought processes, etc.). In this example, the cultural maps allowed for a highly selective awareness of the patterns of "difference" that constituted the professor's extended environment. Not recognized were the "differences" that had been ignored in the earlier metaphorically based cultural experience of thinking of a neutral tool that must be invested with a purpose by the person who uses it.

To connect this discussion of the metaphorical basis of cultural maps to the earlier discussion of liberal ideologies that now guide educational reform, all three forms of educational liberalism, in basing their educational agendas for promoting change on the root metaphor that represents change as linear and progressive, have been unable to articulate how everyday life involves the reenactment and renewal of cultural traditions. All the cultural patterns handed down from the past are part of the ecology of "difference" that act on the actions of others (as Foucault puts it) by empowering, limiting, and in other ways influencing how individuals interact with each other, and with the environment. The degree to which these patterns are taken for granted is what limits the problematic and endless negotiation of meaning in the various forms of cultural communication. It is also what leads academics to overstate the objectivity of the rational process (such as the explanation of the "Ecology of the Internet") and educators to misrepresent the degree to which the individual is an autonomous and self-constituting agent.

Bateson also recognized that the cultural maps that influence awareness are themselves largely unnoticed, as are the consequences of human actions that introduce changes into the structural coupling of natural systems; at one point he notes that "most of the mental process is unconscious" (1972, p. 463). At the end of his life he acknowledged the difficulty of freeing oneself from the epistemology integral to the process of learning to think and communicate in the languages of one's cultural group. "We face a paradox," he wrote in one of his last essays, "in that I cannot tell you how to educate the young, or yourselves, in terms of the epistemology which I have offered you except you first embrace that epistemology. The answers must already be in your head and in your rules of perception" (1991, p. 313). Bateson's understanding of the cultural nature of an individual's way of knowing (conceptual mapping) is most clearly articulated in the earlier quotation about the boundaries of the "total self-corrective" unit. The historical part of the system that "processes information" is the cumulative and multilayered intelligence encoded in the metaphorical language handed down and remetaphorized by successive generations who recognized the outdated and destructive nature of earlier forms of intelligence. But for the most part everyday experience is based on deep and surface level metaphorical constructions that are seldom raised to the level of explicit awareness.

To reiterate, the epistemological aspects of Bateson's thinking are still ahead of what most academics are able to grasp, given that their conceptual maps continue to reinforce the Cartesian view of the connection between language and thought. And his ecological model of knowing, along with its broader cultural implications, is actually more relevant to an ecological world of chaos, disturbance, and disequilibrium than the succession and equilibrium interpretation of natural systems that was widely held during his time.

Primary Socialization

If environmentalists are going to address the dynamic process of how schooling passes on the ecologically destructive ways of cultural knowing, they must understand how socialization occurs, as well as how it can be altered. If the process of socialization had been understood by other reformers, their efforts would have led to more long-term changes. Anthropologists recognize that members of a culture are seldom explicitly aware of the taken-for-granted patterns they share with other members of their group, except when the patterns break down. When conversation turns to this aspect of culture a variation on the old saw that "fish would be the last to discover water" is often cited to make the point that, for all our rational achievements, our shared cultural patterns influence thought and behavior in ways that far exceed our awareness. Indeed, the remetaphorizing of how individualism is to be understood, from being a "subject" in the Middle Ages to an autonomous, individual today, reflects the power of cultural patterns to frame thought and behavior while at the same time continuing to be taken for granted by even the most critically reflective thinkers. In clarifying the dynamics of how individuals learn their cultural patterns without being aware of the deeper layers of symbolic construction, we shall be establishing another part of the argument about how the individual is unconsciously nested in a cultural ecology shaped by the past. We shall also be identifying critical leverage points in the educational and cultural reform process.

While we shall be addressing a cultural process, the framework of vocabulary and theory will be drawn from the tradition of the sociology of knowledge articulated by Alfred Schutz, Peter Berger, and Thomas Luckmann. It should be further acknowledged that only certain aspects of the sociology of knowledge account for how the everyday sense of "reality" is constituted and sustained will be developed here: specifically how the cultural languages that sustain the cultural group's way of experiencing (thinking, valuing, behaving toward) the everyday world become part of the individual's "natural" attitude. Contrary to today's increasing tendency to use genetic inheritance and the evolutionary framework of sociobiology to explain all aspects of human life, from criminal behavior to creative expression, the sociology of knowledge foregrounds the constitutive role that symbolic communication plays. As Peter Berger put it, "the reality of the world is sustained through conversations with significant others" (1970, p. 53). The foregrounding of the importance of the multiple language processes of everyday cultural life does not mean that genetics and the physical environment are not important factors to be considered. Rather, it is more a matter of recognizing that the symbolic foundations of cultural life are not entirely reducible to the genetic code of the individual members of the species. It is also a matter of recognizing that when the genetic reductionist position is adopted we then lose sight of the multiple leverage points that can be utilized to change the taken-for-granted patterns that now influence the modern individual's relationship with the environment. It should also be acknowledged that the following discussion of several key insights derived from the sociology of knowledge does not touch on the complex cultural dynamics of power and solidarity, framing and footing, and explicit and metacommunication that are also part of any interpersonal communication. Nor does it take account of how misunderstanding occurs, even when individuals assume they are using the same vocabulary and grammatical patterns. The discussion here will be limited to explaining four basic aspects of the connection between culture, language, consciousness and behavior that are especially relevant to understanding how individuals learn most of their cultural knowledge at a tacit and contextual level. It is the way in which such cognitive maps and analogue patterns are taken for granted that makes it difficult to recognize that the *experience* of relationships and patterns within the environment are culturally constructed. Understanding how culture is learned both at the implicit and explicit level is vitally important to being able to recognize the nature of the students' dependency on how the teacher or professor guides them through the process of primary socialization. This understanding will also help us to recognize how deep cultural assumptions or root metaphors can be made explicit, which is the first step toward reconstituting them.

Role of Cultural Languages in Constructing and Sustaining Everyday Reality

A person is not born into a culture with all the conceptual categories, patterns of interaction, and self-identity already intact and fully functioning. The patterns of thinking and interaction that separate the Chinese from the middle-class American infant are learned as they participate in the multilayered and interactive communication processes that provide the normative basis of adult life. To put this more succinctly, the world of shared meaning and pattern is learned through the symbolic language processes that connect people with each other, and to the material and institutionalized aspects of cultural life. It is through interaction with others that the language of the body, spoken word, use of space, etc., provide the basis for a shared sense of order, imagination, responsibility, self-identity, and so forth. The constituting power of the cultural language process can be seen in how moving from one language-dominant context to another leads to changes in sense of meaning, identity, and norms of behavior that are taken for granted—like the individuals who change from being students in the classroom to being parents in their own home, or how the experience of anonymity that often accompanies walking down a crowded street changes to a different sense of reality when attending a committee meeting. Differences in language environments lead to the renormalization of taken-for-granted attitudes and explicitly aware thoughts and behaviors. That is, through communication culture is sustained as a living, patterned reality in the life of the individual.

But it is not a sender/receiver model of communication. The design of buildings and other technologies, as well as what is communicated through voice and bodily gestures, encodes and reproduces past cultural norms of intelligence in the experience of the individual—including conceptual categories, ways of understanding the moral dimensions of relationships, use of body language, and so on. In Foucault's terms, the language processes normalize a culturally specific form of individuality and, thus, a sense of subjectivity and self-identity. And while the language processes of cultural life serve to initiate the infant into the shared patterns necessary for meaningful communication, differences in individual perspectives, ways of understanding (and misunderstanding), and sense of self-identity, contribute to minor and even major changes in the coding and normalizing processes of the cultural languages.

Culture, Communication, and the Intersubjective Self

In the sociology of knowledge of Berger and Luckmann, the phrase "intersubjective self" is used to overcome the traditional way of thinking of the individual as separate from society. Instead of representing the individual as an autonomous observer and actor, and society as a collection of individuals, they view the cultural patterns of thought and norms that govern relationships as being internalized—that is, as constitutive and thus as integral to the intersubjective self of the individual. To put it another way, the intersubjective self refers to the internalization of the shared cultural patterns. The sociology of knowledge also recognizes that there are unique aspects of how the individual encounters, interprets, and internalizes cultural patterns. It is this element of difference, both in biographical sequence and elements of personal character, that accounts for a wide range of individualized expression and even resistance to cultural patterns that others take for granted. That is, the biographical uniqueness in the development of the intersubjective self helps to keep in perspective the danger of losing sight of the areas of tension between the normalizing cultural patterns and the sense of personal meaning and integrity. Just as biology can be used to give a deterministic explanation of humans, culture can also be used in equally deterministic ways. The recognition that the life history of each individual involves differences in sequence of cultural events and learning situations helps us to avoid this problem.

Culture as Taken-for-Granted Knowledge

While our educational institutions, as well as the theoretical models of intelligence that serve as the basis of development in areas of technology such as computers, continue to emphasize explicit forms of knowledge, the truth of the matter is that most of our cultural knowledge is experienced at a level that is taken for granted. That is, it is part of our natural attitude toward everyday life. And when it is experienced at this level, we are not aware of reenacting the patterns of our cultural group—like speaking and writing in a subject-verb-object pattern, using shared paralinguistic cues to communicate our attitude toward the person we are interacting with, thinking of ourselves as creating something new, viewing ourselves as separate from nature, and so on. The experience that we take for granted may lead to destructive behaviors that we are not aware of, like the sexist patterns feminists have been attempting to make explicit. It may also involve the reenactment of patterns that do not appear to have detrimental consequences—such as writing from left to right, patterns of greeting others, playing in certain patterned ways. We even take for granted cultural patterns that are essential to the predictability and moral coherence of group life, like driving a car on the correct side of the road, recognizing the rights of others, working to improve the life circumstances of economically marginalized groups, and so forth. These cultural and individual patterns are, as suggested earlier, the basis of tempermental conservatism.

This aspect of cultural life has a number of important implications that relate to the process of education, and for environmental reformers who want to initiate basic changes. First, given such important variables as a shared cultural background, most of what is learned in schools involves initial instruction or reinforcement of the cultural understandings that teachers and curriculum developers take for granted. This has generally gone unrecognized because educators continue to focus primarily on evaluating the students' understanding of the explicit curriculum. When educators have been prodded by outside groups, they become aware of taken-for-granted cultural patterns that are racist and sexist. While most teachers are now sensitive to these specific areas of the implicit curriculum, they continue to pass on to the next generation the patterns that have been taken for granted in their own experience of primary socialization—such as the patterns of thinking and values that frame technological change as progressive in nature, and the environment as a "natural resource."

A second implication is that the individual's taken-for-granted cultural patterns make learning that has genuinely new elements very difficult. This is because the individual's conceptual schemata, which is part of the intersubjective self, is largely based on understandings that are taken for granted; thus the tendency to be aware of what is already familiar—and not to recognize the unfamiliar. As Friedrich Nietzsche put it, *"Rational thought is interpretation according to a scheme that we cannot throw off,"* while elsewhere he observes "In *our* thought the essential feature is fitting new material into old schemas, *making* equal what is new" (1968 edition, pp. 283, 273). What Nietzsche is describing is the power of taken-for-granted beliefs to reinterpret new ideas, experiences, and so forth, in ways that leave undisturbed the guiding cultural epistemology. While it is possible to cite many examples of individuals who have revised certain aspects of their cultural knowledge, there is even more evidence of outright resistance and formulaic interpretations that fit "new material to old schemas." The latter can be seen in the thinking of public school teachers and university professors who currently promote the idea that students be held responsible for creating their *own* ideas.

The Cultural Formation of a Self-Identity

Self-identity is not, in its most formative phase of development, chosen by the young child. The early cultural formation of self-awareness may include so many double binds that, like the Willy Lomans of society, adults may be unable to reconcile the kind of person they want to be with the values and norms upheld by the culture. If the stories woven through daily conversations are about achieving success through economic competition, and gaining power and status in relation to others in the human and biotic communities, the child's self-identity will likely be similarly oriented. As stated earlier, individuals think in the languages learned through interaction with significant others, and the languages encode the metaphors that reflect the cultural group's understanding of the moral nature of relationships. Thus, the development of a self-identity is not just a matter of internalizing the judgments of significant others about who one is in relation to certain cultural settings, as George Herbert Mead suggested. It also involves learning how to center oneself according to the moral norms of the cultural group. There are many instances where being consistent with one's self-identity has led to deviating from the moral norms of the group, but these individuals stand out as exceptions. And even these exceptionally moral individuals unconsciously adhere to conventional moral norms, even as they attempt to raise the level of moral awareness in their special area of concern—like the civil rights leaders who put their lives in jeopardy in order to overturn racial inequality while, at the same time, ignoring the moral norms that have governed relationships between humans and the nonhuman world.

The cultural formation of self-identity is important for environmental reformers to consider for several reasons. First, an individual's self-identity exerts a powerful influence over which kind of evidence relating to the condition of the environment will be considered, as well as which arguments about the nature of educational reform will be taken seriously. The long-held belief that it is the power of rational argument, supported by well-organized evidence, that changes minds is based on a misunderstanding of the primacy of the nonrationally based "reality" constituting processes of culture. Even when individuals are persuaded to consider ways of understanding that diverge from their stock of taken-for-granted knowledge and sense of identity, it is likely that after a short time they will return to their previous way of knowing and being—particularly if the "old reality" is what is being supported through the cultural communication processes. Lasting educational reform thus needs to be based upon the supportive networking of people who help to sustain through their patterns of communication the sense of identity and understanding that are congruent with the new cultural patterns.

A second reason for considering the role that an individual's self-identity plays in maintaining status quo cultural patterns has to do with another insight of the nineteenth century philosopher, Friedrich Nietzsche. The ways in which a culture "normalizes" an individual's self-identity accounts for only part of the reason that deep changes are resisted. Without resorting to the biological determinism argument that is becoming increasingly popular today, there is another aspect of self-identity that needs to be taken into account. Nietzsche's insights into the connections between inner psychological drives and how power is expressed in interpersonal relationships may provide an important clue about why some individuals are able to revise beliefs and values that are the basis of their self-identity, and why others are threatened and reactionary in their response to the need for change. Nietzsche argued that everything humans do, from exercising rational thought to making value judgments, involves the expression of what he termed a "will to power." This unfortunate way of identifying what is an exceedingly complex aspect of human psychology lent itself to serious distortions by Social Darwinist and elitist ideologues who were motivated by the form of power Nietzsche held in the greatest contempt. His way of understanding power is more accurately grasped by going directly to his own statements. "Knowledge," he wrote in 1888, "works as a tool of power." Earlier he wrote in his notebook, "The will to power interprets. . . . In fact interpretation is itself a means of becoming master of something." Later he observed that "it is our needs that interpret the world; our drives and their For and Against." Moral judgments were also seen by Nietzsche to be motivated by this deep psychological drive: "Moral evaluation is an *exegesis*, a way of interpreting. The exegesis itself is a symptom of certain psychological conditions, likewise a particular spiritual level of prevalent judgments: Who interprets?—our affects" (1966 edition, pp. 266, 267, 342, 148).

Nietzsche coined the word "ressentiment" to describe the pathological form of "will to power" expressed in the need to maintain a fixed (and safe) worldview through the act of judging, naming and categorizing, and constructing theories about relationships. And it is this part of his theory that has particular relevance to understanding the role that the individual's self-identity plays in conserving beliefs that are taken for granted—even when they threaten disaster for everybody. Unlike the healthy expression of will to power, which involves the ability to live without the need to compare oneself with others or to gain a sense of self-worth by judging others to be inferior, the ressentient form of will to power both needs to find a basis for denigrating what is different and threatening, and to do it in a way that will not call attention to its mode of expression. Nietzsche described the ressentient person in the following way:

> The man of *ressentiment* is neither upright nor naive nor honest and straightforward with himself. His soul *squints*; his spirit loves hiding places, secret paths and back doors, everything covert entices him as *his* world, *his* security, *his* refreshment; he understands how to keep silent, how not

to forget, how to wait, how to be provisionally self-depre-
cating and humble. (1967 edition, p. 38)

The put-downs, the will to detract from the joy and achievement of others, the expressions of rancor and spitefulness,
are all hallmarks of the ressentient personality rooted in a
deep sense of inferiority and powerlessness that cannot be
acknowledged. But they are often expressed in a way that
makes it difficult to recognize that the poisoning effect of
this type of response is actually intended to compensate for
the ressentient individual's deep sense of inferiority. The
strategy of the ressentient individual is to engage in what
Nietzsche termed a reversal of·values. That is, such individuals often represent themselves as the defender of higher
values, and use these higher values as a way of undermining
the person of action who is the source of threat. It is not that
ressentient individuals actually live by these values; rather
the higher values allow them to occupy the moral highground (at least, during the act of judgment) and thus to
gain a sense of superiority over people whose actions and
ideas are threatening. The reversal of values also occurs
when ressentient individuals uphold higher values that justify their own weaknesses, such as turning the feeling of
"anxious lowliness" into the higher value of "humility,"
transforming the inability to challenge or move away from a
subordinate relationship into the virtue of "patience," cover-
ing up for an inability to think theoretically about relationships into the value of being "practical," and being unable to
take a public stand on the moral wrongness of a foreign policy into standing for "patriotism," and so on. It's not that
these higher values are always groundless. In certain contexts the healthy expression of will to power may involve acting on them—but without calling attention to the fact.
    A number of sociologists, particularly Max Scheler,
Richard Sennett, and Jonathan Cobb have argued that ressentiment becomes more widespread in cultures where the
dominant liberal ideology proclaims the freedom and equality of everybody, while at the same time maintaining the
class barriers that prevent large numbers of people from attaining the level of education and other badges of success

that would enable them to feel equal to others. By representing everybody as being equal and free (that is, as responsible for where they end up in the race for social success and status) the ideology places a burden upon the individual that is often not fully understood or achievable. This burden often leads to feelings of guilt for not having achieved at the same level of others; and the sense of personal guilt, in turn, deflects attention from the systemic sources of inequality. This combination of liberal ideology and class barriers may contribute to transforming the individual's will to power into rancor, spitefulness, and a desire to detract from those who possess the self-confidence to take direct action (Sennett and Cobb, 1973, pp. 254–262).

What are the implications of a ressentient form of self-identity for environmentalists concerned with what students are learning in public schools and universities? Evidence of material and technological progress achieved by rapidly degrading the viability of natural systems will challenge beliefs that many people take for granted, and thus the foundations of their self-identity. As the discrepencies increase between how their culture has taught them to think and the increasingly visible evidence of decline in forest cover, fisheries, and so forth, Nietzsche's observation about the expression of will to power (expressed in the need to interpret and pass value judgments) will become a more prominent part of the public discourse. The destructive expression of will to power will not be directed toward a careful consideration of the physical evidence and trendlines of environmental degradation; rather, it will be directed toward justifying the individual's traditional way of thinking and lifestyle. The interpretations and subsequent value judgments will also be framed in ways that justify the years of deep denial. Ressentiment becomes a factor when the individual's identity and will to power lead to transforming cultural values into moral abstractions that are especially difficult to criticize. Just as ressentient teachers protect the averageness of their own intelligence when confronting especially bright students by using such classroom maneuvers as telling them that having the right answer is not as important as following all the established steps for reaching it, ressentient responses to the challenges posed by the message of environmentalists can lead to similar diversions that serve to camouflage the ressentient individual's areas of weakness. Indeed, who can challenge those who stand for the "Wise Use" of the land without appearing to be outside the bounds of normal moral judgment and common sense?

But it is the mean-spiritedness that goes beyond vigorous debate that is the clearest sign of the ressentient individual. To reiterate Nietzsche's main insight, ressentiment expresses itself in ways that hide the individual's own sense of inadequacies by putting down others who think and act more forthrightly, primarily through the expression of ill-will, rancor, spitefulness, a desire to detract, and so forth. To denounce environmentalists as "false prophets of doom," as Ronald Bailey does in *Ecoscam* (1993, p. 177), involves all the elements of ressentiment: deliberate oversimplification of the ideas and evidence of those who are the source of threat, projection of oneself as the defender of the higher values of rationality and common sense, and the injection of sarcasm and rancor into the evaluation of the opponent's motives. Witness how Bailey summarizes the motives of the environmentalists,

> After the balloon bursts on global warming and it has been incorporated like overpopulation, resource depletion, biotech plagues, and the ozone hole into the conventional wisdom of doom, to what new doom will the environmental millenarians turn next? What new crisis can be conjured up and used to promote their sociopolitical engineering schemes while enhancing their power and influence over the world's governments? (1993, p. 167)

The language of people in the Wise Use and other environmental backlash groups combines an even more pronounced combination of oversimplification and rancor in responding to the efforts of environmentalists. Rush Limbaugh, one of the most visible spokespersons for anti-environmental sentiment, uses language that elevates his immediate sense of personal power (which illustrates Nietzsche's point that judging the other is at the same time a source of self-elevation), is derisive in his representation of all environmentalists, and represents himself as the personal spokesperson of the true will of the American people.

Even within academic circles people protect themselves through ressentient laden responses to the arguments of environmentalists. For example, the suggestion that we might be able to learn from traditional, ecologically-centered cultures is often sidetracked by the claim that they also abused their environment. The categorizing of any discussion of the ecological wisdom of indigenous cultures as "romanticizing" them (which can occur if *all* indigenous cultures were represented as possessing ecological wisdom) is a power play that effectively terminates the discussion, as few individuals are prepared either to challenge the "romanticism" ploy or willing to be labeled as a "romantic" thinker. Other ploys that express the ressentient need to prevail without engaging in a deep discussion of environmental issues include the use of the "everything is relative to your point of view" strategy, and the "we can't go back to the more 'primitive' times when cultures lived in harmony with their environments." The latter ploy is especially interesting because it ignores that a large segment of the world's population is resisting the appropriation and commoditizing of their traditional knowledge of biodiversity by international corporations.

What seems to be an increased effort to undermine environmentalists by labeling them as "ecofascists" should also be understood as the expression of ressentiment. How else can one account for people making this claim when the historical evidence shows clearly that Hitler and his followers used the rhetoric of conservation as part of their justification of racist ideology and extreme nationalism? In perhaps the most authoritative study of this period, *The Environmental Movement in Germany: Prophets and Pioneers, 1871–1971*, Raymond H. Dominich III notes that when the National Socialist party's central newspaper, *Der Volkischer Boebachter*, "discussed conservation, as with almost every issue, it twisted the subject matter around to a nationalist or racist point of view" (1992, 9. 92). Dominick's analysis of a speech by Hitler makes even clearer the fundamental difference between current environmentalists who are being stigmatized with the label of "ecofascist" and the connection between conservationism and National Socialist ideology in Germany. In response to Hitler's statement that "man should never fall into the misconception that he has really risen to be lord and master of Nature . . . rather he must understand the fundamental necessity of the rule of Nature and comprehend even how his own existence is subordinated to these laws of eternal struggle," Dominick observes that when these are read within the context of Hitler's worldview, "like Hitler's numerous other references to Nature they teach Social Darwinism, not preservationism or environmental protectionism" (p. 91). Dominick further notes that "when Hitler invoked Nature, he did so to excuse the ruthless, competitive pursuit of national or racial self-interest, as in these words from a 1931 speech: 'Every healthy Volk sees the right to expansion of its living space as something natural' " (p. 90).

Critics who want to identify environmentalists as having some atavistic connection with National Socialism cannot, if they look at the record, find evidence of any faction within the environmental movement promoting racist or nationalistic ideas. If valuing the importance of living in a responsible relationship with the environment is sufficient grounds for being labeled as an "ecofascist" then the label could just as properly be applied to all indigenous cultures—which is sheer nonsense. Those who want to destroy the environmental movement are engaging in the classic maneuver of the ressentient personality who hides the weakness of his/her own position by claiming the moral highground (in this case, expressing concern about the reemergence of fascism in the guise of environmentalism). Personal identification with the higher values can then be used as the basis for destroying the group that is perceived (but not publically acknowledged) as the personal threat.

There are two important implications of this psychological phenomenon that environmentalists need to consider. As ressentiment grows out of a sense of powerlessness, it is important to recognize that the sense of powerlessness that environmentalists experience in effecting change in people's thinking and behavior can easily turn into rancor and lead to the oversimplification of the opposition's position, as demonstrated in the charge of "ecofascism." Regardless of who introduces ressentient attitudes into the discussion, they tend to polarize people and to deflect the discussion away from what should be the primary issues. Second, awareness that ressentiment may motivate individuals to resist participating in a serious discussion, and not to make the effort to inform themselves about the most important challenge facing us today, may help to put the dynamics of miscommunication in perspective. This clearer sense of what is really going on (that is, why the resentient individual is upholding higher values as a strategy for terminating the discussion or why the exchange is filled with rancor and oversimplifications) may led to different approaches in the discussion—such as exposing the ressentient manuever. This will not change the ressentient individual, but it may enable the larger public to recognize the obstructionist and essentially negative approach. The awareness might also lead to walking away from the ressentient individual, thus saving oneself from a poisonous relationship that is unlikely to lead to a constructive outcome.

Role of Tradition in the Ecology of Mind

The modern way of experiencing oneself as an individual involves, among other cultural patterns that we take for granted, a sense of time that is largely present-centered. The sense of the future is most likely to be measured in terms of upcoming events in one's life and, perhaps, even extend to a concern about the prospects of one's children. Few modern individuals project their concern and sense of responsibility beyond this limited time frame. This attitude toward the temporal dimensions of personal existence also includes the experience of moving away from the authority of tradition—which is seen as an imposition and limitation on personal freedom. Indeed, the modern sense of being an individual (that is, experiencing oneself as the final judge about what should have authority in one's immediate expe-

rience) requires a sense of disconnectedness from the past—
just as it requires a sense of disconnectedness from a sense
of place. The experience of rootlessness, which the modern
individual associates with being "normal," is reinforced
through consumer-oriented media images that equate this
condition with happiness and success. As pointed out earlier, this image of the individual is also promoted through
the use of equally powerful legitimating metaphors by various groups within the educational establishment—from elementary teachers who want to promote an individually
centered form of creativity to university professsors who
equate education with being able to think for "yourself" and
achieving success with becoming economically independent.

Regardless of the sector of mainstream culture that is
being considered, the way in which modern individuals are
dependent upon, controlled, and empowered by cultural
patterns and practices handed down over generations involves a collective myopia that has particularly serious implications—especially for groups concerned with altering
human relationships to our environment. One aspect of
Bateson's understanding of an ecology of mind is that the
cultural schemata influence which information pathways
will be attended to and which will be ignored. The shared
cultural schemata will also influence how the many differences "which make a difference" are interpreted. That is,
the traditions of a culture are immanent in the forms of intelligence expressed as humans interact with each other
and natural systems. To put this another way, an ecology of
mind has a temporal dimension. It may take the form of
past disturbances that alter weather patterns that, in turn,
lead to changes in the growth patterns of the tree being cut
down by an individual who is attempting to turn it into fire-
wood. The temporal dimension of an ecology of mind is also
expressed in the way the individual uses a metaphorical
language that encodes earlier processes of analogic thinking
as the basis for understanding current situations. This temporal aspect of human culture can be understood as tradition—a word still widely misunderstood, even by people
who now speak out in favor of "traditions." What is the
nature of tradition, and why does a more complex and accu-

rate understanding of tradition need to be taken into account when addressing the problem of educational reform? Edward Shils, who has given us perhaps the most balanced and comprehensive understanding of the nature of tradition, explains this historical aspect of culture in the following way:

> Tradition—that which is handed down—includes material objects, beliefs about all sorts of things, images of persons and events, practices and institutions. It includes buildings, monuments, landscapes, sculptures, paintings, books, tools, machines. It includes all that a society of a given time possesses and which already existed when its present possessors came upon it and which is not solely the physical processes in the external world or exclusively the result of ecological and physiological necessity. (1981, p. 12)

He goes on to correct a basic misunderstanding that reifies the modern sense of tradition by representing it as disconnected from the lives of people living in the present.

> Traditions are not independently self-reproductive or self-elaborating. Only living, knowing, desiring human beings can enact them and reenact them and modify them. Traditions develop because the desire to create something truer and better or more convenient is alive in those who acquire and possess them. Traditions can deteriorate in the sense of losing their adherents because their possessors cease to present them or because those who once received and reenacted them now prefer other lines of conduct or because new generations to which they were present find other traditions of belief or some relatively new beliefs more acceptable, according to the standards which these new generations accept. (pp. 14–15)

Like a plant that puts out new roots and branches even as old ones are dying, the traditions of a cultural group undergo change. Some of the changes are too slow, while others are cut short (often by technological innovations) before people understand their importance—like the disappearance of the tradition of craft knowledge, privacy rights, and so forth. While Shils personally favors a cautionary stance toward the emancipatory power of critical reflection, as well as warning against holding onto traditions that are out of touch with the times, he notes that once a tradition has been lost it cannot be recovered in the form it was previously experienced—the implication being that a cultural group should be sensitive to how innovations may impact traditions that still make a contribution to the ecology of community life. The problem of being aware of which traditions can no longer be reconciled with present needs and ways of understanding, and which traditions need to be preserved and renewed in people's lives, is that we are largely unaware of the traditional nature of most of our cultural patterns. As pointed out earlier, what is taken for granted tends to go unnoticed. And most of the traditions handed down from the past exist as the taken-for-granted background of cultural patterns we rely upon as we deal with more immediate concerns. We take for granted that the postal worker will not read our mail or overcharge us while we focus on correctly addressing the letter and dealing with the parking situation at the post office. The multiple ways we are dependent upon, and even empowered by, traditions while taking no special notice of them could be cited endlessly.

The modern problem, as pointed out earlier, makes the challenge of sorting out which traditions to value, and which should be revised or abandoned entirely, even more difficult. The complex messages directed at making individuals think that they are making their own consumer choices, and thus are acting autonomously in all areas of their lives, helps to constitute an erroneous way of experiencing the continuities between the past, present, and future. This experience of disconnectedness while remaining dependent upon traditions handed down from the past becomes a critically important problem for environmentalists who are considering the cultural aspects of the ecological crisis.

Unless the sense of connectedness to the past is part of the individual's taken-for-granted attitude, it is difficult, if not impossible, to develop an awareness of how traditions continue to influence present experience. As suggested earlier, most traditions are carried forward because we depend upon them, and find them meaningful and useful alternatives to other ways of doing things. That we take them for granted makes it difficult to recognize them, or to imagine what it would be like to live without them. Unfortunately, not all responses to past situations that survived over time were ecologically sound at the time of their inception, and many of these traditions have become even more ecologically problematic today. Perhaps the most obvious of many examples is the automobile, which seemed a significant advance at the time, changed the nature of the family unit, encouraged urban sprawl, led to the freeway systems that are now, in some cities, in a near state of gridlock, and framed the mentality of generations of Americans in a way that prevents them from even considering organizing human experience in non automobile dependent ways. But the essential point here is that the attiudes toward present technologies, values, ways of thinking, and so on, that we take for granted can be more easily recognized and put into perspective if individuals are educated to think of how the past continues to influence the present.

Altering the historical and cultural aspects of an ecology of relationships between the humans and the environment involves three areas of decision making. First, participating in the ecology of mind that characterizes present relationships involves becoming aware of and revising traditions that no longer make sense, that were based on a different way of understanding moral responsibility toward others (including nonhuman forms of life), and that undermine the viability of natural systems. Second, we contribute to the scale of disruption occurring in the ecology of relationships if we lack the historical perspective necessary for understanding hard-won cultural traditions. Because of this lack of understanding, and too often a general sense of indifference, we allow important traditions to be overturned by new and highly experimental forms of thinking—such as losing the small businesses that constituted the center of community life in many areas before Wal-Mart-type superstores displaced them. As we become more aware that not all changes in technology and values represent genuine progress, and begin to assess changes in terms of how they contribute to viable relationships between the human and larger biotic community, we will begin to take more responsibility for preserving and renewing traditions that are not ecologically destructive. We are beginning to see more evidence of this type of thinking, but it still represents a minority perspective—one that is easily overwhelmed by the advertising budgets of large corporations.

Third, the modern individual, in seeking one exciting experience after another, appears increasingly rootless and normless. Experiencing oneself as an autonomous individual is culturally learned. That is, the existential sense of temporality is first learned and continually reinforced through the messages and systems that sustain cultural life. If the sociology of knowledge tells us anything, it is that the intersubjective world of the individual (the schemata of understanding, the sense of self-identity, the taken-for-granted domains of experience, etc.) is largely constituted by what is communicated through the culture's technologies, art forms, and other sustaining language systems. The anomic form of individualism is not a result of a defect in the genetic code. It is culturally learned and thus can be culturally reconstituted—which is a basic premise of the advertising campaigns of corporations that continually revise the anomic individual's sense of identity and taken-for-granted attitudes in order to create a demand for their new products. As the corporate elites benefit from a form of individualism that lacks both an historical perspective and a sense of commitment to traditions that contribute to community life, it is unlikely that the processes of primary socialization and reinforcement they control will include these elements. Ethnic groups that have not been entirely overwhelmed by the culture of modernism continue to educate their children to respect their traditions, and to bond with them through community activities. For young people in mainstream culture, the understanding of tradition is too often reduced to carrying forward the patterns associated with special holidays (foods eaten, gifts exchanged, etc.). Whether classroom discussions take place about the complex nature of traditions, including how traditions must

increasingly be understood in terms of their impact on natural systems, depends upon the modern teacher's understanding of the nature of tradition. Unfortunately, most
university level courses reinforce this modern bias and thus
ignorance about the nature of tradition. Furthermore, curriculum materials available in most public school classrooms make explicit reference to tradition only in terms of
holidays and orientations of people who have not yet become modern.

How to educate students about the nature of the continuities that connect their lives with the past, as well as to
future generations, will be addressed in the later discussion
of reforming teacher education. Like the topic of taken-for-
granted beliefs, which many people incorrectly consider
both boring and unimportant, understanding the historical
and cultural aspects of an ecology may not seem as important as reversing the decline of fish populations or introducing wolves into their traditional habitats. But the ability
to understand how past forms of cultural intelligence are
part of today's natural attitude, and to sort out which forms
of intelligence should be further developed and which
should be abandoned as humanly and environmentally destructive, may be even more crucial to the future of our collective well-being.

Toward an Ecologically Centered
Interpretation of Intelligence
and Creativity

The ability of reactionary educators to mask their
ressentient based fear of exposure by appearing to be advocates of highly abstract ideals will not be the only obstacle
environmentalists will encounter as they begin focusing attention on what students are learning in most classrooms.
Another major obstacle is the way in which the modern
view of individualism has influenced how intelligence and
creativity are understood by most educators. This ideologically driven view of individualism is essential to maintaining the Social Darwinist myth that underlies modern

capitalism, which in turn helps ensure that the more romantic ideas of educators will not be seriously challenged by elite groups who possess the real power in society. The growing tendency within the scientific community to turn the understanding of genetic coding into an all-encompassing explanatory framework that accounts not only for all aspects of the individual, but also for cultural differences, further supports the educators' emphasis on the individual as the basic social unit. R. C. Lewontin, who holds the Alexander Agassiz Chair in Zoology at Harvard University, summed up the connection between modern ideology, the emphasis on an extreme form of individualism, and the current extrapolations of genetic research:

> Despite the name *socio*biology, we are dealing with a theory not of social causation but of individual causation. The characteristics of society are seen as caused by the individual properties that its members have, and those properties, as we shall see, are said to be derived from the members' genes. . . . This individualistic view of the biological world is simply a reflection of the ideologies of the bourgeois revolutions of the eighteenth century that placed the individual at the center of everything. (1992, pp. 93, 105)

The popularizers of this new orthodoxy are now explaining to a gullible public how every aspect of human experience, from choosing a mate and making aesthetic choices to criminal behavior, is genetically determined.

Given the increasing authority of scientific explanations to establish the norms of popular understanding, not to mention the power of television talk shows to translate the new deterministic vocabulary into analogies the public can grasp, it is going to be very difficult to remetaphorize the way in which intelligence, creativity, and other icons of the educational establishment are understood. The double bind that environmentalists face is that if they do not address the problem of overturning these modern educational icons their efforts will do little more than contribute to the expansion of scientific approaches to environmental education, thus leaving intact the other areas of curriculum that inculcate the values and beliefs that equate progress with exploiting the Earth's "natural resources." In the following part of this chapter I will suggest how "intelligence" and "creativity" take on an entirely different meaning when framed in terms of the root metaphor of an ecology rather than in terms of the autonomous individual.

An Ecological Way of Understanding Intelligence

Environmentalists who take on the challenge of educational reform will encounter many powerful groups within the educational establishment who still rely upon an individually centered interpretation of intelligence. The most extreme and controversial position was given prominence (again!) with the publication of *The Bell Curve: Intelligence and Class Structure in American Life* (1994). The conclusions reached by the authors, Richard J. Herrenstein and Charles Murray, are so controversial that it would best to quote them directly. In answering the questions "How Much Is IQ a Matter of Genes?" they make the following claim:

> IQ is substantially heritable. The state of knowledge does not permit a precise estimate, but half a century of work, now amounting to hundreds of empirical and theoretical studies, permits a broad calculation that the genetic component of IQ is unlikely to be smaller than 40 percent or higher than 80 percent. . . . For purposes of this discussion, we will adopt a middling estimate of 60 percent heritability, which, by extension, means that IQ is about 40 percent a matter of environment. (p. 105)

Following the public outcry about the use of science to promote Neo-Social Darwinist social policies, *The Chronicle of Higher Education* published an article asserting that the Hernstein and Murray thesis had widespread support within the part of the scientific community that studies intelligence. In fact, fifty-two specialists in the field of intelligence research were reported to have signed a public statement claiming that "intelligence is a general mental ability that can be reliably measured and substantially inherited" (Coughlin, 1995, p. A15).

Although they do not utilize this particular tradition of scientific research, promoters of computer-mediated learning rely upon an equally extreme view of individually-centered intelligence. Marvin Minsky, an important contributor to the epistemological framework that would guide the development of machine intelligence and its educational applications, stated that "there is no singularly real world of thought; each mind evolves its own internal universe." And in an earlier section of *The Society of Mind* (1986) he observed that

> Our conscious thoughts use signal-signs to steer the engines in our minds, controlling in countless processes of which we're never much aware. Not understanding how it's done, we learn to gain our ends by sending signals to those great machines, much as the sorcerers of older times used rituals to cast their spells. (pp. 65, 56)

That this is not an aberrant view of intelligence within the computer education community can be seen in Alan C. Kay's *Scientific American* article, "Computers, Networks and Education" (1991). This influential leader in the field of educational computing represented individual intelligence in the following way:

> Each of us has to construct our own version of reality by main force, literally to make ourselves. And we are quite capable of devising new mental bricks, new ways of thinking that can enormously expand the understandings we can attain. The bricks we develop become new technologies for thinking. (p. 140)

This view of intelligence, as suggested earlier in the discussion of the merging of Neo-Romantic and technocratic ideologies, leads to viewing intelligence as being empowered by massive amounts of data. Data, rather than the cultural episteme encoded and reproduced through the metaphorical language and thought connection, become the basis for students to construct their *own* understanding of relationships and ideas.

Most teacher educators also understand intelligence as an attribute of the autonomous individual. They have even developed a complex list of learning styles in order to highlight modest differences in how individual intelligence is to be nurtured in the classroom: "Constructivist Learning," "Higher-Order Cognitive Strategies," "Individual Learning Styles," and so forth. While an increasing emphasis is being placed on individuals learning to think cooperatively, there has been little effort to understand intelligence in other than individualistic terms. In a publication sponsored by the National Education Association, *Early Literacy: A Constructivist Foundation for Whole Language* (1991), Constance Kamii summed up the view of intelligence that underlies the current proliferation of educational jargon: "Constructivism shows . . . that children acquire knowledge not by internalizing it from the ouside but by constructing it from the inside, in interaction with the environment" (p. 18). Even educators involved in environmental education base their curriculum recommendations on an individually centered view of intelligence. For example David Sobel, who is co-chairperson of the Education Department at Antioch New England Graduate School and a consultant on environmental education, justifies what he refers to as an "authentic curriculum" in the following way:

> Authentic curriculum . . . refers more to the process of movement from the inside out, taking curriculum impulses from inside the child and bringing them out into the light of day, into the classroom. It implies a necessary connection between the subjective, inner lives of children and the objective, external world of schooling. (1994, p. 35)

Robert Sternberg's "triarchic theory of human intelligence" quoted earlier, which represents intelligence as "human information processing," is yet another example.

Although the theorists quoted here might disagree slightly over the classroom and social policy implications of these different theoretical frameworks, they nevertheless would agree on the most important issue—namely, that intelligence must be understood in terms either of the genetic characteristics and architecture of the brain, or the emotive and subjective judgments ("impulses") of the individual. The influence of culture on the form and expression of intelligence is entirely ignored. This totally ideologically driven view of the culturally autonomous individual is what makes their respective theories so deeply problematic. That most other academic disciplines have also been based on this keystone metaphor of modern consciousness may explain why these theories of intelligence have not been treated with the same scorn that the academic community accords to astrology and other spurious modes of inquiry. Another possible explanation is that the long-held tradition of rewarding independent thought, which is viewed both as essential to social progress and to the moral integrity of the intellectual process, has created a supportive environment for the individually centered theories of psychologists and educators.

The most direct and sensible way of reframing how intelligence can be understood is to start with the point central to Bateson's representation of the relational nature of humans, environment, and consciously and unconsciously held cultural patterns. Another way of representing the relational and interactive nature of individual intelligence is to consider how self-identity, thought, and behavioral patterns are constituted and sustained by the language processes of culture—and how culture is interactive with natural systems that provide the essential elements for sustaining life. The notion that individuals can think and act in isolation from culture, particularly when the cultural ways of knowing and communicating have been internalized as part of the individual's natural attitude, is one of the most naive (indeed, absurd) beliefs of modern educators. That the individual can act independently of the environment is equally naive. As Bateson pointed out, it is the individual's actions, along with the differences that make a difference occurring in natural systems, that creates the environment.

This mistaken way of thinking can be put right by recognizing how the intelligence of the individual corresponds to the form of intelligence of other members of the culture. If this were not the case, in terms of the most basic patterns used for understanding relationships, communication with others would be impossible. To put this another way, in learning to speak a common language the members of the culture learn to think and act in terms of the cultural schemata encoded and reproduced in the metaphorical constructions of the language. And because the metaphorical nature of the relationship between language and thought is part of an experience that may have new elements, there is always the possibility of a difference in understanding— particularly when the individual uses an analogue that makes possible a new way of understanding, or, less frequently, bases the process of analogic thinking on an entirely different root metaphor. The cultural nature of intelligence can also be seen in how members of different cultural groups have used entirely different categories for understanding relationships. Studies of the patterns in the language, thought, and behavior of different cultural groups have accumulated to the point where it is difficult to understand why academics have not recognized that the individually-centered view of intelligence is based on the metaphorical constructions of mainstream Western culture. The long list of foreign policy disasters, which have demonstrated time and again that other cultures do not share our understanding of individualism, freedom, democracy, individual property rights, and so forth, should have led psychologists and educators to recognize how ways of thinking that they take for granted are coded in the language processes of their cultural group.

Reforming education in ways that put us on a more ecologically sustainable pathway requires judging the forms of cultural intelligence encoded in technology, language and thought processes, buildings, art forms, etc., in terms of the degree of disruption they introduce into the environment. That is, cultural intelligence, as Bateson points out by using the distinction between the map and territory, must be judged in terms of its ability to recognize how changes in cultural practices introduce changes into natural systems— as well as the implications of changes in natural systems for altering cultural practices. The cultural and conceptual maps, for example, must enable individuals to recognize how 'difference' in natural systems (e.g. ability of different species to reproduce themselves, etc.) are impacted by a particular form of cultural/individual behavior. A useful way of foregrounding the connection between culture and environment would be to think of intelligence as having individualistic, cultural, and environmental dimensions that come into play in the existential experience of understanding relationships and deciding a course of action. These three dimensions should also be part of any view of intelligence that is used as the basis of making educational and social policy decisions. This last point is particularly relevant to the long list of national policies that have led to to the subjugation, and even destruction, of indigenous cultural groups who had evolved this more complex form of intelligence.

Rather than reinforcing in the educational experience of students the Cartesian view of the atomistic individual who is separate from the world that is being viewed and acted upon (which is reflected in the dominance of the personal pronoun, "I see . . .," "I want . . .," "I think . . ."), we should begin to reinforce ways of understanding that foreground the relational and interactive nature of knowing and behaving. This could be called a cultural-ecological form of intelligence. A cultural-ecological view of intelligence actually takes into account how we exist in the world, which always involves interacting with other systems in the environment we find ourselves in. By strengthening a taken-for-granted attitude toward thought and behavior as relational, rather than as autonomous and subjective only, perhaps students will become more aware of the consequences their thoughts and actions set in motion. For readers who are wondering about the practicality of shifting from an individually centered to a more relational, or ecological, form of intelligence I suggest they read Deborah Tannen's *You Just Don't Understand* (1990), which is a study of how individually centered speakers miscommunicate along culturally constituted gender lines. One of the purposes of her book is to help people attend to the nature of the relationships constituted through conversational styles, and to recognize how cultural patterns that we take for granted may contribute to disruptions and misunderstandings in interpersonal communication.

Tannen's study of how cultural patterns influence conversational styles suggests another aspect of a cultural-ecological form of intelligence that should be reinforced in the classroom. The word ecology generally is used to refer to the physical environment, but when it is used in discussions of education it helps to reframe how we think—from a one/many (i.e., the individual is separate from the world being observed and acted upon) to a part/whole way of understanding. Bateson's statement about the total self-correcting unit which evolves through the exchange of information ("difference which makes a difference") is one way of understanding that individuals are never separate from the environment. Bateson's example of how the difference in the cut face of the tree led to differences in the individual's subsequent action illustrates how organisms, given the nature of their own dynamic systems, co-produce the "environment." In other words, the environment is not the stage upon which individuals act out their subjectively determined scenarios. Lewontin makes this point in a slightly different way, and because of the long-standing misconception that represents humans as using their intelligence to manipulate and shape the environment, it would helpful to quote him in full:

> A living organism at any moment in its life is the unique consequence of a developmental history that results from the interaction of and determination by internal and external forces. The external forces, what we usually think of as 'environment,' are themselves partly a consequence of the activities of the organism itself as it produces and consumes the conditions of its own existence. Organisms do not find the world in which they develop. They make it. Reciprocally, the internal forces are not autonomous, but act in response to the external. Part of the internal chemical machinery of a cell is only manufactured when external conditions demand it. For example, the enzyme that breaks down the sugar, lactose, to provide energy for bacterial growth is only manufactured by bacterial cells when

they detect the presence of lactose in their environment. (1992, pp. 63–64)

The Chilean biologists, Humberto Maturana and Francisco Varela, refer to this process of organism and environment undergoing transformation by virtue of their patterns of interaction as "structural coupling" (1992, p. 102). This co-determination or structural coupling can also be understood as a cognitive system. Or as Maturana and Varela put it, "Living as a process is a process of cognition" (1980, p. 13).

If we can overcome the bias of Western humanism that justifies the right of humans to dominate nature on the grounds that only humans possess intelligence, perhaps we can begin to understand that ecological systems, as Bateson suggests, are the unit of intelligence—just as they are the unit of survival. This last point is particularly important because it clarifies why the suggestion that educational reform should be based on an ecological view of intelligence is not ideologically based. Rather, it reflects how ecologists understand that the nature of the environment cannot be explained separate from the behavior of the organisms and other natural systems that act upon each other. But it is necessary to bring into the discussion of an ecological view of intelligence the formative influence of culture—which often tends to be left out of scientists' discussion of the behavior of ecosystems. That is, while we can more easily understand that "living systems are cognitive systems," human participation in these systems is deeply influenced by the interaction, or "co-production," of their individual genetic history, the cultural group's symbolic constructions, and the individualization that reflects the distinctive elements of a lifestyle—including personal interpretations, expressions, sense of integrity, and even expressions of ressentiment.

In terms of education, assessing this cultural form of human intelligence in terms of how it affects the continued viability of natural systems has direct implications for how we understand the responsibilities of educators, and for how we make decisions about the content of the curriculum. As the modern chemically dependent lifestyle and increased demands resulting from a rapidly growing world population continue to introduce changes that are cycling through already stressed natural systems, there is an increasing need to be aware of the different ways in which educators and curricula socialize students to the taken-for-granted patterns of thought and behavior that had their origins in the transition to a modern, commodity-oriented culture. That is, there is a need to shift attention from the development of individual intelligence to assessing the ecological impact (including both the natural environment as well as the human community) of the larger unit of intelligence. Understanding intelligence on this level would involve the biographically distinct expressions of individualized cultural intelligence, the intelligence of past generations encoded and reproduced in the material and linguistic expressions of culture, as well as the interactive patterns in the natural environment. Thinking of educational reform in terms of this larger unit of intelligence (what Bateson refers to as the "ecology of mind") also helps to foreground the importance of a temporal perspective that is sensitive to the different cycles of time in natural systems, and to the prospects for continued survival of the Earth's ecosystems. Some American Indian cultures socialize their children to take responsibility for the consequences of their actions on the seventh unborn generation. The prospects of the mainstream culture adopting this sense of temporal responsibility are slim indeed, but as we begin to move away from an individually centered view of intelligence we will become more aware of the temporal dimensions of our interconnectedness—including our responsibility to future generations.

An Ecological View of Creativity
and Transgenerational Communication

The modern view of creativity is another cultural icon that needs to be remetaphorized in terms of the root metaphor of ecological interdependence. Over the last hundred years or so, creativity has been treated as the touchstone of the modern secular religion being promoted at all levels of the formal educational process, and in nearly all sectors of society influenced by rapid technological change. Like the word "modern," creativity has been associated with individual self-expression and authenticity, and is generally viewed as an essential aspect of humanity that should be expressed as often as possible. Indeed, it has become a mantra of the modern individual, and of educators representing nearly all ideological persuasions. As I point out in a more extended discussion in *Educating for an Ecologically Sustainable Culture* (1995), creativity is seen as the form of human expression that represents the opposite of dependence, conformity, and tradition. Invoking the word today is such a powerful act that it is unnecessary (indeed, inappropriate) to inquire about the need or worth of what emerges from the creative process. And to suggest that creativity occurs in surprisingly formulaic fashions, and often yields equally formulaic results, is unthinkable to the modern individual.

All the elements of the modern way of thinking are present in Sherry Turkle's explanation of the potential of self discovery and self creation in cyberspace. Computer technology, she writes, allows us to experience multiple viewpoints that "call forth a new moral discourse." This is because:

> The culture of simulation may help us achieve a vision of a multiple but integrated identity whose flexibility, resilience, and capacity for joy comes from having access to our many selves. . . . Without a deep understanding of the many selves that we express in the virtual, we cannot use our experiences there to enrich the real. If we cultivate our awareness of what stands behind our screen personae, we are more likely to succeed in using virtual experience for personal transformation. (1995, pp. 198–199)

The progressive nature of whatever is new and ecologically untested, the authority of individual judgment, the relativism of beliefs and values, and the cultural coding process that values starting anew rather than building upon viable traditions, are all present in the above explanation of the educational value of creative art. Especially important today is that this individually centered view of creativity, which encompasses both moral judgment and self-creation, is widely seen as essential to the technological innovation and continued economic growth that are transforming multiple dimensions of face to face relationships that constitute community life into commercial relationships. Witness how Stephen H. Schneider, a scientist and recipient of a MacArthur "genius award," conflates the two:

> Creative dialoguing is one way to get kids involved again in the educational process . . . . It is the unthinking followers and the don't-make-waves types who keep some of our industrial and governmental agencies in neutral. The most successful, innovative companies (i.e., high tech firms) reward creativity, helping to maintain America's competitive edge. (1993, pp. 33, 35)

And Richard Rorty argues that the "social glue holding together the ideal liberal society . . . consists in little more than a consensus that the point of social organization is to let everybody have a chance at self-creation to the best of his or her abilities, and that that goal requires, besides peace and wealth, the standard 'bourgeois freedoms'" (1989, p. 84). These are representative statements that reflect the conventional wisdom of some of our most highly educated people about the nature and value of creativity. Their formulaic statements serve to justify the promotion of a form of creativity that contributes to the experimental orientation of the dominant culture in the areas of ideas, values, and technologies.

As the evidence mounts that our experimentally oriented culture is overshooting the sustaining capacity of fisheries, aquifers, forests, topsoil, and is introducing increasingly adverse chemical changes into biological systems, perhaps it is time to consider how creativity can be understood and experienced if it were based on the root metaphor of an ecology rather than on the root metaphor that equates the creativity of the autonomous individual with progress. In terms of an ecological system, the word "progress" stands out as a culturally based way of expressing optimism that is continually being challenged by unpredictable disturbances in the patterns and cycles of natural systems. Perhaps in thinking about the metaphors that should guide and legitimate educational reform in an increasingly fragile world, we should use the word "sustainability" instead of "progress." But we should avoid using it in a way that suggests that our future is guaranteed. The shift in root metaphors would lead to radical changes in how we understand the connections between creativity and the educational process.

In her book, *What is Art For?* (1988), Ellen Dissanayake makes an important observation about the human need for creative aesthetic expression, and how this need is expressed in traditional cultures. Her insights, however, should be judged separately from her use of sociobiology as a framework for explaining creative aesthetic expression as a survival strategy encoded in the genes of the human organism. The sociobiology part of her argument is problematic for a number of reasons, the three most important being sociobiology's reductionist view of culture, its need for an elite class of scientists who can advance the technology of genetic engineering necessary for eliminating socially disruptive behaviors, and the way in which it gives scientific legitimation to what can be called Neo-Social Darwinism. The latter is especially significant because it provides the moral justification for elite groups working to globalize the capitalistic economic system where competition and survival of the fittest are viewed as the expression of natural selection. Fortunately, Dissanayake's insights about the creative aesthetic dimensions of human experience do not require acceptance of the biological reductionist parts of her argument.

Her insights become even more significant when framed in terms of understanding creative/aesthetic expression as a form of cultural coding and communication about relationships. That is, her main insight that creative aesthetic expression, what she calls the need of "making special," is as necessary to human behavior as breathing and procreation can be justified on comparative cultural grounds. As she describes this universal human need,

Making special implies intent or deliberateness. When *shaping* or giving artistic expression to an idea, or *embellishing* an object, or recognizing that an idea or object is artistic, one gives (or acknowledges) a specialness that without one's activity or regard would not exist. Moveover, one intends by making special *to place the activity or artifact in a 'realm' different from the everyday.* . . . In both functional and nonfunctional art an alternative reality is recognized and entered; the making special acknowledges, reveals, and embodies this reality. (p. 92)

This process of making special, in addition to expressing the artist's transformative skill and sense of meaning, occurs within the belief and value system of the artist's culture. In terms of the modern artist (and most postmodern artists), the emphasis will be on "self-expression" and the unending quest to produce something new and exciting—or at least provocative. And just as modern artists reencode in their work the root metaphors underlying modernity, artists in traditional cultures reproduce in material objects, dance, song, and narrative the metaphorical themes that are the basis of their everyday lives. That is, creative aesthetic expression is a special form of cultural coding. Thus, it should be understood as part of a complex process of cultural communication that reproduces the dominant cultural motifs in ways that provide added perspective and insight, as well as a symbolic framework for the renewal of these motifs in the life of the individual.

The critical questions in terms of understanding the connections between education and the ecological crisis are "What cultural motifs are reproduced through the creative act of 'making special' in modern culture?" and "How do these motifs differ from the cultural reproduction and renewal processes that are part of 'making special' in many traditional cultures?" By framing the question of creativity in terms of cultural coding and renewal processes, we can move the discussion beyond whether a well-known Western artist has made a more significant contribution than the Dogon craftsperson who carves the human and mythical figures on the surface of a granary door or the locally respected carver who creates a mask that will be used in the communal Tigre dance. Understanding creativity as a cultural phenomenon also brings into focus that it is part of an ecology of relationships between cultural and natural systems.

Although we may find the creativity of a modern artist aesthetically moving and intellectually challenging, it too often represents a form of cultural coding and renewal that emphasizes the cultural discontinuities and extreme anthropocentrism of modern subjectivity. When creativity promotes personal interpretation, meaning, anger, and so on, it renews the modern assumption about the progressive nature of change and the authority of subjective experience. In effect, creativity as "making special" makes "special" the new expressions of individual subjectivity—of those who create and of those who interact with the creativity of others. But there is another level of cultural coding and renewal that occurs when "making special" is individually centered. By reinforcing taken-for-granted cultural patterns associated with expressive and utilitarian individualism, the modern form of creativity is increasingly being used to promote the consumer lifestyle now spreading around the world. Elite groups who want to foster the desire to purchase the latest design of a Nike shoe, or promote a new breakfast cereal, use the creative process to establish the connection between the individual's self-concept, the cultural icons associated with success, excitement and youthfulness, and the new consumer product that will add to the corporation's profit margin. The modern approach to creativity thus contributes in a major way to the disruptive and increasingly disconnected ecology of individualism—which is becoming divided into a class of debt-ridden consumers and a smaller class that continually is in search of niche markets to exploit. The irony is that this form of cultural coding and renewal reduces the experience of "making special" to the more passive process of using the consumer product or technique created by the elite groups who now control what constitutes high-status expressions of "making special."

In traditional cultures the process of cultural coding and renewal associated with "making special" is profoundly different. In spite of the wide variation in mythopoetic narratives, technologies, patterns of interaction, and what is made special through craft knowledge and aesthetic sensitivity, it is still possible to make several generalizations about the cultural coding and renewal processes that are widely shared. These common elements, in turn, provide a basis for remetaphorizing "creativity" in ways that foreground the role it can play in helping shift from a technologically oriented consumer culture to one that is more environmentally and community-centered. First, more of the material aspects of cultural life (i.e., clothes, tools, buildings, musical instruments, etc.) are decorated in ways that express the skill of local craftpersons and approaches to "making special." Often the design and use of materials encodes the cultural group's way of maintaining status relationships, communicating about the sense of place and primal events in life, and symbolizing relationships between the human and natural world. What is important about this aspect of cultural coding and renewal is that it renews local knowledge, and thus is not part of the modern process of commodification where profits and product cycles are the dominant considerations.

Second, "making special" in traditional cultures also seems to play a more central role in the process of community renewal. It can be argued that the glitz and idealized images used to sell beer on television are also a community renewal process—which it is. But it is a profoundly different form of community than the forms of community renewed through the use of song, dance, and narrative. The latter involve linking individual members to the larger symbolic world of meaning and relationships. It may take the form of ceremonial propriety in communicating with others, where status differences and social context require enacting and renewing traditional patterns. It may involve the use of the spiritual languages of music, song, dance, and narrative to express a communal sense of thanksgiving for the rain, the bounty of the harvest, the newborn, and the life that has been fully lived. Within the diversity of cultural expression is the common element of using creativity as a central part of a participatory, community-centered, transgenerational experience. That is, "making special" occurs within the context of enabling the members of the cultural group to participate psychologically, physically, and spiritually in the larger symbolic world that represents the group's collective memory and wisdom about the moral nature of relationships. To use Bateson's phrase, the symbolic world that determines how "making special" will be expressed may be an "ecology of bad ideas"—which means the human community or natural system (or both) will be further degraded. Rather, the central concern here is whether "making special" helps to renew the quality of life in the community or, like the modern uses of "making special," fosters both a more anomic form of individualism and the technological/ economic processes that represent consumerism as the main source of human happiness.

Third, many traditional cultures encode in the creative process of "making special" the norms that are to guide human relationships with nature. Dance, song, narrative, carvings, and so forth, not only are used to explain how humans are dependent upon the life-giving forces in the natural world, but also as a means of uplifting the expressions of thanksgiving to a communal level. The cultural group's land ethic is thus sustained in people's lives as a participatory, communal, and spiritual experience. And this bonding experience is given legitimation through the communal reenactment of their way of understanding the primal forces of creation. These traditional cultures, at least those that have evolved a land ethic that defines human needs in ways that are sustainable on a long-term basis, do not use the creative process in a way that makes individual self-expression the ultimate value. Nor does the use of different art forms in communal ceremonies include encouraging the younger members of the culture to reflect critically about what they want to believe and value with regard to their relationships to nature. The nature of their form of cultural coding and renewal, particularly as it relates to passing on the group's land ethic (which is really a survival issue for groups who live within the limits of their bioregion), stands out more clearly when we consider the values that guide the modern individually centered approach to creativity. The art instructor who suggested to students that their creative challenge was to give a number of abandoned Yugo cars a second life is perhaps different only in the scale of the art project from what is the norm, it is not different in terms of the modern values it reinforces. Students painted one Yugo blue and filled it with two thousand tennis balls, while another Yugo was painted and modified to look like a giant toaster—with oversize slices of bread popping up. Other examples of how the modern approach to "making special" reinforces the value of subjective interpretation can be seen in the artist who made shaking hands with the thousands of sanitation workers in New York City her creative act, and the minimalist painting that consists of a framed white painted surface. While modern creative expression is supposed to be "a scream of freedom," as Christo put it, it is a cultural formula for appearing to be unrestricted by cultural norms.

Furthermore, this individualistic approach to "making special" reproduces a cultural orientation that represents the condition of the environment as a matter of personal interpretation. Whether the creative individual chooses to relate to the environment in instrumental terms, if it is even considered, is incidental to maintaining the integrity of artistic expression. When this view of creativity is taught in public schools and universities, and reinforced within the art community, a powerfully destructive form of moral education is being perpetuated. Even those artists who are beginning to recognize the need to represent through their medium of expression the degraded condition of the environment are caught in the double bind where their efforts to illuminate the moral nature of human relationships to nature is dependent upon the judgment of the individual who observes and subjectively decides the meaning of their work.

The difference in the cultural coding and renewal process that separates the modern approach to creativity from how it is used in many traditional cultures brings into focus another educational ideal ("myth" might be a more appropriate word) that needs to be understood in an entirely different way. The earlier discussion of how cultural patterns become part of the individual's taken-for-granted way of experiencing everyday "reality," as well as the discussion of the many ways in which traditions are reenacted and modified, makes it difficult to maintain the view that the best approach to education involves encouraging students to rely upon their own direct experience as the basis of learning. In spite of all the reasons for recognizing this educational ideal as an ideologically driven illusion, it continues to be the most widely held assumption within the educational establishment. Advocates of "inventive spelling," various interpretations of constructivist learning, cooperative learning, computer-mediated learning, and so forth, continue to rely upon this assumption. Indeed, it is often justified on the grounds that any other approach to learning would be undemocratic.

The issue environmentalists need to give careful consideration is whether the reform of public schools and universities will be little more than cosmetic if the keystone idea that students learn best when they rely upon their own experience is not challenged. Both traditional ecologically centered cultures and contemporary environmental thinkers such as Wendell Berry, E. F. Schumacher, Masanobu Fukuoka, and Dolores LaChapelle share the essental elements of a cultural/bio-conservative way of thinking. These elements include: (1) a way of understanding time that is more attuned to the cycles of different life forms that make up the biome; (2) a deep knowledge of the life-supporting characteristics of local natural systems; (3) a nonanthropocentric way of understanding relationships between humans and ecosystems; and (4) a recognition of the vital importance of elders who take responsibility for carrying forward the accumulated knowledge of local systems, as well as the human practices and ceremonies that have been renewed over generations (1995, pp. 165–166).

The last characteristic is the most relevant for understanding the difference that separates "making special" in modern cultures from the more symbolically complex approaches of many traditional cultures. While the best artists in the modern tradition have actually learned from the elders of their respective artistic communities and then gone on to discover their own "authentic" style or voice, at the public school and university level learning to express oneself creatively or in terms of critical thought continues to be represented in a way that makes irrelevant the process of transgenerational communication. This part of the guiding educational ideology is so powerfully binding that it prevents most participants in the classroom from recognizing how the reenactment of cultural patterns, including the reproduction of the epistemic orientation embedded in the metaphorical language of the curriculum, represents the process of transgenerational communication. Encouraging students to "think for themselves," to come up with their own ideas and solutions to problems, and to do their own "navigation" through the data base are also examples of transgenerational communication, but they share the problematic characteristics of other modern antitradition traditions—to use Shils' phrase.

The modern ideological framework, or cultural map, not only puts out of focus the many ways transgenerational communication occurs in social settings, including the classroom, but it also reinforces a way of thinking that explicitly devalues the constructive aspects of transgenerational communication. And by equating various expressions of self-discovery and expression with progress, it introduces confusion both in the thinking of older people about the nature of their reponsibilities to the process of cultural renewal, and in the way youth understand their responsibilities. When teachers tell students that they must make up their own minds, rely primarily upon their own individual or group (usually the same age group) experience, and construct their own ideas from available data, they are contributing to the students' confusion about their relationship with people within the community who are genuine, though often unrecognized, elders. They are also reinforcing the idea that since each generation must avoid the impositions of the previous generation, being a responsible member of the community means looking after oneself. To reiterate a point made earlier, as each generation of youth introduce, live by, and discard ideas and values in the unending quest to be an authentic and self-determining individual, the culture moves down an increasingly experimental pathway. The problem with an increasingly experimental culture is that ecologically sustainable cultural patterns (if we could even recognize them) may be lost as new technologies foster new forms of subjectivity and relationships—and as youth are encouraged by their teachers to focus on their own experience as the source of knowledge. The other problem is that the myth of progress makes it appear unnecessary, both for youth and for the elite groups who promote the technologies that introduce experiments into the cultural ecology, to take responsibility for whether their innovations contribute to long-term ecological sustainability.

Radical educational reform needs to address three specific problems associated with the current orthodoxy of student-centered learning. First, educators should help students understand the many ways in which transgenerational communication occurs—in the language processes of the culture, the material expressions of earlier ways of thinking (i.e., design of buildings, technologies, organization of space, and so on), and in mentoring relationships that are widespread in the culture. Students also need to experience, as well as understand, the renewal role they play when learning from elders. Second, since the culture of modernism equates progress with new ideas, technologies, youth, and so on, there are now generations of people who have grown older without learning what their responsibilities are in the process of transgenerational communication. That is, they have not been mentored in how to be an elder. Nor have many older people learned anything from their years of experience and knowledge accumulation that youth would be willing to learn from. This aspect of the modern crisis is most acutely expressed in the way older people have failed to recognize that the culture they based their lives upon has contributed to the accelerating rate of environmental degradation. If students were to listen to many older people, the message too often would represent success and happiness in material and human-centered terms. That is, they would not see any contradiction in urging youth to live by the belief system that has overvalued technological achievement and undervalued the importance of noncompetitive and nonexploitative relationships.

The difficult challenge that must be faced is how to educate and mentor in ways that help youth recognize that as they grow older they have a responsibility to carefully assess what is worth passing on to the next generations. The philosopher who responded to the question about what he had learned from nearly fifty years of life that was worth passing on to the next generation with the answer that "they should question everything" was simply giving the formulaic answer of the modern thinker. What he associated with wisdom was evidence more of confusion—even irresponsibility hidden by the hubris acquired as part of his training as a philosopher. If we take seriously Alan Durning's restatement of the World Commission on Environment and Development's basic value for a sustainable future as a guide for framing intergenerational responsibility (that is, "each generation should meet its needs without jeopardizing the prospects of future generations to meet their own need" 1992, p. 136), the complexity and responsibility of intergenerational education becomes more obvious. In addition to learning the nature and importance of this process of cultural accumulation and renewal, there is also a need to include in the curriculum, at all levels of the educational process, the wisdom of community members who have followed pathways of personal growth that enabled them to gain the perspective of an elder.

The third challenge is to help students learn how to balance critical inquiry with helping to carry forward the ecologically tested knowledge and wisdom of elders. Critical reflection is essential to identifying destructive and outmoded traditions, and it can also contribute to renewing and adapting traditions to new circumstances. But it needs to be represented in a manner that enables students to recognize that this approach to knowledge is only one of many approaches to cultural renewal. This means not representing it as an activity of an autonomous individual whose decisions are guaranteed by the progressive nature of change. When understood within the context of a cultural/bio-conservative ideology, critical inquiry is more likely to be guided by a sense of responsibility for maintaining relationships essential to the viability of the larger ecology. And as this larger life-sustaining ecology is far less predictable than the myth of progress has led us to believe, there is a need for a sense of responsibility that extends beyond using critical inquiry to promote a disconnected and self-centered form of individualism.

Throughout this chapter, as well as previous chapters, we have been addressing how modern cultural patterns are reinforced in the classroom. From a variety of perspectives the point has been made that it is the taken-for-granted nature of cultural patterns that makes them difficult to recognize—even for professors who supposedly hold themselves to a higher standard of critical reflection. Often these patterns are only recognized by the outsider who has a different set of cultural experiences—including the experience of trying to reconcile the assumptions that have been the basis of modern consciousness with the rate and scope of change occurring in natural systems. Indeed, it is the growing realization that the myths underlying the high-status forms of knowledge taught in the nation's educational institutions cannot be reconciled with the growing body of scientific evidence of damage to the Earth's ecosystems that enables environmentalists to be the outsider who can help educators recognize what they are passing on to the next generation. The challenge in the next two chapters will be to suggest how environmentalists can translate their concerns about the unsustainability of modern culture (now being globalized) into educational strategies for effecting a basic shift in the conceptual and moral foundations of formal education.

Chapter 5

STRATEGIES FOR
EDUCATIONAL
REFORM

As environmentalists become more aware of the connections between the high-status forms of knowledge being promoted by our educational institutions and the degradation of natural systems, their attention will turn increasingly to the challenge of educational reform. However, if their educational reform efforts result only in more environmental studies programs being established, more environmentally oriented scientists being graduated, and more environmental books being added to class reading lists, the basic double binds that now characterize modern culture's relationship with the environment will continue. We need more scientists to study the increasingly rapid changes in natural systems—but scientists who also understand that the downward trendline occurring in the viability of natural systems can only be reversed by making fundamental changes in the symbolic and moral foundations of modern culture. We also need more economists, architects, city planners, and other environmentally oriented experts—but if their expertise continues to be grounded in the root metaphors that are the basis of the modern mind-set their efforts will ameliorate only in patchwork fashion the decline in the sustaining capacity of the environment. Being able to participate in classes where some of the discussions focus on environmental issues would offer students confidence that what is being learned in the long march to a diploma or degree will contribute to their ability to live less environmentally destructive lives—but treating environmental books

199

and discussions as add-ons to courses still anchored in modern cultural assumptions will only add to the larger phenomena of collective self-deception that the paramount
issues we face must be judged on an individual basis.

The suggestion that environmentalists should focus attention on how educational institutions are linked to the
cultural sources of environmental abuse, as well as to how
the high-status forms of knowledge promoted by these institutions undermine the belief systems of ecologically centered cultures, is not expected to lead to a unified approach
to educational reform. Nor is there the expectation that the
various groups making up the environmental movement
can reach agreement either on the nature of the cultural beliefs and values that should be the basis of an ecologically
responsive form of formal education, or a common educational reform strategy. The efforts will be diverse, conflicting, and may even include reinforcing deep cultural
patterns that have contributed to the environmental problems we now face. Thus, the following discussion of strategies for reforming public schools and universities is meant
more as a set of guidelines, like reference points on a compass, for helping align what is being learned in the classroom
with the characteristics of ecologically centered cultures. But
this process of alignment should not be interpreted as borrowing from or copying other cultures; rather, it is more a
matter of finding within the context of our culturally diverse society approaches to cultural development that enhance the sense of ecological citizenship rather than the
unending quest for profits and personal freedom—perhaps
two of the most powerful images of modernity now being
globalized.

Before discussing specific steps that are most likely
to result in fundamental educational reform, it would be
useful to summarize a number of key points from earlier
chapters that should be kept clearly in mind as essential
reference points. Changing the deep conceptual and moral
foundations of a culture—especially the assumption that
equates technological progress with the highest expression
of human evolution—is about as difficult as attempting to
steer an iceberg. Nothing will happen quickly, and what is

often the most resistant to changing directions is that which lies below the surface level of awareness. As we know from past efforts to initiate deep changes in the dominant culture, there may be more of a sense of total futility than immediate evidence of success. And the efforts will not always be supported, or even understood. Thus, it is also important to understand the forms of resistance that will be encountered. The reference points for assessing how the dynamics and cultural content of the educational process, as well as the forms of resistance, both need to be continually considered as an essential part of any reform effort. That is, to cite one example, efforts to change the curriculum need to be based on an understanding of the teacher's control over how the language of the curriculum may reproduce the more problematic thought patterns from the past. At the same time, the reform effort needs to take account of the many possible forms of resistance, such as the humanities professor who equates his enthusiasm for outdoor activities and his deep love of nature as a personally sufficient response to being a good environmental citizen—while ignoring the anthropocentric values and ways of thinking reinforced in the courses he teaches.

A review of earlier chapters, as well as other books that address the cultural bases of environmental degradation, quickly reveals highly prescriptive arguments that do not fit the general rules of critical discourse long associated with the exercise of academic freedom. The right to pursue different lines of inquiry, to advance any explanation in the hope that the sustaining evidence will be discovered, and the right to use public resources to investigate whatever seems of interest to the professor, have traditionally been seen as essential to advancing knowledge and to uplifting the human condition. Unfortunately, the rate of environmental change, as well as the scale of damage—such as the collapse of the Grand Banks fishery, the world-wide extinction of species now estimated at 1000 times the normal rate, and the destruction of habitats that were the basis of subsistence cultures—now confront us with a new set of realities that can no longer be reconciled with the old assumptions about academic freedom being the seedbed of human progress. The modern understanding of academic freedom must now be reconstituted in ways that foreground human dependency on increasingly stressed ecosystems. As the educational reform efforts of environmentalists will be criticized on the grounds that they involve the imposition of a new standard of political correctness on what is being learned in classrooms, and on the intellectual processes in general, it is absolutely essential that the myths surrounding the liberal tradition of academic freedom be fully understood. Only then will it be possible to reframe the limits and responsibilities connected with the exercise of academic freedom in a way that contributes to an ecologically sustainable future.

Summary of Guidelines for Ecologically Centered Teaching

Primary Socialization

Unlike the more contextual learning that occurs in the everyday world, learning about culture in the classroom is more often dependent upon talking, reading, and manipulating abstract images. There is also a greater emphasis on developing the student's capacity to think about particular aspects of culture that are the focus of the curriculum. At the university level, the ability to perform in accordance with professional intellectual standards is an increasing part of the curriculum. But even in the more professionally oriented departments, students must first be socialized to the language that will, in turn, normalize their thinking. Central to this process of primary socialization are the cultural encoding and reproduction characteristics of the language process that are mediated in terms of the teacher's past socialization, including socialization with only minor variations in the epistemic patterns that their teachers have taken for granted—and their teachers' teachers. To reiterate a key point: when the student is learning something for the first time, and the teacher (used here to refer both to the public school teacher and university professor) is a significant other in that moment of liminality, the student is in a dependency relationship—even when the teacher is encouraging students to do their own thinking. The following aspects of primary socialization must be seen as influencing whether the student acquires the language that contributes to communicative competence, or to the more limited language that reproduces taken-for-granted cultural patterns. Understanding how primary socialization influences which aspects of culture will be learned at an explicit level, and which will become part of tacit understanding or ignored entirely, is as essential for the teacher as an understanding of the Constitution is for lawyers, and human anatomy for doctors:

1. The language framework acquired during primary socialization (i.e., the vocabulary and theory that explains relationships) provides the initial basis of the student's understanding—and this moral and conceptual schema will influence subsequent understandings. It is, therefore, imperative that teachers give special consideration to the following: whether the complexity of the language reflects the complexity of the area of culture that is being learned; whether the language is abstract or contextualized in ways that relate to the student's cultural experiences; and whether the metaphorical encoding of the language reproduces earlier ways of thinking that are environmentally destructive. With regard to the latter aspect of language, the teacher needs to give special attention to how the root metaphors influence the explanation of new phenomena, both in advancing knowledge and in introducing students to new understandings. The teacher also needs to give special attention to the conceptual schema or template of understanding encoded in the iconic metaphors that seem, at first glance, conceptually and morally nonproblematic.

2. Primary socialization involves a constant interplay between the explicit knowledge that is being introduced to students, and the background cultural understandings that may be taken for granted by the students and the producers of the curriculum materials (books, videos, software, etc.). There is also a need for teachers to continually assess which aspects of the knowledge and practices that they

take for granted are being made problematic by social changes. Knowing when to make explicit the implicit cultural patterns, and when to leave them at the implicit level of awareness, is perhaps one of the most difficult yet important aspects of teaching. As many readers are still under the influence of Enlightenment thinking that holds that everything should be subjected to critical reflection, I want to reiterate two points: not all traditions are oppressive and thus in need of being politicized; and, secondly, a dominant characteristic of ecologically centered cultures is that they understand which cultural patterns must be passed on to the next generation at the taken-for-granted level—often through narrative and communal ceremonies.

3. When something is being learned for the first time, the dependency of the student upon the significant other necessitates that special attention be given to when the appearance of facticity and objectivity in the curriculum needs to be put in an historical perspective, and understood as an interpretation based on the author's culturally influenced way of knowing.

If teachers do not understand how they mediate the cultural reproduction and renewal process, as well as how altering the patterns of primary socialization contributes to the development of the students' communicative competence, the "greening" of the classroom will be little more than a mixture of culturally contradictory messages.

Root Metaphors and Other Symbolic Maps

Root metaphors that were the basis of high-status knowledge that co-evolved with the Industrial Revolution, and continue today to influence nearly all areas of the public school and university curriculum, include the following:

1. A mechanistic way of understanding life processes that is expressed in such varied words and phrases as "mental mechanism," "data-based decision making," "architecture of the brain," "genetic engineering," "creative spark," "checks and balances," "feed-back systems," "cyberspace," and so forth.

2. A view of change as linear and progressive in nature. This part of the dominant conceptual and moral schemata is expressed in the unquestioned acceptance of the positive connotation of such words and phrases as growth, change, new, experimental, creative, innovation, development, virtual reality, and so on.

3. A view of the individual as the basic social unit and of life as a constant Sisyphean struggle to escape from the influence of all traditions. This culturally specific view of the individual is expressed when moral judgments, creativity, and intelligence are considered to be either the responsibility or an attribute of the autonomous individual. Words and phrases such as "think with data," "think for yourself," as well as the legal principle of copyright, are only a few of the many expressions of the modern view of individualism.

4. An anthropocentric way of understanding human relationships with nature. This root metaphor is expressed in the use of such words and phrases as "natural resource," "our world," "my property," and so on. It is also the basis of high-status knowledge that underlies biotechnology, human history that is written from a perspective that does not consider the impact of human activity (including what are regarded as great achievements) on the viability of natural systems, literature that does not situate the human experience in terms of the influence or condition of the environment, and a view of intelligence that does not take account of other life forms of cognitive information systems that humans interact with and are dependent upon.

5. The view of science as the most powerful and legitimate source of knowledge, including knowledge of the origin of life. Scientific cosmologies now being advanced represent human existence either as purposeless, or as an accidental outcome of chemical changes that survived and evolved in response to equally accidental changes occurring in other systems. Scientific cosmologies that retain the Western view of linear progress now represent humans as on the verge of being replaced by computers in the evolutionary process (Moravec, 1988; Stock, 1993). Science, which now functions both as a root and iconic metaphor, encompasses the other root metaphors associated with modern high-status knowledge. It also provides the knowledge that leads to powerfully new and culturally experimental techno-

logies, while at the the same time undermining the meta-
narratives that serve in more traditional cultures as the
source of wisdom and moral judgment about whether technologies should be introduced into the culture.

Whether the public school and university curriculum
continues to be part of the problem or part of the solution
can, in part, be determined on the basis of whether these
root metaphors are encoded and reproduced in the language
and thought processes encountered in the classroom. Reform efforts that broaden the course reading list, or add an
environmentally oriented course to the traditional course
offerings will not lead to changes in the deep epistemic
foundations of modern culture. If the reform effort is to be
genuine, it must expose the connections between the existing root metaphors and the environmentally and communally destructive practices of modern culture. The reform
effort must go beyond public criticism and exposure. It must
also help educators understand how to base the curriculum
on ecologically centered root metaphors, and how to shift
from the current cultural pathway that emphasizes individualism, technological mastery of nature, and the equating of
a consumer life style with personal success, to a pathway
that emphasizes the noncommodified relationships within
the community and environment.

Summary of Characteristics of Ecologically
Centered Cultures

As suggested earlier, cultures cannot be retrofitted with
a new symbolic infrastructure. But history provides examples of cultures that have changed the foundation of their
belief systems. The once stratified and fixed world of Me-
dieval society, the belief that the earth was at the center of
the universe, and the divine right of kings, were all challenged in ways that led to basic changes in the deepest
symbolic foundations of cultural belief and practice. Like
the growing evidence that human abuse of the environment

is diminishing the prospects of future forms of life, these earlier defining events that led to fundamental changes in the regime of truth and distribution of power that were taken for granted, is confronting us with a similar challenge (and opportunity) to change the basis of the dominant paradigm. The following summary of cultural patterns is noteworthy because it foregrounds the areas of symbolic development emphasized by cultures that recognized the need to live within the sustaining capacities of the local bioregions. As these areas of cultural development have been tested and refined, in some cases, over thousands of years, we should view them as a legacy of human achievement that can be used as a guide for changing the aspects of cultural development that have been given a privileged status in the West for the last three hundred years. The following summary should be viewed as a set of general guidelines for long-term sustainability, and should be part of any discussion of what can take the place of anthropocentrism, the drive to bring more of the world into the market economy, and the other mythic foundations of modern, high-status culture:

1. Cultural development in the area of mythopoetic narratives should represent humans and other forms of life that make up the natural world as equal participants in a sacred, moral universe. New mythopoetic narratives that explain the origin of the universe and forms of life on this planet must be judged, in part, in terms of how they represent humankind's moral relationships to other forms of life.

2. Metaphorical thinking should be rooted in an understanding of the reciprocal relationships between cultural practices and the natural world. Metaphors derived from images of machine (including computers) or that represent humans as superior, dominant, and more evolved, will continue to frame human thought in environmentally destructive ways.

3. The cultural way of experiencing temporality should take for granted the recognition that the past and future

are important sources of authority in making current decisions. This view of connectedness should be based on a complex understanding of how the present is influenced by traditions in both positive and negative ways, as well as on a deep sense of responsibility to the generations that follow.

4. The process of transgenerational communication must, in part, be guided by the wisdom of elders—women and men who possess a deep sense of responsibility for carrying forward and renewing the cultural traditions that contribute to equitable and self-reliant communities that are ecologically sustainable.

5. Technologies must contribute to enhancing the skills of the members of a community, the quality of their relationships with each other, and reflect the principles of ecological design—which mean that they must be suited to local needs and be based on an understanding of the characteristics of local ecosystems.

6. The ideological and epistemological orientation should be ecologically centered, and should stress conserving patterns of social interactions that overcome the sense of scarcity in human relationships, aesthetic expression and communal rituals, and mutual sharing of skills and responsibilities. The need to develop cultural traditions that allow the environment to regenerate correlates with the need to reverse the modern trend of expanding the scope of economically and technologically mediated relationships— which the various interpretations of liberalism continue to legitimate. The phrase cultural/bio-conservatism is meant to emphasize that regeneration of the community cannot be attained by further degrading the environment.

It may appear redundant to summarize the areas of cultural development shared by communities that avoided treating nature as needing to be brought under human control. But the earlier experience of reading about the characteristics of ecologically centered cultures is likely to have receded to the margins of awareness as seemingly more pressing issues compete for attention. Neither our everyday experiences nor classroom-based education challenge us to consider the characteristics of ecologically sustainable cultural patterns. The nearest we come to confronting the issue of sustainability is in the area of species extinction (there is something about the disappearance of old growth forest and salmon runs that cuts through the mesmerizing effect of the continual stream of technological innovation), and in dealing with the technical challenges of coping with the mountains of waste resulting from our consumer lifestyle. Recycling, legislation that protects the environment from the more extreme forms of abuse, and monitoring the status of different ecosystems, while important, have not led to questioning how our educational institutions continue to perpetuate the deep cultural assumptions that reduce the efforts of environmentalists to being little more than stopgap efforts. Highly educated elites are still manipulating the public into becoming a growth market for the next generation of technological innovation. As the modern trend of commodifying every niche and sector of daily life continues to be equated with progress and the good life, the formal educational process, from elementary grades through graduate school, is coming increasingly under the influence of the business and technological elites. The paradox that goes unnoticed is that while the restructuring of corporations is resulting in a massive reduction in the work force, the influence of restructuring on public schools and universities has resulted in justifying curriculum reform on the grounds that it will create the competitive work force needed in the 21st century. While the business community and educators increasingly use environmentally oriented language to give legitimacy to environmentally destructive practices, there is no evidence of widespread and systematic attention being given by the educational establishment to the ecologically sustainable cultural patterns and relationships that should be nurtured. This lack of attention to what is possible, within the context of our own Western traditions, makes it all the more imperative that these concerns become as central to the public discourse as the Cold War was to the post-World War II generation.

Forms of Resistance that
will be Encountered

Environmentalists will encounter many forms of resistance to their efforts to challenge the ways in which public schools and universities promote the most extreme expressions of modernity. The most pervasive resistance will take the form of temperamental conservatism that is part of the educator's natural attitude toward everyday cultural patterns. Indeed, this form of resistance can be found even today within the various groups that make up the environmental movement. As temperamental conservatism is a basic aspect of human life, there is no one strategy that can be counted upon to raise beliefs and behaviors that are taken for granted to the level of critical awareness. Over time this aspect of cultural embeddedness changes, at different rates for different individuals, and for a wide range of reasons. As the classroom often leads to challenging beliefs that are taken for granted, often in ways that not even the teacher is aware of, we shall focus on two other forms of resistance that must be addressed by environmentalists. The first relates to the issue of academic freedom and, ironically, to how academic freedom can be used to thwart critical discussions on the reactionary nature of what is being taught in public school and university classrooms. The second form of resistance is rooted in the long tradition of ignoring the cultural basis of academic disciplines that serve both as the well-spring for the legitimation and promotion of high-status knowledge.

Academic Freedom and the Issue
of Political Correctness

Just as the educational reform efforts of feminists, ethnic groups, and religious conservatives are now being criticized for imposing a test of political correctness on what can be taught in public school and university classrooms, environmentalists will face similar criticisms in the future. The voices raised in defense of academic freedom may even drown out environmentalists who challenge the intelligence of passing on to the next generation the cultural patterns of thought that have integrated the myth of technological progress with the myth that happiness is to be attained through the pursuit of individual self-interest. To many observers, it might even appear that the vigorous and widespread defense of academic freedom is protecting a higher value that transcends the concerns of environmentalists. The defense of academic freedom is often eloquent, even while it may denigrate the moral and intellectual standing of groups that want to protect certain beliefs and values from being relativized by the intellectual process, or that want to protect what they regard as sacred from "objective" inquiry that will supposedly add to the storehouse of human understanding. If they are to avoid feeling caught in the double bind where efforts to reform environmentally destructive cultural patterns are represented as undermining one of the primary foundations of human progress, environmentalists will need to keep reminding themselves that academic freedom is part of a specific cultural tradition, and has always involved implicit criteria of political correctness.

The effort here to clarify the issues surrounding academic freedom should not be interpreted as an appeal to abandon this valuable tradition. Nor should it be dismissed as part of the strategy of capitalism for promoting hegemonic culture, as Marx argued. Rather, the need is to reframe the moral and intellectual parameters within which it is exercised. The suggestion that restrictions should be placed on the process of free inquiry may lead the more naive academics to see this suggestion as in conflict with the idea of academic freedom, and an invitation for other groups to define the limits of inquiry in ways that protect their own beliefs and traditions from critical scrutiny and theorizing. Why the establishment of a new set of moral and intellectual parameters does not make a sham of academic freedom, and why the efforts of environmentalists to reconstitute the guiding moral framework (which is not different from what other groups have successfully achieved over the last several hundred years) needs to be explained more fully. And this can be achieved by keeping in mind the following characteristics of academic freedom:

1. Academic freedom is a distinctly Western tradition. And like Janus, the Greek god that faced in opposite directions, it has contributed to genuine improvements in the human condition while at the same time undermining the authority of many cultural groups' beliefs—particularly traditional cultural groups that attempted to resist being drawn into the orbit of modernity. While academic freedom has been both constructive and destructive in terms of its influence on mainstream and minority cultures, it also has the distinctive feature of being most closely associated with the technocratic and emancipatory forms of liberalism. These forms of liberalism have been used to legitimate the educator's messianic drive to make critical reflection the basis of emancipating individuals from the influence of their cultural traditions. Basically, the liberal values that both provide the legitimation for academic freedom and, in turn, are strengthened by its achievements include: (i) the autonomous individual; (ii) the belief that new ideas and values (including technological innovations) are the basis for uplifting humanity; (iii) an anthropocentric perspective on human relationships with nature; and (iv) the belief that the inquiry process is a humanistic and essentially secular activity that should not be limited by what cultural groups regard as sacred.

What is important to keep at the center of any discussion of how to reconcile academic freedom with the cultural imperatives that the environmental crisis now forces us to recognize is the close connection between the present view of academic freedom and the messianic way modern values and thought patterns are being globalized. To make this point more directly, the close connection between academic freedom and the promotion of high-status knowledge needs to be kept in mind when the defenders of academic freedom use the metaphors of "progress" and the "good of humanity" as the moral basis of their defense.

2. Academic freedom is often represented as the unimpeded search for a better and more accurate way of understanding. It is also represented in terms of the liberal image of an open model of inquiry that is conducted on a level playing field where opposing interpretations will have an equal chance to prevail. In recalling Alvin Gouldner's observations about the rules that govern the intellectual process, we find that the rules involve politically

correct guidelines that ensure that the outcome is not determined by the weight of the cultural group's historical
experience or the wisdom of elders. Rather, the outcome is
determined in terms of the participant who has the most
elaborated speech code and the economic resources to conduct research that can be used to buttress the innovative
theory or argument being advanced. As Gouldner points
out, cultural groups who ground their speech in tradition,
sacred texts, or other forms of cultural authority are not
seen as advancing knowledge claims that have any credi-
bility. The rules that govern this supposedly culture-free
mode of critical discourse, and which are identified most
closely with academic freedom, include: (i) a concern with
justifying assertions; (ii) the use of a mode of justification
that does not fall back on the authority of tradition, religious beliefs, or elders; (iii) an open forum where minds
are swayed on the basis of evidence and the power of argument (1979, pp. 28–29). Clearly, tacit and contextual understandings, as well as communally based knowledge,
will have no standing in the competitive arena of critical
discourse, which has a close similarity to Adam Smith's
way of understanding the ameliorative effects of economic
competition that occurs between individuals. A further
similarity is that both the ground rules of critical discourse
and Smith's economic model of human behavior assume
that all the participants meet on an even playing field,
which is sheer nonsense when the form of discourse privileged by the ground rules is considered.

What Gouldner's observations put in focus is how the
ground rules of critical discourse ensure that academic
freedom serves the interests of the intellectual and technological elites who view the deauthorization of tradition
as clearing the way for a more progressive and often culturally experimental development. Academic freedom also
protects inquiry that challenges the foundations of long-
standing cultural orthodoxies—as I am am doing here.
Again, it should be emphasized that I am not making an
argument for the elimination of academic freedom, but
rather to change the moral framework that guides the educational and scholarly activities within universities.

3. That academic freedom has always been framed by a
set of cultural assumptions and values that marked the
boundary between appropriate and inappropriate inquiry

can be seen in its close connections with liberal traditions of thought, and the norms that have governed the areas of cultural experience that were to be taken seriously. This brings us to the central issue that environmentalists should understand: namely, that political correctness is not a new imposition. The criteria of political correctness has always been an integral aspect of the ideological and epistemological biases that represent the cultural and class orientation of the dominant groups within the academic community.

4. There have always been moral norms and intellectual biases that have marked the boundaries within which academic freedom has been exercised. Often the boundaries are so taken for granted that they only become recognizable when they are crossed, as in the example of scientific experiments conducted on prisoners during World War II and experiments on individuals and groups who lacked the power to protect themselves—such as the African Americans who were deliberately infected with syphilis and prison inmates who were used to test the effects of radiation. That these attempts to advance human understanding (a phrase that hides the Janus nature of academic freedom) were subsequently viewed within the larger academic community as morally reprehensible indicates the shared moral conventions that, when upheld, limit the scope of academic freedom. That the moral norms change over time can be seen in how the physical remains of American Indians, which are considered as sacred within their own cultural groups, were collected for scientific study, and then stored away in dusty drawers like so many other scientific specimens. Efforts to force the scientific community to recognize that what is regarded as sacred, even by marginalized groups, places limits on the inquiry process have partially succeeded in getting the remains returned to the appropriate groups. Other examples of the moral conventions that have long been recognized, or that have changed in recent years, can easily be cited as evidence that academic freedom has never meant total freedom to experiment and question. The arguments about the limits of biotechnology, which Andrew Kimbrell documents in his remarkable book, *The Human Body Shop: The Engineering and Marketing of Life* (1993), are, in part, about

the moral limits of academic freedom. Similarly, spokes-persons for rejecting the Western idea of development, which is gaining increasing support in Third World countries, are really challenging the Western view of academic freedom—which they view as legitimating the imposition of a materialistic and exploitative view of wealth onto cultures that have developed complex forms of intangible and communal wealth (Sachs, 1992). Examples of how the limits of academic freedom vary within the mainstream academic community can be seen at the departmental level where fear of being censored or passed over for promotion reflects an awareness of what the dominant faculty members regard as significant inquiry—and what is not worthy of scholarly attention and reward. Indeed, one of the ironies that surrounds current protests over the ability of previously powerless groups to establish new moral parameters for the exercise of academic freedom is the fact that the moral boundaries have continually reflected the perspective of the faculty group in power. Heated debates about the limits of academic freedom are often avoided by ensuring that faculty holding significantly divergent views are not hired.

Ecology as a New Moral Basis of Academic Freedom. Academic freedom has about the same moral standing among educators as the Hippocratic Oath has within the medical community. It symbolizes a moral responsibility to use the intellectual process to promote human progress and enlightenment, which has most often meant overturning beliefs based on unexamined conventions of thought and practice. And, like the doctor's commitment to engage in ethical behavior, it has been compromised in many ways. A strong case can even be made that academic freedom has provided the protection to develop technologies and ways of thinking that have increased our ability to exploit the environment, and to lay the basis for a more consumer-driven lifestyle. The evidence for this criticism of academic freedom can be found in how the inquiry process and legitimating moral framework have so often been based on the root metaphors underlying the modern and environmentally disruptive form of thinking. It also provides protection, as mentioned earlier, for criticizing how it has been used to legitimate cultural practices that are pushing the Earth's ecosystems to the verge of collapse.

As part of a strategy to reform public schools and universities, environmentalists should answer the criticism that they are imposing a new regime of political correctness with the argument that there is a need to radically change the moral guidelines that have always been integral, though largely implicit, in the exercise of academic freedom. To return to several points made earlier, language is used to communicate about relationships; since relationships have a moral dimension (that is, determining which behaviors are appropriate in the relationship), language encodes the largely taken-for-granted moral schemata shared by other members of the language community. The language used in scholarly inquiry, research, and technological development reproduces the moral orientation (and blindness) of the cultural group—even when the inquiry process leads to challenging widely held conventions of thought and behavior. Efforts to change the deep metaphorical foundations of modern culture—from being human centered to ecologically centered, and from measuring the standard of living in terms of rising consumer expectations and technological innovations to assessing the quality of life in how widely the intangible forms of wealth are communally shared—are also efforts to change the moral framework that serves as the accepted parameters for the exercise of academic freedom. Instead of justifying academic freedom on the basis of contributing to social progress and emancipation from ignorance (both of which have been understood in terms of the modern bias against low-status forms of knowledge), it should now be justified on the grounds that it provides the protection needed for questioning ecologically destructive cultural patterns, and for passing on to the next generation the forms of knowledge, values, and practices that contribute to a sustainable future.

When academic freedom is understood as essentially a moral issue, rather than as the basis of human progress—a phrase that combines two godwords that are beyond challenge within the high-status knowledge community—it then becomes possible to reframe the discussion of political correctness. In short, it is not academic freedom that is being challenged here, but the moral framework that is both encoded in the language and beliefs that are taken for granted by the person who is exercising it. When the moral framework is changed from being based on the root metaphors underlying modern culture to root metaphors that represent how humans are nested in culture, and cultural systems are nested in life-sustaining natural systems, then inquiry that leads to forms of knowledge and technologies that are destructive of these interdependencies would be viewed as immoral. The shift in how the taken-for-granted moral values frame the intellectual boundaries within which academic freedom is exercised can be seen in the recent change in the public's attitude toward smoking. The gradual recognition that smoking and the incidence of cancer are linked has led to reframing the moral boundaries for the conduct of scientific research. The same arguments were made in defense of academic freedom in the years when scientists willingly conducted research that benefitted the tobacco industry that are now being made in a changed climate of opinion where scientists would no longer consider undertaking research that would contribute to disguising the presence of addictive drugs in cigarettes. This shift in the taken-for-granted moral framework led to redefining the boundary lines of academic freedom, and the scholar who crosses the redefined boundary for personal gain faces being censored by colleagues.

As there have been no fundamental changes in the moral and mythic framework that currently legitimates the use of academic freedom to advance ecologically destructive high-status knowledge, the university and professional reward systems continue to value inquiry that leads to the development of technology that further deskills workers and, increasingly, displaces them entirely, and of communication techniques that increase the effectiveness of advertising. It also continues to reward the teaching of philosophy courses that represent rational thought as free from the influence of culture and the constraints of the natural environment, to courses in an increasing number of disciplines that represent data (which is really a degraded form of knowledge) as the basis of individual empowerment and social progress. Indeed, the use of academic freedom to promote ecologically destructive forms of high-status knowledge is its most dominant characteristic today. As environmentalists begin to examine how the high-status knowledge being advanced in universities contributes to the globalization of the modern cultural agenda, and as they begin to promote ecologically based forms of knowledge, relationships, and technologies, they will be helping to establish an ecological moral framework that shares the characteristics of cultures that possess the wisdom to make the environment and the prospects of future generations the centerpiece of their moral framework.

Cultural Pattern of Ignoring the Influence of Culture

There is a connection between the moral misuse of academic freedom and the lack of awareness in most disciplines of how every aspect of human existence is an expression of a cultural ecology that has developed over centuries. But the cultural part of the problem, like the example of academic freedom, needs to be understood in terms of the distinctive challenges it poses for environmentalists, particularly if environmentalists are to address the deepest and most unconscious levels of resistance to radical educational change.

The culturally influenced sources of resistance to shifting from a modern, individually centered approach to education to one that foregrounds self-limitation, in all its modern forms, for the sake of others—including the biotic community—will be both varied and pervasive throughout the university community. The resistance needs to be seen as a reactionary response; that is, an attempt to hold onto the conceptual and moral patterns that gave modernity its messianic energy. The reactionary response may take the form of professors resisting educational reform out of a desire to justify a career of scholarship that helped to reinforce the myths of progress and an anthropocentric worldview. Reactionary professors may also attempt to protect their source of research grants. Resistance may also take the more banal form of professors wanting to think and teach within the theoretical framework they acquired during their graduate years. But as the recent impact of feminist criticism of higher education demonstrates, even professors who exhibited the above expressions of resistance were influenced to make changes—at least on the surface. Unfortunately, the degree of change now being forced upon us by declines in the sustainable characteristics of natural systems cannot wait for this generation of academics to retire. As the next generation of academics is likely to contribute only new interpretations rather than replace the deep conceptual foundations of high-status knowledge, environmentalists should not be misled by self-serving explanations that "intellectuals" are the best qualified to recognize their own misconceptions.

For now, it is important to clarify further why the cultural habit of ignoring the influence of culture is a generally unconscious yet powerful source of resistance to reforming the cultural premises underlying all levels of education. As suggested earlier, the education of philosophers, scientists, economists, psychologists, and even newly established groups of experts such as environmentalists—to cite only a few of the disciplines that have remained isolated from the insights of anthropologists and cultural linguists—involves increasingly specialized bodies of knowledge that have been based on the assumption that the individual is the basic social unit. This foregrounding of the individual made it difficult, if not unnecessary, to understand how the cultural ways of knowing (including the values appropriate to how different relationships are understood) are encoded in the semiotic systems that sustain the everyday sense of reality, as well as in the language used to organize and advance high-status forms of knowledge. The liberal bias of academic disciplines discussed in an earlier chapter also makes it difficult to recognize that the modern agenda for uplifting other cultures to the Western standards of rational thought and individual self-determination is a culturally specific way of thinking. As can be seen in the writings of Allan Bloom, Mortimer Adler, and William Bennett, so-called conservative academics failed to recognize that their own educational prescriptions are influenced by the same culturally specific assumptions that are the basis of the liberal thinkers they criticize—the two most central being an anthropocentric view of human relationships with nature, and a view of progress as linear and driven by rational thought.

If we follow the cultural pathway of basing the knowledge passed onto the next generation on the assumption that the individual is the basic social unit (even as science is now transforming this assumption in a way that makes the gene the basic unit that determines thought, behavior, and thus culture), environmentalists will continue to have difficulty in getting both the public and educators at all levels of schooling to recognize that the ecological crisis is largely cultural in nature. The lack of a deep cultural perspective was evident at the 1995 conference jointly sponsored by a consortium of nine seminaries and theological schools in the Boston area and the American Association for the Advancement of Science. The main purpose of the conference was to explore how science-based environmental courses could be incorporated into the study of theology. The moral discourse taking place within various religious communities, it was thought, could be further strengthened if the new ethics relating to population and consumption issues were based on the findings of science. While the growing number of environmental dialogues between scientists and theologians is an important development, framing the problem in a way that excludes examining cultural assumptions about the nature of progress, individualism, and intelligence helps to ensure that the more fundamental sources of the double binds that we now face, whose roots can be traced back to the basic beliefs of the Judeo/Christian tradition, will not be examined. This example of interdisciplinary dialogue also highlights that a knowledge of the connections between the mythopoetic beginnings of Western culture (including how its epistemic orientations continue to be reproduced in the language used to advance high-status knowledge in the sciences) might have led both theologians and scientists to reflect on how recent scientific explanations of the origins of the cosmos, the earth, and human life undermine the theologically based cosmologies that are supposed to give authority to the new ethics limiting population and consumption, which are to be taught in local places of worship. The double bind exemplified in this well-intentioned effort is a manifestation of the problem discussed in an earlier chapter: namely, the lack of understanding of how science, for all its genuine achievements, is the basis of the rapid pace of technological innovation that, in turn, requires a high level of consumerism. It is also a contributing factor in the worldwide spread of modernity, which makes it difficult for many cultures to maintain traditions not oriented toward consumerism and individualism.

It would be relatively easy to bring together theologians for the purpose of discussing the cultural and religious roots of the modern view of progress and other cultural assumptions that are contributing to the ecological crisis. But getting scientists to participate in such a discussion, either at the local or national level, would be difficult, if not impossible. Because the basic unit of human reality is not recognized as cultural in nature, scientists tend to view environmental issues as essentially questions of good or bad science, and to ignore the importance of the cultural assumptions that exert such a profound influence on how cultural groups relate to the environment. The irony is that if the cultural dimensions of the ecological crisis are not resolved, the most spectacular achievements of science such as the deep space probes, understanding the basic structure and properties of matter, and the Human Genome Project, will seem rather expensive intellectual undertakings that have little relevance for addressing the scale of social disruptions that lie ahead. Indeed, the cultural and thus educational dimensions of the ecological crisis are both more critical to averting ecological collapse, and more difficult to deal with in terms of effecting genuine change; yet they continue to be peripheral concerns because of the long tradition of not recognizing that individual thought, as well as the discourses of the sciences, economics, philosophy, and so on, are embedded in the symbolic systems of a modern culture that is now mistakenly being represented as the universal standard.

Some readers might object to my criticism that the disciplines (with the exception of anthropology and certain specializations within linguistics) are not based on a deep understanding of our own culture—and how it differs from those that are ecologically centered—does not take account of the widespread efforts to incorporate multicultural education into all levels of formal education. While efforts to address the issues surrounding this reform effort are complex and well-intentioned, multicultural education largely leaves students in the public schools with little more understanding of cultural differences than they would gain from a tourist industry approach to developing appreciation of diversity. Because it is such a contentious issue on university campuses, it is largely limited to adding the writings of minority authors to course reading lists and to the course offerings of the ethnic studies department. In short, multicultural education, like environmental studies, is an add-on to the curriculum, and thus does not challenge the cultural assumptions that underlie the high-status forms of knowledge that lead directly to professional careers in the fast changing mainstream of modern culture.

The resistance of highly educated members of the public to addressing the cultural roots of the ecological crisis reflects the resistance of their public school teachers and professors to recognizing that what they are teaching is based on culturally specific assumptions that represent human progress as being on a pathway that is independent of the fate of the environment. The failure to recognize the cultural basis of thought and values, including how the value of individual choice is one of the keystones of modernity, also has had an adverse effect on the thinking of philosophers within the environmental movement. The writings of Warwick Fox and Arne Naess marginalize the importance of the cultural language systems that constitute and sustain the everyday sense of "reality," which leads them to overemphasize the importance of the rational judgment of the individual. Even Aldo Leopold made the mistake of making the "land ethic" dependent upon the individual's rational understanding of why behavior should "preserve the integrity, stability, and beauty of the biotic community" (1972 edition, p. 262). Ecologically centered cultures, by way of contrast, developed in diverse ways that encoded the common understanding that all the language systems of the culture (everyday discourse, dance, song, narratives, visual arts, architecture, technologies, and so forth) were repositories of knowledge that needed to be renewed in ways that reflected changes occurring in the environment, and passed on to the next generation. While they may lack the ability to make explicit their guiding assumptions in the detached critical style so valued in the West, they do not think of themselves as autonomous individuals who are free to adopt whatever stance seems personally appropriate toward the semiotic systems that sustain cultural life, and to view themselves as independent observers.

Immediate and Long-Term Strategies for Effecting Educational Reform

There are as many pathways to educational reform as there are societal starting points and individual interpretations of the problem. The use of academic freedom to protect reactionary thinking, as well as the ethnocentrism that obscures differences that exist in cultural ways of knowing, stand out as the most prominent sources of resistance within the academic community. In light of these forms of resistance, two generalizations can safely be made that have special relevance to a discussion of immediate and long-term strategies for changing the deep cultural foundations of high-status knowledge promoted in university classrooms and through scholarly publications. The first relates to the extreme sense of individualism manifested in the professor's right to determine the content of courses and the focus of scholarly activity. This cowboy attitude may not always lead to success within the domain of departmental politics, but when expressed in terms of "nobody is going to tell me what I can teach or write about," it becomes a problem that cannot be overlooked.

The second generalization that can be supported by the historical record emphasizes the shifts in the orthodoxies that have governed the appropriate way to think in the different disciplines. Indeed, this characteristic of the academic community caught the attention of Friedrich Nietzsche, which in 1884 led him to write in his notebook that "the scholar is the herd animal in the realm of knowledge" (Kaufmann, 1968, p. 226). This proclivity represents one of the ironies of the university. While professors militantly defend their scholarly freedom they have demonstrated an equally strong tendency to find validation and strength by working within what is the currently accepted explanatory framework. Stephen Jay Gould's *The Mismeasure of Man* (1981) documents how this herd mentality was manifested in the scientific racism that was dominant in academic departments (especially anthropology, psychology, and the other sciences concerned with ranking individuals and cultures on the basis of "intelligence") at the turn of the last century. More recent examples of this herd tendency can be easily cited: structuralism, poststructuralism, analytic philosophy, Marxism (which produced its own sub-paradigmatic frameworks), deconstructionism, postmodernism, and, now, the reemergence of sociobiology. The new interpretative framework often represented a genuine improvement over what was being replaced. But it also served to give a new form of legitimacy to cultural assumptions that were basic to the interpretive framework being replaced, such as the anthropocentric way of thinking about human and nature relationships, and the view of change as progressive in nature—both of which were essential to all of the orthodoxies cited above. The earlier explanation of how the deep cultural assumptions are encoded and reproduced through the language processes essential to teaching and scholarship suggests that this phenomena is, to a certain extent, an inevitable aspect of any specialized discourse. Perhaps the more important point is that the herd tendency within the academic community can be utilized as part of a reform strategy. That is, many of the specific recommendations that will be made in subsequent pages for turning universities into more ecologically responsive institutions will have a multiplier effect because of the tendency of most academics to adapt their teaching and writing to how the frontier of their field of inquiry is being defined.

The problem for environmentalists is that this bandwagon phenomena may take even more nihilistic directions,

such as the shift from viewing the individual as the basic social unit to explaining cultural norms, individual attributes,
and even intelligence itself as genetically determined. An
even more nihilistic academic trend is to explain evolution
in terms of the merging of humans with machines (a hybrid
that Donna Haraway refers to as a "cyborg") as preliminary
to the full realization of a "postbiological world." Given
these possibilities, the immediate task is to bring to public
awareness the diverging human and environmental trendlines by juxtaposing the scientific evidence of the degraded
state of the environment (along with defensible projections
of human demands on the environment over the next
two decades) with the assumptions underlying high-status
knowledge in the different disciplines and professional
schools. Given the increasing public awareness of the importance of the environment, exposing the theories and policy implications that are being promoted in our institutions
of higher learning might lead to the kind of public reaction
that followed the exposure of widespread racism and sexism
in universities. The historical record indicates that universities have too often been unable to reform themselves, but
that they do respond to public pressure and changing priorities for the funding of research. Thus, the following recommendations should be seen as part of the primary strategy
of highlighting the double bind of promoting high-status
knowledge that is currently contributing to the globalization of cultural patterns directly associated with specific
forms of environmental degradation.

*Public Exposure of What is Being Taught
and the Theories that Guide Research*

Which classes are still based on the cultural assumptions that have contributed to ecologically and culturally destructive practices in the past? Does the research paradigm
take account of the moral nature of human relationships
with the nonhuman world? Who benefits from the forms of
knowledge promoted in classrooms and research settings?
What will be the impact on cultural groups that have developed more in the areas of community and environmental

responsibility? Do the forms of knowledge promoted in universities have self-limiting guidelines that recognize the rights of other forms of life as well as the rights of the seventh unborn generation? Does the process of learning itself foster a natural attitude toward market driven relationships? These are just a few of the questions that should be part of an ecological audit of the gains and losses connected with the high-status knowledge that is the centerpiece of transgenerational communication in our nation's universities. I used a similar series of questions as the basis of examining what is being taught through high school textbooks (1993, pp. 117–153), and the findings were more alarming than I originally thought possible. Similar efforts to document the assumptions and models of thinking being passed on through the university classrooms needs to be undertaken, and the findings made public. In some disciplines, such as psychology, philosophy, economics, political science, and history, the anthropocentric and other root metaphors basic to modern consciousness will be readily apparent—at least to observers who do not take them for granted as part of their own conceptual and moral framework.

Being able to recognize what is ecologically and culturally problematic about the increasingly specialized languages used to advance the "frontiers" of the sciences will be more difficult. At first glance, it may seem that clarifying the cultural and ecological implications of computer-mediated thinking will be relatively easy when compared to articulating the changes that will be introduced into the environment as a result of globalizing technologies and economic policies based on genetic research, the new materialistic models for explaining complexity in self-organizing systems, and so on. But when theorists begin to extrapolate, as is now beginning to happen, the implications of chaos theory for understanding local ecosystems, the most recent findings of brain research for making pedagogical and curricular decisions, and the ramifications of over four billion years of evolutionary life processes on earth for contemporary economic and moral behavior, the task will become much easier. The immediate challenge is to follow the example of ecologically oriented thinkers, such as George Sessions in philosophy, Herman E. Daly in economics, and Donald Worster in history, in exposing the deep cultural assumptions that continue to be embedded in even the most advanced areas of high-status knowledge.

Just as gender bias was exposed by feminists who were more than able to hold their own with the preeminent scholars within their fields, as well as by students and others who acted from a more immediate and common-sense basis, exposing the nihilism and the ecological destructiveness of cutting edge thinking is a responsibility that must be shared on as wide a basis as possible. The immediacy and scale of the ecological crisis should awaken more people to the need to take responsibility for bringing the various forms of high-status knowledge into an enlarged moral discourse on what constitutes the appropriate cultural expectations and relationships with the natural environment.

Getting the Message to University Administrators and Governing Boards

The men and women who occupy the top of the academic pyramid cannot be approached in the same way that environmental activists in the Northwest get their message across to the U. S. Forest Service. Sit-ins and other confrontational tactics, while appearing heroic, are less likely to effect the desired changes in administrative leadership priorities than approaches that better fit the patterns of discourse to which they are accustomed. University presidents and related administrators, as well as members of the governing boards, are generally drawn from the strata of society that has benefitted most from the modern emphasis on the integration of science, technology, and economic activity. That is, in most instances these will be the people most threatened by the message that the high-status knowledge they have committed themselves to advance out of deep sense of public responsibility is threatening life on the planet. This group's social status is significant for another reason that should be taken into account in determining what might be the most effective strategy for influencing them. With few exceptions, university presidents, and espe-

cially members of governing boards, experience the plenitude of the mainstream technological and consumer oriented culture in a way that is different from most other
strata of society. Whereas the poor and, increasingly, the
lower middle class are constantly bombarded with the complex visual message systems that remind them of the abundance of consumer items available (shopping malls and
television commercials give no hint that the sources of the
seemingly endless supply of consumer items are shrinking
at a rapid rate), university administrators and members of
governing boards actually take for granted the plenitude as
a part of everyday life. In short, they experience the com-
forts, aesthetic tastes, conveniences, and status-conferring
characteristics of modern culture not found in the garish atmosphere of shopping malls.

Thus, the initial attempt to reach them with the message that the university is contributing to the perpetuation
of the mythic structures of modernism that are beginning to
unravel has to be thought out and packaged in a way that
will fit the limited time frame they might give to an issue so
different from the budget and policy issues they are accustomed to addressing. For environmentalists to make a ver-
bal presentation at a board of governors meeting, or at a
meeting with the university president and advisors, would
be largely a waste of time. The presentation within the context of other agenda items that appear more pressing, like
budget allocation issues related to the use of new computer
technology that will further integrate the state system of
higher education or making decisions about the appoint-
ment of a new university president, would distort its true
significance while giving the top leadership of the university the false sense that they have fulfilled their responsibility by allowing environmental issues to be on the agenda.
A far more effective approach would be for an environmentally oriented foundation to invite the board of governors
and top administrators down to the level of deans of major
units of the university to a two or three day retreat held in
an environment that has few outside distractions.

The ideal scenario would be to have well-known scientists give presentations that would provide an overview of

the changes taking place in natural systems, similar (yet with more specificity) to the overview presented in the Union of Concerned Scientists' statement, "World Scientists' Warning to Humanity" that was sent in 1993 to the heads of governments and international agencies. The presentation should also include projections of how the current growth in world population will further impact the Earth's ecosystems. These presentations should be followed by equally well-known social scientists who explain the connections between high-status forms of knowledge being advanced by universities, the cultural patterns that have an adverse impact on the environment, and the consequences of globalizing this high-status knowledge for cultures that have taken less economically and technologically driven approaches to development. The increasing discrepancy between the upward trendline in human demands on the environment and the downward trendline in the viability of natural systems, as well as the limited time line now being estimated as the window of opportunity for turning things around, will challenge attending administrators and governing board members to confront the leadership decisions that most have escaped through a combination of personal self-denial about the existence of an environmental crisis and being immersed in a discourse that highlights the connections between universities and social progress. Ideal scenarios are seldom a realistic possibility, particularly when the need is for environmentalists to change the thinking of administrators of so many universities (even the trendsetting universities represent a significant number). A practical suggestion would be to have videos of scientific and culturally oriented presentations that could be used at the retreats.

    What should environmentalists expect to come out of this effort to educate university presidents and others in leadership positions about the need to address the educational implications of the ecological crisis? As we are in the beginning phase of questioning how our cultural patterns are threatening the environment, and have only limited understanding of some of the characteristics of ecologically sustainable patterns, it is impossible to give more than a partial answer. As the word "crisis" is being used here in the sense of imminent and possibly irreversible danger to many people alive today (and as posing a threat the next generation will be even less able to avoid), it seems reasonable to expect leadership in setting new guidelines that would not distort already underfunded budgets or limit the university's role in ameliorating the effects of ignorance. The new guidelines should, among other things, rectify the current practice of basing new knowledge on ignorance of the human dependency on natural systems, and on the greed of the present generation. More specifically, universities need to establish guidelines that discourage the current "publish or perish" atmosphere that pressures untenured faculty members to devote time to research and writing on issues that are often of minor significance. Presidents and deans, with the blessing of the board of governors, could simply rescind the use of scholarly publications as the main criterion for promotion and tenure. When viewed in terms of whether scholarly publications really contribute to improving people's communal and spiritual lives, it is difficult to see what would be lost if publishing were delayed in the professor's career until expert knowledge within a specific field of inquiry could be balanced with wisdom about genuinely important relationships and values. If free of the need to write the articles and books required for promotion and tenure, professors would then have the time to participate in conversations about how to reconstitute the metaphorical foundations of their disciplines (how to motivate them will be discussed later). Ironically, as long as promotion and tenure are based on an impressive list of publications, professors will make this a higher priority than the dangers their children face from the deepening ecological crisis.

A second change that needs to be initiated by leadership at the higher levels of the university is the resetting of the university's intellectual and moral compass. Because only a few university presidents and academic deans have made the cultural dimensions of the ecological crisis central to their way of articulating the mission of the university, environmentally oriented courses and faculty now have only a peripheral and not fully respectable standing within the various disciplines (with the exception of certain fields of science). The pressure to work within the discipline's current definition of high-status knowledge will constantly pull faculty in a multitude of directions. Those in positions to set university priorities should constantly remind faculty that if they do not contribute to reversing the present cultural and environmental trendlines, their theories, mathematical models, and discoveries about past events, will have no immediate or enduring significance.

A third area of policy change should address resource allocation within the university: that is, decisions about which departments will be allowed to atrophy or disappear altogether, and which departments should be strengthened or created. Hopefully, changing the mind-set at the top of the university pyramid (and it will take more than one retreat) would also lead to setting priorities for hiring new faculty, and for bringing speakers to campus. Presidents and academic deans now encourage (with only limited success) the hiring of faculty who contribute to gender and ethnic balance. Environmentalists need to pressure university administrators to articulate policies that will "green" the faculty. The case also needs to be made that women and ethnic minority faculty members are more likely to contribute to an understanding of the ecological and communal importance of cultural patterns that are less technologically and consumer-oriented.

Reaching the Faculty

The diversity of faculty interests (not to mention personality traits) makes it difficult to suggest a single approach to achieving the goal of reconstituting the conceptual and moral foundations of discipline-based knowledge. In my more optimistic moments I like to think that the recent announcement that scientists are now in agreement that global warming is occurring, and that modern technologies are the primary cause, would lead scholars across North America to come together on their respective campuses to discuss the implications for their fields of inquiry. If this were to happen there would be no need for environmentalists to direct their energies to challenging the moral indifference and conceptual double binds that now exist on university campuses. But it is not happening, and there is no evidence that the hubris and self-legitimating conceptual frameworks that equate scholarly inquiry, regardless of how arcane the topic is, with human progress have been brought into question by this quantum leap in the significance of environmental change. While the indifference that prevails among most members of the academic community can be explained on the grounds that it is genuinely difficult to think in ways that do not assume a human-centered world, the progressive nature of change, and that the individual is the primary agent of moral and rational judgment, a more accurate assessment suggests a parallel between the indifference that characterizes most of the American academic community and the indifference, indeed complicity, of most German academics during the Nazi regime.

Given the depth of and varied reasons for the widespread indifference toward considering how the ecological crisis brings into question the moral and intellectual underpinnings of all academic disciplines, as well as the arguments within the disciplines, the question becomes one of determining the most likely leverage points for effecting change. I am going to suggest four strategies that go beyond the recommendations in the *Blueprint for a Green Campus*. However, before discussing them I want to reiterate the two most important questions that need to be considered: (1) How can the characteristics of ecologically centered cultures be used to reconstitute the modern assumptions that currently underlie what is learned in the classroom and perpetuated in nearly every area of academic research? (2) How can we introduce a more ecologically centered morality into the language of the curriculum and scholarly research? If we keep in mind Hannah Arendt's distinction between internalized forms of authority and the external and coercive character of authoritarianism, reconstituting the root metaphors of the academic disciplines in terms of ecological sustainability becomes then a matter of shifting the taken-for-granted basis of authority in a way that will help avoid the suffering and dislocation that will accompany the extreme changes now being predicted for natural systems. That is, one of the dangers that we face in the scale of changes occurring in natural systems is that in order to cope with the socially disruptive consequences governments will be forced to adopt more authoritarian measures. If we can change the moral codes embedded in the languages of the culture, which partly can be done through the process of primary socialization that educators mediate, there is a greater possibility of the taken-for-granted cultural patterns becoming the source of authority for a more ecologically sustainable lifestyle than what will emerge from a centralized political process.

The first strategy that I am recommending should take account of the proclivity of most academics to revise their thinking and focus of research in ways that take account of the continual shifts in what constitutes the accepted paradigm of understanding. This proclivity suggests that one way for environmentalists to have the greatest effect would be to engage the intellectual trend-setters and especially prominent scholars in the different disciplines in a discussion of how to reconcile the direction that thinking is taking in their special fields with the evidence of rapid environmental degradation. For example, if trend setting scholars like Robert Sternberg in psychology, George Lakoff in linguistics, Jacques Derrida in philosophy, and Clifford Geertz in anthropology were invited to a retreat where the trend-lines of modern consumption and population growth were juxtaposed with the changes occurring in natural systems, it might lead to fundamental rethinking of how the foci of these respective disciplines need to be redirected. The danger in suggesting these particular scholars as examples of intellectual trend-setters is that the internecine struggles within the disciplines will lead many academics to claim that these particular scholars are no longer in the forefront of the field. While there will seldom be agreement about who represents the leadership in a field of inquiry, there are, nevertheless, scholars who exert an influence that extends beyond their specialized areas of study—and it is these individuals that environmentalists must engage in a sustained examination of the cultural implications of the ecological crisis. To make this point in another way, whenever possible efforts to engage faculty in the reconceptualization of the conceptual and moral assumptions that underlie high-status knowledge should take account of their ability to influence other scholars.

A second strategy is for environmentalists to organize retreats or on-going seminars held on campus where faculty discussions of the cultural implications of the ecological crisis can be given a specific focus through the use of videos and other media that clearly document the extent of the crisis. The goal of these discussions, in addition to addressing the conceptual and moral continuities between the Industrial Revolution and modern (and postmodern) ways of thinking, should be to understand how the characteristics of ecologically sustainable cultures can open up new lines of inquiry and teaching. A second goal would be to examine how the forms of knowledge and relationships emphasized in more traditional ecologically centered cultures may represent constructive alternatives to the nihilism and destructive relationships that are increasingly overwhelming what have been viewed as the positive aspects of modernity. If the initial discussions are allowed to drift in accordance with each faculty member's level of interest and background knowledge, the whole effort is likely to engage the interest of only those faculty who already are taking seriously the environmental crisis. Like the initial presentations to university administrators, the discussion needs to be framed by a clear and succinct presentation of the extreme disjuncture between the cultural trendlines being exacerbated by the globalization of modernization and the trendlines that reflect the decreasing viability of natural systems. The success of this strategy will depend largely upon the university administration establishing that these discussions are of paramount significance to the future of the university, and that faculty participation will be given more weight in tenure and promotion decisions than scholarly publications.

A third strategy is to help redirect faculty research into areas that make a contribution to understanding the extent to which different cultural groups have maintained convivial and non-consumer-oriented traditions that either have been ignored and undervalued because of the emphasis on high-status knowledge. Often these traditions take the form of community celebrations, the passing on of folk knowledge and skills, sharing community-centered responsibilities, forms of play, rituals and ceremonies that contribute to the spiritual centeredness of the community, and so forth. There is a genuine need to have a better understanding of the many activities and relationships that contribute to the well-being of community life, and that are not dependent upon the commodifying process that occurs in mainstream culture. As scholars help recover the ability to recognize the alternative forms of community relationships and activities, there is a greater likelihood that this understanding will be carried over into what is learned in university classrooms. Again, the success of the strategy will partly depend upon the redirection of economic resources which, in turn, will require a shift in the funding priorities of private foundations, governmental agencies, and the university itself.

The fourth strategy should address what has been a traditional source of pride of university professors: namely, that their success as teachers is dependent primarily upon their thorough knowledge of their field of inquiry. If we consider the ecologically destructive cultural assumptions that professors reinforce as they teach their subject areas, it is then difficult to take seriously the claim that professors do not need to understand the cultural dynamics of the pedagogical process. Like public school teachers, professors are engaged in the process of primary socialization as they introduce students to new areas of cultural knowledge—especially when the class represents exposure to knowledge that is on the cutting edge of the field. Being able to recognize how the language processes they mediate reproduce the deepest cultural assumptions and patterns of thinking is as essential for the professor as it is for the elementary grade teacher. The other aspects of primary socialization, including how the cultural patterns that govern metacommunication in the classroom, are also essential to understand if the professor is to avoid the traditional patterns of classroom discourse that lead to representing what is being learned as objective and thus as universally shared. Environmentalists should help clarify how part of the problem of generalizing modern cultural patterns, where students are often being influenced by the reified thought patterns of their professors, can be traced back to the professor's lack of understanding of how the cultural episteme is reproduced though the metaphorical constructions of the language that, in turn, influence thought patterns that are taken for granted. This cultural schemata of understanding, like the anthropocentric and other patterned ways of thinking discussed earlier, may even be the basis of new insights that serve to further hide the taken-for-granted conceptual and moral framework that underlies the professor's field of knowledge. In addition, there is a genuine need to establish ways in which faculty can learn to recognize how the language processes in the classroom reproduce the metaphorical constructions that encode an earlier pre-ecological way of thinking and moral sense of relationships. Workshops, retreats, and mentoring in how to become aware of the deep taken-for-granted cultural patterns being reinforced in the process of teaching and learning are all possibilities that should be explored.

Student Involvement in the Greening of the University

It is unfortunate that the retired members of society (that is, the people who do not have to worry about career choices being thwarted because of political activism) do not take an interest in how universities contribute to the areas of cultural development most closely associated with overreaching the sustaining capacities of the environment. While there are many retired people who are active within the environmental movement, it appears that students again will have to carry the burden for the kind of direct political action that needs to complement the efforts to change the conceptual and moral priorities of university faculty and administrators. In addition to the present existence of student environmental organizations that are networked together, there is a need for students to recognize the connection between the power they now possess on university campuses and the need to challenge the legitimacy of courses that promote ecologically destructive values and ways of thinking. There are several reasons that students are in a unique position to effect fundamental change in the area of the curriculum. Many students are already knowledgeable about environmental issues, and often bring to their classes perspectives that diverge significantly from their professor's underlying value framework. Until recently, however, students were more vulnerable to the consequences of raising questions that challenged the foundations of the professor's knowledge, such as challenging the philosophy professor about the culture-free view of rational thought that has long been a staple of the field, and the economic professor's inability to think of a healthy economy in terms other than growth. The balance of power on campuses is now undergoing important changes due to the increasingly restricted levels of funding of university budgets. As universities become more dependent upon student tuition, students are increasingly in the driver's seat in terms of critical areas of the university curriculum. This increasing economization of the curriculum has led to changes that earlier would have been viewed by faculty as compromising the essential intellectual foundations of the students' education. Currently, if students, for whatever reason, do not enroll in sufficient numbers in a course, it is quickly dropped or modified in order to retain sufficient "student credit hours" necessary for making it economically viable. While the traditional arguments about distribution requirements that ensure breadth in the students' undergraduate courses have not entirely disappeared (partly for reasons connected with the ideology underlying the discipline and with protecting departmental budgets), increasingly new courses are being offered because they are perceived as "capitalizing" on what students are interested in. And with the possibility of students being able to take courses over the Internet there will be even more pressure to base curricular decisions on a market model.

Students need to become more aware of the power of refusal they can now exercise, and begin exercising it by not taking courses that are based on ecologically destructive cultural patterns of thinking—in the same way that students now refuse to take courses that are based on explicit expressions of patriarchical thinking. Courses that are based on anthropocentric metanarratives, on reductionist theoretical frameworks that promote the power of elite groups, on an instrumental and individually centered moral framework, to cite the most obvious examples, need to be challenged. Not enrolling for a course will have undesirable consequences in terms of the student credit hours "generated" by the department, but this silent form of refusal may be incorrectly interpreted by faculty (e.g., the course was offered at the wrong time of the day, or it was offered at the same time as a required course). The politics of refusal need to be expressed in a more public way by using the campus newspaper, leaflets, and other forums to expose the reactionary content of the course. These actions are less likely to be misinterpreted, as the threat of a further decline in enrollment will quickly get the attention of both the faculty and administration. A more constructive consequence is that public exposure of course content that reinforces the mythic underpinnings of modern culture will help foster discussion among faculty and students about the forms of knowledge that are relevant to the kind of cultural transformation that must now be undertaken. If the course is part of a group requirement, then more coordinated efforts will be needed in order to force faculty to revise the requirements. The recent success of students in challenging sexist and racist content in courses should serve as a source of optimism about the efficacy of student action. Challenging the modern biases that are undermining both the environment and other less commodified cultures will be more difficult, but the consequences of not acting represent an entirely different magnitude of importance.

Chapter 6

GREENING COLLEGES
OF EDUCATION

Throughout the last century public schools have been thrust into the role of saving the nation from one perceived threat after another. They have seldom made the contribution expected of them, and now after many decades of uneven achievement there is a more mature awareness of the influence that public schools have on the process of social reform. While public schools are limited in their ability to take a leadership role in initiating social changes, no genuine reform effort on a national scale can succeed if the values and beliefs taught in public schools represent an oppositional point of view. The national gains made in the area of human rights for minority groups have been supported by the efforts of teachers who used the curriculum to raise the students' understanding of why discrimination in all its forms of expression diminishes the well-being of society. Granted, the consistency and effectiveness of this effort was and continues to be uneven. Discrimination continues to be highly visible in the low quality of education available to many ethnic minorities, especially in urban areas. In assessing the public schools' role in this reform effort, it is important to recognize that the positive contribution came about primarily because of outside political pressure. As pointed out earlier, awareness of racial and, later, gender discrimination did not arise from within the teaching profession. But many teachers were quick to change the curriculum in response to the criticism of outside political activists. Another characteristic of public schools needs to be noted: namely, that teachers who attempt to support the

larger social reform efforts often depend upon the visibility
of outside political activism at the national level, as well as
upon the ability of activists to articulate the moral justification for the reforms, in order to justify to their administrators and colleagues the changes they introduce into their
curriculum.

   This brief overview of the mixed achievements and vul-
nerabilities of public schools has a number of implications
for the various groups that make up the environmental
movement. The first is that the eventual success of shifting
away from a technological and consumer-oriented culture
needs to be supported through an educational process that
will introduce the younger generation to the forms of knowledge and values essential to living in more self-reliant and
ecologically sustainable communities. The second is that
environmental groups need to help clarify for teachers, administrators, and curriculum developers the full implications of David Orr's observation that "all education is
environmental education"(1992, p. 90), and focus attention
on the the causal relationship between the adverse changes
occurring in the environment and cultural practices that
need to be more fully understood. The examination of these
cultural practices, as well as the identification of alternatives that do not have a negative impact on the environment, are essentially educational activities that should be
at the center of the public school curriculum.

   As environmentalists begin to examine what is being
taught in the public schools, they will find that a small minority of teachers are already attempting to raise their students' awareness of the environment. They will also find
that many more teachers are concerned about the future implications of a degraded environment for their own lives, but
that this concern has not led them to consider how their
courses may be preparing students to take for granted a receptive attitude toward the high-status forms of knowledge
that now threaten our collective future. While environmentalists will find a few outstanding examples of students
being encouraged to examine the causal relationships between changes occurring in local ecosystems and cultural
practices, most of what passes for environmental education

is restricted either to the elementary grades—where it usually takes the form of using the rain forest as the theme that serves as the basis of an integrated approach to teaching art, social studies, writing, and so forth—or to science-oriented classes where students learn about habitat restoration and how to monitor changes occurring in local streams and other natural settings.

While these are important beginnings that should be further encouraged, especially since they represent the efforts of a small minority of public school teachers, such approaches to environmental education involve serious shortcomings that the teachers themselves are often unable to recognize. That is, they frequently reproduce the double binds inherent in addressing environmental issues by using the modern values and patterns of thinking that are largely responsible for the very environmental problems that students are learning to solve. Just as the minority of environmentally conscious teachers reproduce the double binds that characterized the thinking of their professors, these same double binds are being reproduced in the way students are being taught to think about rain forests, wetlands, and the importance of recycling. Unfortunately, the contradictory nature of promoting both environmental education and a modern form of consciousness cannot be overcome by the teacher's good intentions, and the consequences for students and the rest of society will be long lasting. This phenomena can be seen in the elementary grades where teachers involve students in an integrated curriculum with an environmental focus, while at the same time reinforcing the importance of creative ideas, individual thought and group "brainstorming" (both of which suffer from basing ideas on the limited experience of young students), and finding the best technological solution. When the environmental problem being studied exists in some other part of the world, another characteristic of modern consciousness is reinforced—namely, the modern proclivity of projecting onto a threatened ecosystem halfway around the world the diagnosis and solution dictated by Western values and assumptions. What these elementary students will not learn about is the complex nature of tradition (including how traditions have co-evolved in response to changes in the local habitat), the difference between oral-based communities and print-based publics and networks, the characteristics of elders and how to participate in the renewing of their communal and ecological wisdom, and how language encodes and reproduces earlier forms of metaphorical thinking—including the mythic nature of earlier root metaphors. If students do not have the opportunity to learn about these aspects of culture, which can begin in the early grades if the concepts are contextualized in terms of the students' own cultural experiences, they will not have the conceptual reference points necessary for being able to make explicit at a later time in their lives the aspects of modern consciousness that are ecologically problematic. At the high school level the moral and conceptual double binds take an even more extreme form as science-based approaches to environmental education are increasingly based on the extreme modernist assumptions of critical pedagogy.

The assumptions central to critical pedagogy appear to have a progressive orientation toward social justice issues, which lead socially and environmentally conscious teachers not to question them. However, as these assumptions were the basis of the Industrial Revolution, and continue to provide the legitimation for the globalizing of high-status knowledge, it is necessary to examine them more closely. Otherwise, there might be a tendency to use the marriage of environmental education to the assumptions underlying critical pedagogy as the model for reforming those areas of the public school curriculum that do not presently address environmental issues. The word "critical" highlights what is supposed to be the main classroom activity. Peter McLaren explains that the teacher's responsibility is to "first, encourage students to develop a *pedagogical negativism*—to doubt everything, and to try to identify those forms of power and control that operate in their own lives." After all taken-for-granted patterns of the students' lives have been questioned and thus politicized, teachers are to "assist students in *making a judgment* about these forms of power and control." Teachers can then transform critical questioning into student empowerment by the simple act of framing the question in terms of "What can be used to promote empowerment, and what must be discarded?" (1989, p. 233). Henry Giroux, perhaps the second most important educational theorist after Paulo Freire, states both the goal and process of critical pedagogy in the following way:

> Critical educators must provide the conditions for students to engage in cultural remapping as a form of resistance. That is, they should be given the opportunity to engage in systematic analyses of the ways in which the dominant culture creates borders saturated in terror, inequality, and forced exclusions. At the same time, students should be allowed to rewrite difference through the process of crossing over into cultural borders that offer narratives, languages, and experiences that provide a resource for rethinking the relationship between the center and margins of power as well as between themselves and others. In part this means giving voice to those who have been normally excluded and silenced. (1992, p. 209)

And in a recent interview featured in the *Harvard Educational Review*, Paulo Freire states that "one of our challenges as educators is to discover what historically is possible in the sense of contributing toward the transformation of the world, giving rise to a world that is rounder, less angular, more humane, and in which one prepares the materialization of the great Utopia: Unity in Diversity" (1995, p. 397).

In a surprisingly superficial assessment of the cultural mediating characteristics of cyberspace, Michael Peters and Colin Lankshear view the Internet as expanding the possibilities for individuals to emancipate themselves from the oppressive hold of cultural traditions. Ignoring both cultural differences in ways of knowing (including Third World cultures resisting the Western economic model of development) and the computer's role in the commoditization of knowledge and relationships, these two critical theorists hold out the following promise of a digital based liberation of subjectivity:

> Within postmodernity . . . this ideal of the media based upon the model of lucid self-consciousness yields to an ideal

in which emancipation is based on oscillation and plurality. Here the key to emancipation is found in the plurality and complexity of 'voices': an emancipation consisting in disorientation which is, at the same time, a liberation of dialect, local differences, and rationalities, each with its own distinctive grammar and syntax. (1996, p. 60)

In addition to its tendency to divide the world into the neat and morally unambiguous categories of emancipatory and oppressive practices, there are a number of other characteristics of critical pedagogy (now termed "critical literacy") that should be of special interest to environmentalists who are concerned about the process of educational reform. First, critical pedagogy retains the extreme form of anthropocentric thinking that was characteristic of the Marxist and Enlightenment thinkers who Freire and his followers are chiefly indebted to. Second, the view of change as inherently progressive in nature is essential to their argument that critically based "transformations of the world" represent an advance over what now exists. That is, their view of history assumes that it is possible to make a radical break with the past, and that each generation, with the assistance of teachers schooled in the methods of critical pedagogy, will continue to separate themselves from the oppressive conditions created by the previous generation. Indeed, Freire writes about the need for each generation to rename the world. Their writings do not address how this view of continual revolution can be reconciled with the cultural/bioconservatism of cultural groups that are attempting to resist the modern view of development, with its emphasis on integration into the world economy, computer networks, and anomic individualism (Sachs, 1992). Third, the emphasis on critical reflection as the basis of determining the authority of ideas and values, as we have discussed earlier, foregrounds the authority of the autonomous individual and the modern idea that decisions should be made on the basis of the individual's immediate experience. Fourth, traditions that represent hard-won achievements essential to sustaining self-reliant and just relationships within communities and between communities and the environment are to be "deconstructed" through the process of doubting everything, which the critical pedagogy theorists view as preparing the way for the "materialization of the Great Utopia." Also missing in their thinking is a more complex understanding (and appreciation) of the importance of elders, and the recognition that critical reflection may be only one of many ways important knowledge and values are learned, renewed, and passed on to the next generation.

Environmental education teachers are not the only ones to combine the reinforcement of modern values with teaching students a technological way of thinking about environmental management, but the special aura of legitimacy associated with those areas of the curriculum that claim some scientific basis makes it even more difficult to recognize the double binds—even when they should be apparent to most observers. Witness how the assumptions about a human-centered world and an experimental approach to human relationships with nature provide the conceptual and moral basis for an educational software program called *Sim Earth*. The manual explains the objectives of the program, as well as how it should be used in the classroom. It also claims that James Lovelock's Gaia hypothesis provides the conceptual framework for student decision making. Addressing students directly, the manual states that the when using *Sim Earth* they will be "in an experimental mode. You [the student] are given unlimited energy to mold *your* planet. This allows *you* to set up any type of planet in any state of development, and then introduce any new factor *you* want and see what happens" (italics added, 1990, p. 2). To cite another example, the software program , *Environmental Education Toolbox*, is justified on the grounds that it fosters student-centered, experimental inquiry. That is, "it promotes the 'constructivist' view of learning" (1994, p. 16). As an examination of environmental curricula will reveal, what might be seen at first glance as model approaches to incorporating environmental issues into the public school curriculum often turn out to be the most problematic. What needs to be given special attention is the ideology that is reinforced along with the scientific content of the lesson. The background ideology is especially important because it will influence whether students understand and experience their relationship with the environment in terms of an experimental lifestyle based on high-status knowledge and technologies, or whether they will be open to learning from elders and to thinking within the community-based language that encodes the moral relationships with the environment that must be observed.

A Source of the Problem: Colleges of Education

While the reasons public schools continue to reinforce modern values and conceptual patterns are too complex to be attributed entirely to a single cause, colleges of education (the umbrella term I will use for referring to teacher education programs and other graduate studies in education) must be held to a higher level of accountability, and thus responsibility. The widespread lack of awareness that the ecological crisis raises fundamental questions about what is being taught in colleges of education is a problem that exists across the country. A related shortcoming shared by even the most prestigious colleges of education is that most public school teachers do not understand the complexity of the cultural processes that are integral to how they guide students through the process of primary socialization. When classroom teachers do not recognize how past forms of metaphorical thinking are reproduced in the language of the curriculum, how modern ways of thinking lead to a completely distorted understanding of the nature of tradition, how high-status knowledge and values differ from cultural patterns that have been categorized as low-status (and thus not worth learning about), and how different forms of technology privilege certain forms of knowledge and relationships over others, colleges of education must be held directly responsible. The argument might be made that if professors in other parts of the university were to address these issues in their courses then students going into teacher education programs would not be as dependent upon what is taught in colleges of education. As this observation suggests, the responsibility for public school teachers' failure to recognize how their efforts to raise environmental awareness are often justified in terms of the nihilistic values and conceptual patterns of modernity can be placed on many doorsteps. But the control that education professors have over the content of the professional courses, in both teacher education and graduate degree programs, suggests that they have a unique responsibility that is not being recognized. It also suggests an area of the university that environmentalists need to give particularly close scrutiny.

As environmentalists begin to give close attention to what is being taught in public schools, it will become apparent that high school teachers are more concerned with the knowledge of content areas, while in the early grades the knowledge of content takes more of a backseat to promoting social skills and a positive self-concept. Another widely shared characteristic of teachers at all levels is the liberal ideology that foregrounds a human-centered perspective, individualism, a secular, scientific form of reductionist thinking, and the continual search for new and experimental ways of thinking. Students going into teacher education programs will already have experienced nearly sixteen years of formal education based on these assumptions; their professional courses will further cement the connections between liberal assumptions and teaching methods. These criticisms should not be interpreted as applying to all education courses. Some are taught by highly educated and thoughtful professors, and their courses are as intellectually challenging as the best courses offered in other parts of the university. Again, it needs to be emphasized that the dominant characteristics of colleges of education are the primary focus here.

Close scrutiny of colleges of education will reveal other characteristics that have special significance for the development of effective reform strategies. Perhaps the most important is the way in which the liberal ideology that underlies modernity has evolved into three distinct approaches to education. To reiterate the differences discussed in Chapter 3, the technocratic tradition of liberalism leads to an emphasis on the use of classroom management techniques, continual efforts to align the curriculum with the kind of work force that business elites view as essential for competing in a global economic environment, and the increased use of computers as a way of delivering the curriculum. This conceptual and moral framework is couched in the rhetoric of scientific and technological progress, meeting individual and culturally diverse needs, and constructivist learning theory.

Education students will encounter in their other professional courses neo-romantic liberal assumptions about the child's ability to learn from direct experience, the need for the child to experience her/his own sense of freedom, and the need to inculcate the importance of valuing equally all points of view, as long as they are held by caring and authentic individuals. In still other education classes, students will be given a different set of prescriptions for ensuring that schools contribute to social progress. Reading Dewey and Freire, as well as educational theorists influenced by the latest intellectual fad sweeping though academic departments—Marxism, critical theory, deconstructionism, postmodernism, and cultural studies, to identify some of the more prominent shifts in emancipatory thinking—will leave many education students with a messianic sense of purpose. But they will have little opportunity to clarify how such metaphors as "resistance," "empowerment," "border-crossing," "decoding texts," and "struggle for freedom," are to be applied in classrooms where their own students represent different cultural backgrounds. Ironically, Christian fundamentalists, the elite business community, and members of libertarian groups that oppose all forms of government regulation (to cite just three examples) can all claim that other social groups are limiting their sense of freedom, and that these metaphors could be used to justify their respective approaches to overcoming the forms of domination they are struggling against.

Education students learn that these ideologically driven vocabularies are often course-specific, and that they may even be used in the same course without the professor pointing out the contradictions or that these context-free metaphors have little relevance for deciding how to respond to the often conflicting public demands that will be made on them when they become public school teachers. One of the unfortunate consequences of this surface exposure to conflicting vocabularies for thinking about the purpose and process of education is that few teachers will possess the solid theoretical basis necessary for thinking critically about the seemingly endless stream of educational panaceas that sweep through the educational establishment, leaving teachers too exhausted to keep in focus the social challenges that do not lend themselves to formulaic thinking. For example, learning how to identify which of the seven forms of intelligence a student possesses and how to adjust the curriculum accordingly, how to manage the classroom in terms of the goals of "outcome-based" education, how to keep a portfolio of the student's work, and how to adapt the curriculum to "brain-based" teaching techniques, to note the most recent panaceas that keep teachers focused on techniques rather than on the cultural content of the curriculum, contributes to a professional atmosphere where efforts to draw attention to the paramount importance of cultural patterns that threaten the viability of the Earth's ecosystems will be seen as yet another demand being placed on overworked teachers. In effect, the Tower of Babel atmosphere which colleges of education create leads to reducing everything to the same level of momentary significance.

The succession of educational fads that compete for the attention and energy of the public school teacher often has its origin in the diversity of theoretical frameworks extrapolated from the different streams of educational liberalism, as well as from "scientific" discoveries that focus on the psychological and learning patterns of the individual. With deans of colleges of education now largely playing the role of business managers, this diversity of perspectives is one of the primary reasons that environmentalists will find resistance within education faculties to engaging in a sustained discussion of the educational implications of the ecological crisis. The authority of the professor's subjective judgment, and often superficial knowledge of recent developments in related academic disciplines, become the deciding factor in what will be discussed in any depth. Mostly, faculty meetings address procedural matters connected with committee reports and making program adjustments in response to

changes in the larger university bureaucracy. Given the difficulty of intellectual and moral leadership emerging from
within colleges of education around environmental issues
(even when these issues are related to the future of life supporting systems on this planet), the possibility of a sustained and in-depth discussion will be dependent upon
outside pressure being brought to bear in a manner that
highlights the reactionary nature of what students are
being exposed to. The education professor's desire to be on
the cutting edge of the latest expression of modernity have
left them with a nearly phobic reaction to anything that is
labeled as backward or reactionary. Criticisms that their
various approaches to promoting the culture of modernism
should now be understood as backward and reactionary
may get their attention long enough for environmentalists
to present the evidence of how the diverging cultural and
natural system trendlines are connected.

These characteristics of colleges of education suggest
two primary questions that will be basic to the success of efforts to introduce a combined cultural and ecological perspective into teacher education programs, and into the
graduate studies of people who will be in educational leadership positions. They are: "What specific changes should
environmentalists attempt to introduce into colleges of education?" and "What forms of intervention are most likely to
succeed?" Over the years, many outside groups have called
for the reform of teacher education programs and, indirectly, graduate studies in education. Their general lack of
success suggests just how difficult reform will be, and thus
why environmentalists need to have a clear understanding
of their own reform agenda. They also will need to understand how to match their reform agenda with the potential
sources of support within colleges of education.

Reform Priorities for Changing Ecologically
Destructive Cultural Patterns

The nature of what teachers do suggests the direction
that the reform of colleges of education should take. When
professors of education represent teaching in terms of mak-

ing decisions about how to utilize different strategies for motivating, managing, and evaluating students, they are addressing only those aspects of teaching that seem to be the primary concern of beginning teachers. A more fundamental part of teaching is that it involves mediating how students will learn to think about the aspects of culture presented in the curriculum, while at the same time influencing which areas of cultural experience will not be reflected upon. There are many examples of areas of the student's personal experience that cannot easily be made explicit because the educational process has not provided the language for naming and thinking about the relationships that make up the experience. These educationally marginalized areas of cultural experience later represent the areas of adult life where destructive taken-for-granted patterns continue to dictate the rhythm of daily life because they cannot be articulated and reconstituted. For example, most people who have gone through public schools learn to think of technology as a neutral tool, even though their experiences with different technologies are mediated in complex existential and cultural ways. That is, their experiences with different forms of technology are far more complex than how they think about them. Often otherwise highly educated individuals will state that technology is like a tool, and that it becomes good or bad depending upon the purpose that the user gives it—which is the standard explanation that is given in textbooks and by most teachers who reproduce the explanations that were previously taken for granted and passed along to their teachers.

Another example of the influence of the teacher's mediating role in influencing which aspects of culture will be learned at the explicit level (and understood in terms of a conceptual schemata that may hide the culturally constructed nature of what is being learned), and which aspects will be learned at the level of implicit and pre-verbalized understanding, can be seen in the statements made by Steven Pinker, who is a professor of linguistics at MIT and the author of the best selling book, *The Language Instinct*. In making his argument against theorists who overestimate the importance of language (he refers to them as linguistic determinists and his examples are taken from the first half of this century), Pinker states his own position that "thoughts are trapped inside the head of the thinker" (1994, p. 67). He further suggests that while waiting for scientists to locate the gene responsible for what he calls the "language instinct," we should recognize that "language is no more a cultural invention than is upright posture" (p. 18). Pinker's own inability to recognize that he is continually interacting with thought processes that have become embodied in such varied expressions of material culture as the layout of streets, the design of buildings, the postage stamps he uses, and so forth, is an example of how explicit knowledge is always framed against a background of taken-for-granted cultural patterns and assumptions. This highly educated individual's very complicated theory about the nature of thinking and the role of language actually reproduces the simplistic explanations heard over and over in public schools: namely that thinking is located in the head or brain of an autonomous individual. The lasting influence of teachers' own classroom instruction can also be seen in the fifth grade textbook explanation that work involves receiving a salary, which remains part of the schemata of understanding that underlies the omission of "housework" from the gross national product. These examples of the teacher's inability to recognize when the content of the curriculum is problematic are more critical to helping reformers recognize the collective problems we face than the current emphasis on teaching techniques and emancipatory visions.

It is the teacher's role in mediating how the student will learn to think about many areas of the culture that suggests what the primary concerns of environmentalists should be. The emphasis on learning teaching techniques, which is especially dominant in the professional education courses for elementary teachers, needs to be subordinated to an understanding of how the curriculum reproduces past cultural ways of thinking. The following characteristics of culture are especially important to the teacher's professional decision making about how the content of different courses may influence the student's understanding human/ nature relationships. For readers interested in how these aspects of culture can be used as the basis of the courses and student-teaching experience that are the core of the teacher's professional education, I would suggest that they read *Responsive Teaching: An Ecological Approach to Understanding Classroom Patterns of Language, Culture, and Thought* (Bowers and Flinders, 1990). The following is a list of what teachers need to understand in order to take a cultural approach to ecological literacy. The list is intended to serve as a guide for environmentalists who may be encountering for the first time the liberal rhetoric used to legitimate the technocratic and emancipatory traditions of modernism promoted in colleges of education, and who do not fully realize how this rhetoric obfuscates the cultural and environmental issues that must now be addressed.

What Teachers Should Understand About Culture, Community, and Ecology

1. *The different ways cultural knowledge and values are encoded, reproduced, and renewed.* Teachers should understand the differences between spoken and written communication, the metaphorical nature of the connection between language and thought , the cultural storage and renewal role of the visual arts, song, dance, and mythopoetic narratives.

2. *How individual intelligence can be understood as cultural and ecological in nature.* Teachers should understand the origins of the Western view of intelligence as an individual attribute, the differences between modern expressions of intelligence and forms of intelligence valued in ecologically centered cultures, the ways in which the language systems of a culture reproduce earlier forms of intelligence, and the educational implications of Bateson's use of the "map and territory" metaphor for explaining how the modern form of intelligence leads to seeing the environment in terms of a natural resource.

3. *The ways in which cultural patterns are handed down from the past, revised, discarded, and new traditions started.* Teachers should understand the different ways

the present is linked to the past, the differences between a fashion and a tradition, the ways in which some traditions empower while other traditions limit human and communal possibilities, the different expressions of anti-traditions and how they can lead to the loss of hard-won traditions. This more complex view of tradition is essential to helping students understand the dynamics both of ecologically unsustainable and sustainable cultural patterns, as well as why some cultures are more successful in developing complex symbolic systems that do not degrade the environment.

4. *The differences between high- and low-status forms of knowledge, values, technologies, and forms of relationships.* Teachers should understand the assumptions that are the basis of high-status knowledge, which cultural groups benefit and which groups are disadvantaged by this distinction, which forms of knowledge tend to be more community and ecologically centered, and why high-status knowledge contributes to forms of commoditization that displace communally shared knowledge and relationships with expert systems.

5. *How cultural patterns that have been categorized by our educational institutions as low-status may be more consistent with a cultural / bio-conservative ideology.* Teachers should understand the nature of convivial traditions of cultural groups in the community, how these noncommodified forms of relationships contribute to more connected and interdependent lives, and the connections between valuing the intangible forms of wealth and ecological sustainability.

6. *How technologies mediate both the personal and cultural dimensions of experience, and how they can be assessed in terms of impacting the viability of human and biotic communities.* Teachers should understand how the nature of a technology influences the selection of certain cultural patterns for amplification (and the loss of others), how technology can provide the analogues encoded in the process of metaphorical thinking and thus create a technological form of consciousness, and the differences between modern, high-status, and indigenous technology. As David Orr continually reminds us, teachers should also understand how the principles of ecological design can be used as a basis for helping students assess the human and environmental impact of technologies.

This list covers the preliminary knowledge necessary for recognizing how to make the thought processes encoded in various forms of curriculum materials, including classroom discourse, a genuinely educational experience. Updated versions of ways of thinking inherited from the Industrial Revolution that are widespread in the curriculum at all levels can be turned into a powerful educational experience, but only if the teacher is able to recognize the assumptions that underlie the thought patterns and values, and knows how to frame the discussion in terms of some of the more important differences that separate modern cultural patterns from those of more ecologically oriented cultures. In fact, being able to recognize how to broaden a discussion by bringing in related cultural issues that students have not considered suggests the need to link a deep knowledge of culture to methodology courses that are now the dominant feature of most teacher education programs.

Courses that introduce students to the classroom implications of different theories about the nature of intelligence would also be radically improved if based on understanding what is outlined in the above list. Not only would teachers then be able to put the current liberal view of intelligence in its proper historical and cultural context, they might also be able to recognize how the cognitive scientists' explanation of intelligence in terms of the firing patterns of neurons is really laying the basis for the view of intelligence that economically benefits the computer industry. Courses in educational philosophy would need to change from the current liberal emphasis on individual emancipation, rationally based moral decision making, and individually centered caring and spirituality, to a more comparative study of how educational issues are framed by different cultural approaches to moral, political, economic, and ecological issues. Instead of reading anthropocentric educational philosophers such as John Dewey, Paulo Freire, and their current interpreters, students would read authors such as Gregory Bateson, Charlene Spretnak, Dolores LaChapelle, Wendell Berry, and Ivan Illich. In history of education classes, attention would be given to the ways in which educational changes have been influenced in the past by elite groups interested in promoting the high-status forms of knowledge that underlie modernization. There would also be an emphasis on understanding how changes in educational policy undermined the more self-reliant traditions of orally based communities. Educational historians have focused almost entirely on the struggles between different elite groups to use the schools to achieve their vision of modernity, but the cultural groups that were attempting to hold onto their traditional sense of community have largely been ignored. How educational reforms throughout American history have been influenced by changing perceptions of nature would also be a relevant focus of inquiry.

By making culture the basis of teacher education and graduate studies in education, rather than the themes foregrounded by the different interpretations of educational liberalism, it would then become obvious that the computer education courses would have to shift from their current noncritical instruction in learning how to use different forms of software in different areas of the curriculum, to learning how to recognize the cultural assumptions that are reproduced both in educational software programs and in computer-mediated communication. There might even be room for a course titled "Educational Computing, Ideology, and the Ecological Crisis." Such a course could examine the forms of cultural knowledge and relationships marginalized by this technology, and why computers should still be viewed as a Cartesian technology (even in the age of parallel processing and advances in the interactive nature of computer technology). Teachers might then be better able to help students understand how the hype that surrounds this culture-changing technology obscures the fundamental moral and political issues connected with the extension of this technology in more areas of community life.

Strategies Most Likely to Contribute to Greening Colleges of Education

Years of criticism of education courses by discipline-based academics as well as by private foundation reports have led to the recent elimination of four-year teacher education programs at many universities. Continuing criticism, as well as reductions in support of higher education generally, are now leading in some states to shifting the professional education credential process away from colleges of education entirely. The new trends include the certification of the teacher's professional knowledge on the basis of national competency examinations, and the state assuming more authority for determining the combination of undergraduate courses and work experiences that should qualify a person to be a classroom teacher. To date there is little evidence these trends will lead to increased knowledge of the cultural-mediating role of the teacher, or that the ecological crisis has profound implications for what should be included in the professional education of teachers. This withdrawal of support for colleges of education has created an atmosphere of general uncertainty among education faculty. Given this self-doubt (and rising concern about the budget balancing strategy of eliminating the weakest units in the university) there may now be a greater receptivity to finding new ways to justify the role of colleges of education. But whether education faculty can begin to frame educational issues in terms of the cultural patterns that are threatening the environment is still an unanswered question.

Most professors of education continue to be in denial that the media accounts of mounting scientific evidence of the downward trendline in the sustaining characteristics of natural systems have any relevance to what is being taught in education classes. But there is another aspect of the problem that needs to be recognized. In giving talks at universities across the country I have often met education faculty who are genuinely concerned about what is happening to the environment. Partly because they represent a small minority within their faculty, and partly due to their unfamiliarity with thinking about educational issues within a conceptual framework that is centered on the relationship of culture to its ecosystem, there is a general sense of uncertainty expressed about how to change the deep conceptual basis of their courses. Another characteristic that needs to be taken into account is that, with only two exceptions that I am aware of, there is no intellectual leadership being given by deans of colleges of education on the need to address the ecological crisis. This combination of the majority of education faculty being in deep denial, the environmental concerns of the small minority of education faculty being undermined by the liberal convention of treating every point of view as being equally tolerated—as long as nobody exhibits the bad manners of insisting that their issue should be discussed in depth by the entire faculty, and the failure of deans to create the conditions around which a sustained discussion of cultural and environmental issues is possible, makes reform of colleges of education a daunting challenge indeed. However, before total discouragement sets in, it is important to keep in mind that colleges of education which exhibited these same characteristics responded to public pressure to address gender and racial issues. As in other social institutions, the changes were slow in coming and uneven in terms of their depth, but the changes have now reached the point where few education courses are taught from a consciously patriarchal or racist point of view. Given the evidence that change is possible, environmentalists should set as their goal that over the next five to ten years all education courses will address some aspect of how formal education can contribute to a more ecologically sustainable future.

The following strategies are the most likely to succeed in addressing the problem of denial, the conceptual and ideological double binds, and the sense of uncertainty about how to think about educational issues within metaphorical frameworks that situate the individual within culture, and culture within natural systems.

1. *There must be public exposure of the extreme modernist assumptions and values taught in most education courses.* The emphasis on change, individual and group authorship of ideas and values, and human-centeredness not only makes a travesty of the educator's commitment to cultural diversity, it also lays the moral, conceptual, and psychological foundations for creating a generation of anomic and rootless individuals who will be more easily manipulated by business and technological elites. What is being taught in most education courses as well as what passes for schol-

arship in educational publications needs to be brought to the public's attention in ways that highlight how much of the conceptual and moral legacy of the Industrial Revolution continues to be the basis of teacher education courses.

2. *The development of cultural and ecological literacy among education faculty needs to take several forms.* The habit of basing the conceptualization of educational issues and teaching methodologies on liberal assumptions makes it difficult for even the more environmentally-conscious faculty to break from this tradition—indeed, some environmentally-concerned education professors do not even recognize the contradiction. The need is for workshops and retreats that will enable education faculty to discuss over a sustained period of time the pedagogical and curricular implications of the ecological crisis. These settings should also provide guidance on how to recognize the cultural coding and reproduction processes connected with the use of metaphorical language in different areas of the public school curriculum. Faculty should also learn how to introduce into their teacher education courses concrete approaches that can be implemented in the classroom for examining how cultural patterns and traditions of different groups in the community can be studied from an ecological perspective. These workshops and retreats need to be organized in a way that ensures a deep understanding of the cultural processes that teachers mediate, and of the curriculum issues related to the differences that exist between how high- and low-status forms of knowledge and how technologies influence community and environmental relationships.

As there has been little written on a cultural approach to ecological literacy, and there are no examples of teacher education programs that are entirely based on culturally- and ecologically-centered courses and classroom experiences, the establishment of several model teacher education programs becomes even more essential. These model programs would help demonstrate the connections between multicultural and environmental issues. They would also show how cultural criticism, which should be an essential part of education courses, needs to be balanced with the ability to recognize and incorporate into class discussion examples of ecological and community sustaining traditions. The ideal scenario would be to have these model teacher education programs established as part of colleges of education that have high national visibility. Finding faculty who are accustomed to thinking in terms of the connections between cultural patterns and ecological sustainability (especially since the discussion of ecological sustainability within the context of a modern culture is just beginning) could be a serious problem. Funding of model programs will also pose a difficult challenge. But the millions of dollars required to set up these programs would represent an insignificant expenditure compared to the wide range of costs connected with the environmentally destructive pathway we are currently on. The proposal for setting up a national network of workshops and retreats, as well as several model teacher education programs, could easily be funded by private foundations committed to addressing the role that public education can play in helping to reverse the cultural and natural system trendlines.

3. *There needs to a way of sharing ideas and successful classroom practices on a national basis.* Establishing a journal that addresses the cultural and educational dimensions of the ecological crisis may sound out of date, given the current growth in electronic communication. Regardless of the medium to be used, there is a need to provide some form of in-depth exchange of ideas and exemplary practices among education faculty who are attempting to make the transition from an Industrial Revolution way of thinking to a cultural and ecological approach to education.

4. *The establishment of several model graduate programs is also needed if the next generation of education professors are going to avoid the reactionary thinking that is the hallmark of this generation.* When students ask me about graduate schools of education that offer specialized programs of educational study based on a cultural and ecological paradigm, I am unable to do anything more than suggest several universities that have a professor or two whose writings touch on cultural issues related to the environment. Studying with these professors would be important, but there is a need for graduate programs of study that take an interdisciplinary approach and that offer a wide range of education courses that are taught from a combined cultural and ecological perspective. Over the last three years, the School of Education at Portland State

University has succeeded in creating within an existing Masters program a focus area called Education, Culture, and Ecology. All of the education courses that students may elect to take, with topics ranging from learning theory to issues in curriculum, have been greened. More recently, seven faculty members have established an interdepartmental program of doctoral study around the theme of Community and Environmental Renewal. Because of continuing cutbacks that reflect the state of Oregon's unwillingness to fund higher education at previous levels (funding has declined by nearly 30 percent over the last decade), these limited efforts to establish conceptually coherent and in-depth approaches to graduate level study of education may not survive, or be allowed to develop in a way that would make them a national model. Along with York University in Canada, the graduate programs at Portland State University represent important advances beyond the heavily science based approaches to graduate study in environmental education that a number of universities now offer, and thus provide important insights into how to avoid organizing a program of study that incorporates the double bind of basing a technological approach to environmental education on the liberal view of the individual as a constructor of knowledge.

The proposal that model graduate programs be established will more likely become a reality if there is sufficient pressure from environmental groups. While the experience at Portland State University demonstrates the possibility of faculty reordering their priorities in ways that allow for the reconfiguration and greening of existing courses (thus avoiding the need for new funding), circumstances that allow these changes to occur are quite unique. And they are not likely to be duplicated at other universities. In addition to the need for outside pressure, there is also the need for environmentally-oriented foundations to use a system of matching grants to encourage education faculty to make the needed changes in their graduate programs.

Concluding Observations

Two of the purposes of this book were to lay out the general conceptual direction that educational reform should take, and to identify the double binds as well as leverage points that need to be considered as part of a reform strategy. Until there is agreement within the diverse factions that make up the environmental movement that the reform of public school and university level education should be made a high priority, going further into the specifics of any one area of educational reform would not be particularly useful. I would like to end the discussion of educational reform strategies with the observation that the connections between what is being learned in public schools and universities, and the cultural patterns that are contributing most directly to overshooting the sustaining capacities of natural systems, are perhaps best summarized in the following quotation from Gregory Bateson: "In no system which shows mental characteristics can any part have unilateral control over the whole. In other words, *the mental characteristics of the system are immanent, not in some part, but in the system as a whole*" (1972, p. 316).

This could be interpreted to mean that the cultural forms of consciousness reinforced in the educational institutions that help advance high-status forms of knowledge are immanent in the system of dams that obstruct the migration of salmon, in the air that carries the chemicals that are altering the forms of life that exist in the soil, lakes, and rivers, and in the shopping malls that depend upon subsistence culture being economically and technologically "developed" in ways that integrate them into a commodity-oriented economy. The arguments being made here for changing the form of culture reinforced in our educational institutions are really arguments for changing the form of mind that is becoming increasingly "immanent in the system as a whole"—which should be the concern of all environmentalists.

REFERENCES

Adler, Mortimer. 1982. *The Paideia Proposal: An Educational Manifesto*. New York: Macmillan.

Athanasiou, Tom. 1996. *Divided Planet: The Ecology of Rich and Poor*. Boston: Little, Brown.

Bailey, Ronald. 1993. *Ecoscam: The False Prophets of Ecological Apocalypse*. New York: St. Martins Press.

Barber, Benjamin R. 1992. *An Aristocracy of Everyone: The Politics of Education and the Future of America*. New York: Oxford University Press.

Bateson, Gregory. 1972. *Steps to an Ecology of Mind*. New York: Ballantine.

———. (edited by Rodney E. Donaldson). 1991. *Sacred Unity: Further Steps to an Ecology of Mind*. New York: Harper Collins.

Bellah, Robert, Madsen, Richard, Sullivan, William M., Swidler, Ann, and Tipton, Steven M. 1985. *Habits of the Heart: Individualism and Commitment in American Life*. Berkeley: University of California Press.

Bennett, William J. 1989. *Our Children and Our Country: Improving America's Schools and Affirming the Common Culture*. New York: Simon and Schuster.

Berger, Peter. 1970. "Marriage and the Construction of Reality." In *Recent Sociology: Patterns of Communicative Behavior*. Edited by Hans Peter Drietzel. New York: Macmillan, pp. 49–72.

Berger, Peter, Berger, Bridgett, and Kneller, Hansfried. 1974. *The Homeless Mind: Modernization and Consciousness*. New York: Vintage Books.

263

Berry, Wendell. 1983. *Standing By Words*. San Francisco: North Point Press.

— — —. 1986. *The Unsettling of America: Culture and Agriculture*. San Francisco: Sierra Club Books.

Biehl, Janet. 1991. *Rethinking Ecofeminist Politics*. Boston: South End Press.

Bloom, Allan. 1987. *The Closing of the American Mind: How Higher Education Has Failed Democracy and Impoverished the Souls of Today's Students*. New York: Simon and Schuster.

Bloom, Harold. 1994. *The Western Canon: Books and Schools for the Ages*. New York: Harcourt Brace.

Bloom, Irene. 1985. "On the Matter of Mind: The Metaphysical Basis of an Expanded Self." In *Individualism and Holism: Studies in Confucian and Taoist Values*. Ann Arbor, MI: Center for Chinese Studies, pp. 294–308.

Bookchin, Murray. 1990. *Remaking Society: Pathways to a Green Future*. Boston: South End Press.

Bowers, C. A. and Flinders, David. 1990. *Responsive Teaching: An Ecological Approach to Classroom Patterns of Language, Culture, and Thought*. New York: Teachers College Press.

Bowers, C. A. 1993. *Education, Cultural Myths, and the Ecological Crisis: Toward Deep Changes*. Albany: State University of New York Press.

— — —. 1995. *Educating for an Ecologically Sustainable Culture*: *Rethinking Moral Education, Creativity, Intelligence, and Other Modern Orthodoxies*. Albany: State University of New York Press.

Budiansky, Stephen. May 13, 1996. "Academic Roots of Paranoia." *U.S. News & World Report*, pp. 33–34.

Chalmers, David J. 1995. "The Puzzle of Conscious Experience." *Scientific American* (December): 80–86.

Coughlin, Ellan K. 1995. "Intelligence Researchers Issue Statement on 'Mainstream Science'." *The Chronicle of Higher Education* (January 5, 1995). p. A15.

Crick, Francis. 1994. *The Astonishing Hypothesis: The Scientific Search for the Soul*. New York: Charles Scribner's Sons.

Daignault, Jacques. 1992. "Traces at Work from Different Places." In *Understanding Curriculum and Phenomenology and Deconstructed Text*. Edited by William Pinar and William Reynolds. New York: Teachers College Press, pp. 195–215.

Daly, Herman E. 1991. *Steady-State Economics*. Washington, D.C.: Island Press.

Derrida, Jacques. 1987. *The Post Card: From Socrates to Freud and Beyond*. Chicago: University of Chicago Press.

Devall, Bill, and Sessions, George. 1985. *Deep Ecology: Living as If Nature Mattered*. Salt Lake City: Gibbs Smith.

Dissanayake, Ellen. 1988. *What Is Art For?* Seattle: University of Washington Press.

Dominick, Raymand H. III. 1992. *The Environmental Movement in Germany: Prophets and Pioneers, 1871–1971*. Bloomington: Indiana University Press.

Foreman, David. 1991. *Confessions of an Eco-Warrior*. New York: Crown Trade Paperbacks.

Freire, Paulo. 1974 edition. *Pedagogy of the Oppressed*. New York: Seabury Press.

Freire, Paulo, and Macedo, Donaldo P. 1995. "A Dialogue: Culture, Language, and Race." *Harvard Education Review*. Vol. 65, No. 3 (Fall): 377–402.

Foucault, Michel. 1982. "The Subject and Power." In *Michel Foucault: Beyond Structuralism and Hermeneutics*, by Hubert L. Dreyfus and Paul Rabinow. Chicago: University of Chicago Press.

Fox, Warwick. 1990. *Toward a Transpersonal Ecology*. Boston: Shambhala.

Garson, Barbara. 1989. *The Eclectronic Sweatshop: How Computers are Transforming the Office of the Future into the Factory of the Past*. New York: Penguin Books.

Geertz, Clifford. 1973. *The Interpretation of Cultures*. New York: Basic Books.

Giroux, Henry. 1992. "Resisting Difference: Cultural Studies and the Discourse of Critical Pedagogy." In *Cultural Studies*. Edited by Lawrence Grossberg, Cary Nelson, and Paula Treichler. New York: Routledge: pp. 199–212.

Goldsmith, Edward. 1993. *The Way: An Ecological World View*. Boston: Shambhala.

Goodenough, Ward H. 1981. *Culture, Language, and Society*. Menlo Park, CA: Benjamin/Cummings Publishing Co.

Gouldner, Alvin. 1979. *The Future of Intellectuals and the Rise of a New Class*. New York: Seabury Press.

Hamilton, William. 1994. "The Metaphysics of the Curriculum." *Holistic Education Review*. Vol. 7, No. 2 (Summer): 12–20.

Harvard Business School. 1995. *Harvard Business School MBA Program*. Cambridge, MA.

Heilbroner, Robert. 1972. "A Radical View of Socialism." Social Research. Vol. 39 (Spring): pp. 1–15.

Heinz Family Foundation. 1995. *Blueprint for a Green Campus*. (monograph).

Herrenstein, Richard J., and Murray, Charles. 1994. *The Bell Curve: Intelligence and Class Structure in American Life*. New York: Free Press.

Illich, Ivan. 1971. *Deschooling Society*. New York: Harper & Row.

Jacobsen, Robert L. 1995. "The Coming Revolution." *The Chronicle of Higher Education*. (April 27): A27–29.

Kamii, Constance. 1991. "What Is Constructivism?" In *Early Literacy: A Constructivist Foundation for Whole Language*. Edited by Constance Kamii, Maryann Manning, Gary Manning. Washington, D.C.: National Education Association, pp. 17–29.

Kay, Alan C. 1991. "Computer, Networks and Education." *Scientific American*. (September): 138–148.

Kimbrell, Andrew. 1992. "Second Genesis: The Biotechnology Revolution." Intercollegiate Review (Fall): 11–18.

Leopold, Aldo. 1970 edition. *A Sand County Almanac*. San Francisco: Sierra Club/Ballantine.

Lewontin, R. C. 1992. *Biology as Ideology*. New York: Harper Perennial.

MacIntyre, Alasdair. 1984 edition. *After Virtue: A Study in Moral Theory*. Notre Dame, IN.: University of Notre Dame Press.

Mander, Jerry. 1978. *Four Arguments for the Elimination of Television*. New York: Morrow Quill Paperbacks.

———. 1992. *In the Absence of the Sacred: The Failure of Technology & the Survival of the Indian Nations*. San Francisco: Sierra Club Books.

Marler, Peter. 1994. "Born to Talk?" *Natural History* (Summer): pp. 70–72.

Maturana, Humbert R, and Varela, Francisco J. 1980. *Autopoiesis and Cognition: The Realization of the Living*. Holland/Boston: D. Reidel.

———. 1992. *The Tree of Knowledge: The Biological Roots of Human Understanding*. Boston: Shambhala.

Maxis, and Wright, Will. 1990. *Manuel for SimEarth*. Orinda, CA.: Maxis.

McLaren, Peter. 1989. *Life in Schools: An Introduction to Critical Pedagogy in the Foundations of Education*. White Plains: Longmans.

McLaren, Peter, and Lankshear, Colin. 1993. "Critical Literacy and the Postmodern Turn." In *Critical Literacy: Politics, Praxis, and the Postmodern*. Edited by Colin Lankshear and Peter McLaren. Albany: State University of New York Press, pp. 379–420.

McLaughlin, Andrew. 1995 "The Heart of Deep Ecology." In *Deep Ecology for the 21st Century*, edited by George Sessions. Boston: Shambhala, pp. 85–93.

Minsky, Marvin. 1988. *The Society of Mind*. New York: Simon & Schuster.

Moravec, Hans. 1988. *Mind Children: The Future of Robot and Human Intelligence*. Cambridge: Harvard University Press.

Naess, Arne. 1989. *Ecology, Community and Lifestyle*. Cambridge: Cambridge University Press.

Nash, Roderick F. 1989. *The Rights of Nature: A History of Environmental Ethics*. Madison: University of Wisconsin Press.

Nietzsche, Friedrich (1968 edition). *Will to Power*. New York: Vintage Books.

———. (1967 edition). *On the Geneology of Morals*. New York: Vintage Books.

Norgaard, R. 1985. "Coevolutionary Agricultural Development." *Economic Development and Cultural Change*. Vol. 32, No. 3. pp. 34–46.

Norberg-Hodge, Helena. 1992. *Ancient Futures: Learning from Ladakh*. San Francisco: Sierra Club Books.

Orr, David. 1992. *Ecological Literacy: Education and the Transition to a Postmodern World*. Albany: State University New York Press.

———. 1995. "The Ruling Class." *Real World*. Vol. 11 (Spring): 4–5.

Peters, Michael, and Lankshear, Colin. Winter 1966. "Critical Literacy and Digital Texts." *Educational Theory*. Vol. 46, No. 1, pp. 51–70.

Pinker, Steven. 1995. *The Language Instinct: How the Mind Creates Language*. New York: Harper Perennial.

Polanyi, Karl. 1944. *The Great Transformation*. New York: Farrar & Rinehart.

Pound, Ezra. 1951 edition. *Confucius: The Great Digest, The Unwobbling Pivot, The Analects*. New York: New Directions.

Rorty, Richard. 1989. *Contingency, Irony, and Solidarity*. New York: Cambridge University Press.

Rosenau, Pauline Marie. 1992. *Post-Modernism and the Social Sciences: Insights, Inroads, and Intrusions*. Princeton: Princeton University Press.

Sachs, Wolfgang (editor). 1992. *The Development Dictionary: A Guide to Knowledge as Power*. London: Zed Books.

Sale, Kirkpatrick. 1995. *Rebels Against the Future: The Luddites and Their War Against the Industrial Revolution*. New York: Addison-Wesley.

Schneider, Stephen H. 1993. A Better Way to Learn." *World Monitor*, Vol. 6, No. 4: 30–38.

Scollon, Ron, and Suzanne Wong Scollon. 1991. Working Papers on China, Literacy, and American/East Asian Intercultural Communication. Haines, Alaska (unpublished manuscript).

Sennett, Richard, and Cobb, Jonathan. 1973. *The Hidden Injuries of Class*. New York: Vintage Books.

Sessions, George (ed.) 1995. *Deep Ecology for the 21st Century*. Boston: Shambhala.

— — —. 1995. "Postmodernism and Environmental Justice: The Demise of the Ecology Movement?" *The Trumpeter*, 12, 3, pp. 150–154.

Shils, Edward. 1981. *Tradition*. Chicago: University of Chicago Press.

Shiva, Vandana. 1985. "Monocultures of the Mind." *The Trumpeter*. Vol. 10, No. 4, pp. 132–135.

— — —. 1993. *Monocultures of the Mind: Biodiversity, Biotechnology and the Third World*. Penang, Malaysia: Third World Network.

Snyder, Gary. 1990. *The Practice of the Wild*. San Francisco: North Point Press.

Sobel, David. 1994. "Authentic Curriculum." *Holistic Education Review*. Vol. 7. No. 2 (Summer): 33–34.

Sperry, Roger. 1985. "Changed Concepts of Brain and Consciousness: Some Value Implicatons." *Zygon: Journal of Religion and Science*. Vol. 20, No. 1: pp. 25–36.

Sprady, William. 1992. "Outcome-Based Education." In *A Leader's Guide to School Restructuring: A Special Report of the NASSP Commission on Restructuring*. Reston, Virginia: National Association of Secondary School Principals, p. 62.

Spretnak, Charlene. 1991. *States of Grace: The Recovery of Meaning in the Postmodern Age*. San Francisco: Harper.

— — —. 1994. "Critical and Constructive Contributions to Ecofeminism." In *Worldviews and Ecology: Religion, Philosophy, and the Environment*. Edited by Mary Evelyn Tucker and John A. Grim. New York: Orbis Books, pp. 181–189.

Staats, Arthur W. 1994. "Psychological Behaviorism and Behaviorizing Psychology." *The Behavioral Analyst*. Vol. 17, No. 1 (Spring): 93–114.

Sternberg, Robert J. 1992 edition. *Metaphors of Mind: Conceptions of the Nature of Intelligence*. New York: Cambridge University Press.

Stock, Gregory. 1993. *Metaman: The Merging of Humans and Machines into a Global Organism*. Toronto: Doubleday Canada.

Suzuki, David and Knudtson, Peter. 1992. *Wisdom of the Elders: Honoring Sacred Native Visions of Nature*. New York: Bantam Books.

Tannen, Deborah. 1990. *You Just Don't Understand: Women and Men in Conversation*. New York: Ballantine Books.

Tawangyowma, Carolyn. 1988. Comments to the press reprinted in *The Indigenous Voice: Visions and Realities*. Edited by Roger Moody. London: Zed Books.

Toulmin, Stephen. 1990. *Cosmopolis: The Hidden Agenda of Modernity*. New York: Free Press.

Turkle, Sherry. January 1996. "Who Am We? *Wired*. 4:01, pp. 148–152, 194–199.

Wilson, David. 1994. "Humanist Wins Praise for Book on the Role of New Technologies." *The Chronicle of Higher Education* (October 5): A22.

Rohwedde, W. J. and Alm, Andy. 1994. *EE Toolbox Workshop Manuel: Using Computers in Environmental Education*. Ann Arbor, MI.: School of Natural Resources and Environment.

Wolkomir, Richard. 1994. "We're Going to Have Computers Coming Out of the Woodwork." *Smithsonian* (Summer): 82–93.

OTHER BOOKS BY
C. A. BOWERS

The Progressive Educator and the Depression: The Radical Years

Cultural Literacy for Freedom

The Promise of Theory: Education and the Politics of Cultural Change

Elements of a Post-Liberal Theory of Education

The Cultural Dimensions of Educational Computing: Understanding the Non-Neutrality of Technology

(with David Flinders) *Responsive Teaching: An Ecological Approach to Classroom Patterns of Language, Culture, and Thought*

Education, Cultural Myths, and the Ecological Crisis: Toward Deep Changes

Critical Essays on Education, Modernity, and the Recovery of the Ecological Imperative

Educating for an Ecologically Sustainable Culture: Rethinking Moral Education, Creativity, Intelligence, and Other Modern Orthodoxies

INDEX

Social Ecology, 20
Sociology of Knowledge, 173;
  intersubjective self, 157–
  158; taken-for-granted
  knowledge, 158–160
Sommers, Christina Hoff, 134
Sperry, Roger, 48
Spretnak, Charlene, 20, 72,
  132, 136
Sprady, William, 88
Staats, Arthur, 63
Sternberg, Robert J., 62–63,
  178, 233

T
Tallories Declaration, 12–13
Tannen, Deborah, 181–182
Tawangyowma, Carolyn, 44–45
Taylor, Frederick W., 120
Tradition, 73–74, 116–117,
  168–174, 253–254
Transgenerational communica-
  tion, 5, 195–197, 208
Tufts University Environmen-
  tal Literacy Institute, 12,
  15

Turkle, Sherry, 185

U
Union of Concerned Scientists,
  49, 229
Universities, 5–10;
  computers, 52–60;
  humanities and social sciences, 61–77;
  modernizing orientation,
  38–39;
  professional schools, 77–9;
  sciences, 39–52

V
Varela, Francisco, 183
Viereck, Peter, 133

W
Watt, James, 130
Weizenbaum, Joseph, 53
Wise Use, 165
Worster, Donald, 227